The Golden Tapestry

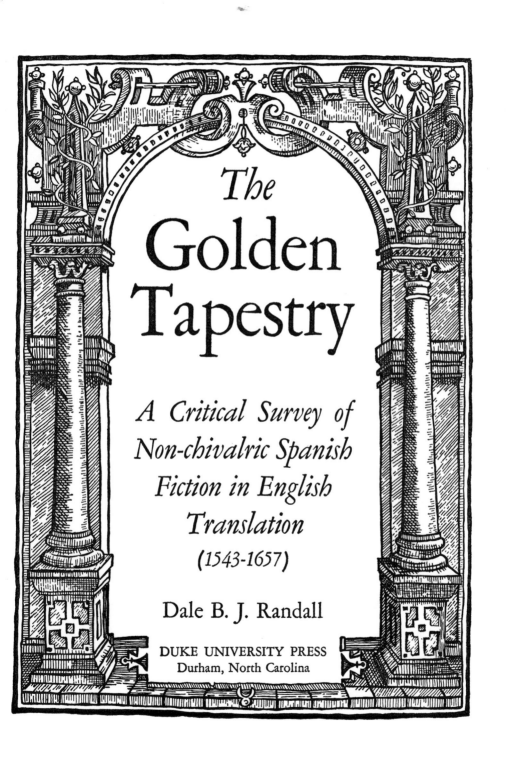

The
Golden
Tapestry

A Critical Survey of
Non-chivalric Spanish
Fiction in English
Translation
(1543-1657)

Dale B. J. Randall

DUKE UNIVERSITY PRESS
Durham, North Carolina

© 1963, Duke University Press

Library of Congress Catalogue Card number 63–13313
Cambridge University Press, London N.W.1, England

Printed in the United States of America
by Kingsport Press, Inc., Kingsport, Tenn.

To my father

Preface

I should like to direct my first prefatory words to those who dislike fancy titles. Although I admit a leaning toward phrases which stimulate the imagination, the present book, in order not to confuse booksellers, cataloguers, and potential readers, was for some time destined to have a factual label, but only until it was discovered that no accurate label was brief enough. (The present subtitle is evidence.) Hence the extravagance.

As a glance at the book soon reveals, it lacks a general bibliography. Realizing that I could not possibly hope to record all of my debts, I have settled for moderately complete documentation in the footnotes. This at least has the advantage of juxtaposing a number of valuable commentaries and the various subjects on which they have proved helpful to me. It has the disadvantages of overemphasizing the value of some works, of minimizing the value of certain others, and of leading to the omission of still others. The virtual omission, for instance, of *A List of English Tales and Prose Romances Printed before 1740* (London, 1912), by Arundell Esdaile, is not an oversight but an implicit acknowledgment that the ground covered by this pioneer and relevant to my own work has now been re-surveyed by Charles C. Mish in his much more recent *English Prose Fiction* (Charlottesville, Va., 1952).

It seems best to say a word, too, on the editions of the many narratives I discuss. I have tried to work always from first editions or microfilms of first editions, failing sometimes, of course, as when it came to the first *Lazarillo* or, more strangely, to Lope's *Pilgrime of Casteele*. It follows that my debt to librarians is unusually great.

Among the many librarians to whom I am indebted are Miss Florence E. Blakely and her staff at the Duke University Library, Mrs. Flora D. Colton at the University of Pennsylvania Library, and Miss Dorothy E. Mason and her staff at the Folger Shakespeare Library. Among libraries extending special courtesies are the British Museum, the Bodleian Library, the Library of Congress, the Libraries of Harvard University, the Huntington Library, and the libraries of Sion College, Dulwich College, Worcester College (Oxford), and the Société Jersiaise.

vii

Most particularly I should like to express my appreciation for the help of Professors Nicholson B. Adams, Arthur B. Ferguson, Weston Flint, John L. Lievsay, Charles C. Mish, and George Walton Williams, each of whom was good enough to read and comment helpfully on either part or all of the present study when it was still in manuscript form.

For assistance or encouragement at various earlier stages of my investigation I should like also to express appreciation, though in no way inculpate, Professors Werner P. Friederich, Otis H. Green, and M. A. Shaaber.

Professor William A. Jackson, who shared with me his notes for the revised *STC,* deserves special thanks. His help gives weight to some of the bibliographical information which is scattered in my text, notes, and appendixes. Among other researchers to whom I am grateful for answers to specific inquiries are Professor Celeste Turner Wright, Miss Clara Louisa Penney, and the late Professor J. Milton French.

For generous financial assistance I thank the Duke University Council on Research.

Having presented now a couple of rationalizations and a great many thanks, perhaps I should use my final prefatory words to acknowledge that bibliographical accuracy of the sort attempted in this book is a frustratingly relative matter. In fact, having caught myself so often in such a variety of errors, I can only hope that most of the original grand total of errors have at last been weeded out. My apologies for those that remain.

D. R.

Contents

The Golden Tapestry

Chapter I

Introduction

Don Quixote believed that a book and its translation are like the two sides of a tapestry. The one is clear, well-ordered, and meaningful; the other, blurred in outline, marred by thrums and knots.[1]

Writing during the Golden Age of Spanish literature—which came at about the same time as the Golden Age of English literature, including English translation—Cervantes endowed his mad knight with some perfectly sane doubts about the limits of translation. Furthermore, both before and after Cervantes, English writers repeatedly expressed the doubts that they, too, had about transferring the literature of one land into the language of another. In 1582 George Whetstone turned to history for an earlier version of Cervantes' tapestry figure, declaring that he who

is the Troucheman of a Straungers Tongue, may well declare his meaning, but yet shall marre the Grace of his Tale: And, therefore, Themistocles, the noble Captayne and Philosopher of Athens, compareth suche forced Speaches [translations], to Tapistrie Hangings rowled vp: which, beyng open, appeare beautifull: and fowlded, reserue their Vertue, but lose their showe. . . .[2]

Later Englishmen such as James Howell, Leonard Digges, Humphrey Moseley, and Nathaniel Waker felt the same way, and even thought the

1. *El ingenioso hidalgo Don Quijote de la Mancha* (I, 1605; II, 1615) was translated into English by Thomas Shelton, Pt. I being printed in 1612, Pts. I and II together in 1620. Unless otherwise specified, the 1620 edition will be cited, and for convenience the English form "Quixote" will be used throughout.

In the passage referred to here, Don Quixote says that translating is "iust like looking vpon the wrong side of Arras-Hangings: that although the Pictures be seene, yet they are full of threed ends, that darken them, and they are not seene with the plainenesse & smoothnesse, as on the other side . . ." (II, 427).

The simile had appeared earlier in Spanish in Luis Zapata's introduction to his translation from Horace, *El arte poética* (Lisbon, 1592), A2ʳ (now available in facsimile [Madrid, 1954]). According to Villegas, it also appeared in the writings of Diego de Mendoza (Esteban Manuel de Villegas, *Las eróticas* . . . [Madrid, 1774], II, a4ᵛ).

2. *An Heptameron of Civill Discourses*, Aiiiᵛ. This story of Themistocles (*ca.* 525–*ca.* 460 B.C.) furnishes the sanction of antiquity to the comparison.

simile of the tapestry worth repeating.[3] Ultimately, as such men saw, complete translation is impossible. On the other hand, by the accident of our placement in time, we may add to this insight the fact that translation during the English Renaissance was of the greatest importance, aesthetically, intellectually, linguistically, and even politically.

England's early native fiction was unpromising. During the reigns of Henry VIII, Edward, and Mary it consisted mainly of a few jestbooks and romances.[4] In fact, it showed scarcely any indications of developing until the latter part of Elizabeth's reign, and even then, as Ernest Baker has observed, writers had only "the vaguest and most confused apprehension of the problem to be solved; whether the main object was the story or the moral, the incidents or the picture of life." There was room for good translations, and Baker goes on to indicate the "value of the tutelage and discipline afforded by translation from experienced foreigners."[5] Put most simply, translations prompted nearly all the literary fashions of the time, and occasionally even furnished the means of turning foreign works into masterpieces of English art.

It is customary for literary historians to say that Italy poured a great amount of fiction into the stream of English consciousness, and that France functioned both as a tributary and as a reservoir for other countries; and it is widely held that Spain made a contribution which was varied and rich.[6] Our concern here, however, is that the extent of the Spanish offering has never been measured. There have been important studies of individual translators and translations, even of the picaresque genre as a whole, but there has not yet been a synthesis to clarify the over-all Spanish contribu-

3. Howell, *Epistolae Ho-Elianae,* ed. Joseph Jacobs (London, 1890), p. 329; Digges, tr. *Gerardo the Unfortunate Spaniard* (1622), A2ʳ; Moseley, publisher of the English version of Scudéry's *Artamenes* (1653), I, verso of third leaf after title page; and Waker, tr. *The Refin'd Courtier* (1663), A8ᵛ. Other men used other figures to impugn translation. To Roger Ascham a translation seemed an "euill imped wing" by which the unlearned might attempt a low, uncertain flight; or it was "a heuie stompe leg of wood" (*The Scholemaster* [1570], p. 51ᵛ).

4. For a listing see Sterg O'Dell, *A Chronological List of Prose Fiction in English Printed in England and Other Countries 1475–1640* (Cambridge, Mass., 1954).

5. *The History of the English Novel* (London, 1929), II, 14–15. Baker later obscures his stand, however, by stating that the "practical effect" of the translations was small (II, 55–56).

6. The most indispensable work on the subject is Fernand Baldensperger and Werner P. Friederich, *Bibliography of Comparative Literature* (Chapel Hill, N. C., 1950). Annual supplements appear in *Yearbook of Comparative and General Literature.*

tion.[7] It has never been indicated, for instance, that between 1543 (the date of the first English printing of a Spanish narrative) and 1657 (the date when the last of the great picaresque books was turned into English) there were over a hundred English titles, editions, and issues of translated Spanish fiction. Averaging roughly one per year, these certainly constitute a respectable and important record.[8]

This study, therefore, attempts to suggest the nature and extent of the Spanish fiction—especially the non-chivalric fiction—that was imported for Renaissance English readers.[9] It begins with a rapid glance at the knowledge of Spanish in England, and then considers briefly the aims and problems of translators, but its chief subject is the works themselves. More or less chrono-

7. I refer to such helpful but intentionally limited sources as T. P. Harrison, "Bartholomew Yong, Translator," *MLR,* XXI (1926), 129–139; Edwin B. Knowles, "Cervantes y la literatura inglesa," *Realidad,* II (1947), 268–297; and P. E. Russell, "A Stuart Hispanist: James Mabbe," *BHS,* XXX (1953), 75–84. Broader in scope but rare are articles such as these: Rudolph Schevill, "On the Influence of Spanish Literature upon English in the Early 17th Century," *Romanische Forschungen,* XX (1907), 604–634; J. Moreno-Lacalle, "Influencias españolas en la literatura inglesa," *Bulletin of the New England Modern Language Association,* XII (1922), 10–18; Salvador de Madariaga, "Paralelos anglo-españoles," *Ensayos anglo-españoles* (Madrid, 1922), pp. 143–190; Arturo Farinelli, "España y su literatura en el extranjero," *Ensayos y discursos de crítica literaria hispano-europea* (Rome, 1925), I, 45–108; John W. Barker, "Influencia de la literatura española en la literatura inglesa," *Universidad,* XXIII (1946), 594–610; and P. E. Russell, "English Seventeenth-Century Interpretations of Spanish Literature," *Atlante,* I (1953), 65–77. Among longer works one might cite Frank W. Chandler, *Romances of Roguery* (New York, 1899); John Garrett Underhill, *Spanish Literature in the England of the Tudors* (New York, 1899); Martin Hume, *Spanish Influence on English Literature* (London, 1905)—to be used with caution, as is the same author's "Some Spanish Influences in Elizabethan Literature," *Transactions of the Royal Society of Literature,* Ser. 2, XXIX (1909), 1–34; James Fitzmaurice-Kelly, *The Relations Between Spanish and English Literature* (Liverpool, 1910); E. G. Mathews, "Studies in Spanish-English Cultural and Literary Relations, 1598–1700," unpublished Ph.D. dissertation (Harvard, 1938); Remigio Ugo Pane, *English Translations from the Spanish: 1484–1943* (New Brunswick, N. J., 1944)—which should be supplemented, e.g., with Mathews' review, "English Translations from Spanish: A Review and a Contribution," *JEGP,* XLIV (1945), 387–424; Antonio Pastor, "Breve historia del hispanismo inglés," *Arbor,* IX (Madrid, 1948), 549–566; and Gustav Ungerer, *Anglo-Spanish Relations in Tudor Literature* (Berne, 1956).

8. For a complete listing see *Appendixes B* and *C.*

9. The chivalric romances played a significant role in the Anglo-Spanish relationship, but since they constitute a formidable topic in themselves and are treated elsewhere, I have elected to discuss them quite briefly (Ch. IV, pp. 53–57, and *Appendix C.*)

logically it presents the various genres leading up to *Don Quixote,* and after that historic point, where narratives begin to grow more numerous, it groups them as Byzantine romances, *novelas,* and satiric-realistic fiction. After a few preliminary observations, in other words, it surveys both the translations and the originals of the non-chivalric Spanish fiction that was produced during the Anglo-Spanish Renaissance.

Chapter II

Now Steps Castile Language In

The Spanish Language in England

English Interest in Spain

In 1066 one Walter Giffard returned from a pilgrimage to Santiago de Compostela, bringing a gift horse from Alfonso of Galicia to William of Normandy; and on this steed sent from Spain, William rode to victory over Harold at Hastings.[1] In later times Chaucer included in his masterwork an English knight who had fought in Spain, an English seaman who knew the ports of Spain, and an English businesswoman who had made a pilgrimage to Spain. Though we sometimes forget the fact, Chaucer's patron, John of Gaunt, even claimed to be King of Castile. In short, drawn by diplomacy, war, commerce, and religion, to say nothing of Spain's universities, the English for many years had various kinds of contact with Spain.[2] Perhaps surprisingly, therefore, it was not until the Renaissance that the Anglo-Spanish relationship became noteworthy in linguistic or literary ways.

Coming to the English throne in 1485, Henry VII proved to be an ambitious and businesslike king who kept his eye on the main chance. Because he hoped to establish his family among the powerful ruling houses of Europe, he formulated the plan of marrying his oldest son, Prince Arthur, to the daughter of Ferdinand and Isabella. It was natural that he should look to Spain; the Spanish monarchs were likely to be interested in the help that he could offer in a project they hoped to carry out in France. At any rate, the royal pair did accept Henry's offer, and in 1489 he affixed his name to the Treaty of Medina

---

1. Noted by James Fitzmaurice-Kelly, "Some Correlations of Spanish Literature," *RH,* XV (1906), 59. In William's forces, by the way, although they owed him no allegiance, there were a number of Spanish lords.

2. A helpful analysis of this contact is given by John W. Barker, "Influencia de la literatura española en la literatura inglesa," *Universidad,* XXIII (1946), 594–610.

del Campo, agreeing to invade northern France in exchange for a marriage. In 1503, however, after the premature death of Prince Arthur left the Spanish princess, Catherine, a widow, another treaty had to be made. This one arranged for Catherine's marriage to Arthur's twelve-year-old brother Henry, and in due time, as the queen of Henry VIII, Catherine became an important figure in the cultural relations between her native and adopted lands.

At the time of Henry's marriage to Catherine and for some time after he set her aside, such Spanish influence as there was continued to be courtly in the main. The translations of the period are indicative: Antonio de Guevara's moralistic *Golden Boke* (1535) is a Spanish mirror for magistrates; Diego de San Pedro's *Castell of Love* (*ca.* 1548) is a handbook for rhetorically-inclined, patrician lovers; and the English version of Fernando de Rojas' *Celestina* (*ca.* 1530) has an interpolated aside in which a character reveals the quality of his audience by asking them pointedly, "How sey ye my lordis se ye not this smoke/ In my maisters eyes y^t they do cast"?[3]

As the well-known story goes, Henry eventually began to think about a divorce from his Spanish queen, partly because she had produced no living heir but Mary, partly because she always remained so attached to everything Spanish, and partly because he had fallen in love with one of her attendants, Anne Boleyn. The outcome is known to every schoolchild. Henry had his way, and England's diplomatic relations with Spain became unimportant, remaining thus until the reign of Catherine's daughter.

When Mary came to the throne in 1553, she was already in the habit of asking advice from Spanish ambassadors, and when Prince Philip of Spain landed at Southampton in 1554, Spain certainly may be said to have resumed her significance to Englishmen. Yet the marriage of Philip and Mary proved barren, both in literary and other ways. Not only were most of the English undazzled by the brilliance of the Spaniards, in fact fearful of their peaceful invasion, but knifings occurred in the royal palace itself.[4] Outside the palace

---

3. *A New Cõmodye* . . . , also called *The Interlude of Calisto and Melebea*, Malone Society Reprints (London, 1908), ll. 469–470.

4. In the *Calendar of Letters, Despatches and State Papers Relating to the Negotiations between England and Spain,* XIII, ed. Royall Tyler (London, 1954), 60–61, we may read the sentiments of a Spanish gentleman writing on October 2, 1554: "The English hate us Spaniards, which comes out in violent quarrels between them and us, and not a day passes without some knife-work in the palace between the two nations. There have already been some deaths, and last week three Englishmen and a Spaniard were hanged on account of a broil."

and against the advice of the canny Spaniards, who saw that it would weaken their position, Mary began to pile faggots for those of her countrymen who refused to accept the Spanish religion.

When Mary died (1558) and Elizabeth ascended to the throne, the new queen found that her widower brother-in-law was suing for her hand, too. Although Elizabeth's acceptance of Philip would have relieved tension in Europe in some respects, Philip had become the lay leader of the Counter Reformation and was scarcely the man to smooth away wrinkles from the troubled brows of the English. Hatred of Spaniards, dating back to the bloody reign of Mary, had by this time become too strong. When at last Elizabeth made public her decision to refuse Philip, the pope responded by excommunicating her and declaring her deposed. Then, together with Philip, he plotted to put Mary of Scotland on the English throne. Though neither Philip nor Elizabeth was ready for open war, the Spanish embassy in London seethed with plans. Philip did some harassing with his negotiations in Scotland and his expedition in 1580 "to conquer Ireland to the Popes vse," but it was not until 1586 that he actually began to prepare his famous fleet—"the greatest Nauy that euer swam vpon the Seas"[5]—for an attack on England herself. Bolstered with pious hope the expedition sailed in 1588, and such ships as the English *Bear, Bull, Revenge,* and *Dauntless* demolished such Spanish vessels as *Nuestra Señora, La Trinidad, La Concepción,* and *Santa María.* Neither England nor Spain was ever quite the same afterward.

During the closing decades of the sixteenth century, and particularly after English pride had been stirred by the defeat of the Armada, there was a continuing interest in Spain and a substantial increase in the number of books translated from Spanish. Among these, significantly, there was an increase in the percentage of works rendered directly from their originals, without the aid of intermediate versions.[6] Moreover, translations from Spanish were beginning to be read in the lower levels of society. Besides the courtly *Diana,* and besides *Lazarillo de Tormes* and the Spanish romances of chivalry, which could be enjoyed by both velvet and cloth breeches, Englishmen for the first time could buy such practical translations as *The Arte of Navigation* (1581)

5. Francis Bacon, *Considerations Touching a Warre with Spaine* (1629), pp. 23, 26.
6. John Garrett Underhill, *Spanish Literature in the England of the Tudors* (New York, 1899), p. 346. See also Underhill's bibliography of translations, pp. 375–408.

from Pedro de Medina, and *The Serjeant Major* (1590) from Francisco de Valdés. It was perfectly natural that Gabriel Harvey should jot in his copy of *The Spanish Grammer* (1590), "Praecipue Linguae hodiernarum Negotiationum Anglicarum; *Francica,* et *Hispanica.*" In short, during Elizabeth's time as in Catherine's, England's concern with Spain was both courtly and literary, though it was also practical, political, commercial, and religious.

After James I succeeded Elizabeth in 1603, one of his first moves was to make peace with Spain. Tolerant in matters of religion, James had respect for Spain—perhaps too much respect—and in the spring of 1605 appointed the Earl of Nottingham, who had commanded the English against the Armada, to sail with five hundred Englishmen on a mission of good will. In 1613, with the arrival in England of Gondomar, Spain's new ambassador, James became even more friendly to the southern power. Spain, for her part, was willing to accept the overtures of England because she wanted to lure the English away from the German Protestant Alliance and because, as much as ever, the northerners were a nation to be won back to the Roman church. In fact, Gondomar encouraged the idea that James's son Henry might be married to the daughter of Philip III. Henry himself stoutly refused to think of such a match, declaring that "two religions shall not lie in my bed,"[7] but James, heartened by the ardor of his other son, Charles, and by Buckingham, became more and more agreeable to the idea of another Spanish marriage. His enthusiasm wavered but gradually increased until the time it occurred to him that Spain not only would want the children of such a marriage to be Catholics, but that she also would insist on a suspension of the English penal laws against Catholics. James was beginning to see the true state of affairs in 1620, when he learned that a Spanish army had marched into the Palatinate of his son-in-law, Frederick V of Bohemia. The Spanish had duped him.

Although the English were ripe for a war against their old enemy, James had trouble raising funds, and, while he was still undecided, the resourceful Gondomar came at him again, trying to make him believe that even yet the Spanish troops would be evacuated from the Palatinate for the sake of a marriage alliance. Such was the state of affairs in 1623 when young Prince Charles and Buckingham conceived the idea of slipping out of England in false beards so as to woo the Spanish princess in person. From the time he arrived, however, the romantically inclined young prince was given a diet that was rich in theology and lacking in wooing. When it became quite clear

7. Noted by M. A. Gibb, *Buckingham* (London, 1935), p. 64.

even to him and Buckingham that a marriage was unlikely unless he became Catholic, and that even then the Spanish troops would remain in the Palatinate, he and Buckingham returned to England, angered and eager for war. The English were wild with delight to see their prince still a bachelor, and the French ambassador could no longer complain that "the whole Court is Spanish."[8]

During these decisive years toward the close of James's reign there was not only an increased interest in the study of Spanish, as we shall see, but an increased effort on the part of English translators. The booksellers' shelves were fairly burgeoning with a variety of Spanish works, including the first translations of the complete *Don Quixote, Persiles and Sigismunda, The Pilgrime of Casteele, The Rogue, Gerardo,* and *The Pursuit of the Historie of Lazarillo de Tormez.* In fact, the evidence tempts one to call this not only a period of intense political interest in Spain, but, literarily speaking, the richest period in the entire Anglo-Spanish relationship.

For all that, when James died in 1625, the great if short-lived popularity of his successor stemmed partly from the fact that he was known to be anti-Spanish. In the year of his coronation, under Buckingham's incompetent direction, Charles sent an expedition of eighty ships to Cadiz, the very port where Drake had pounced on the Armada before it sailed almost forty years before. But Buckingham was no Francis Drake, and the project was a failure.

When an empty purse and troubles at home forced Charles into inaction abroad, he at least succeeded in making a temporary peace with Spain. In 1655 there was official, grumbling reference to "a prevalent Spanish Faction, always in the Council of the late King and his Father," both of whom, it was felt, were "too much addicted to the Spaniards";[9] and Cromwell himself, who went to war with Spain in 1654, warned in 1656 that, even then, "Spanish interest at home is a great piece of your danger."[10] Finally, in 1657, the termi-

---

8. John Nichols, *The Progresses . . . of King James the First* (London, 1828), I, 473. Earlier it had also been reported that the queen herself was *"meerly* Spanish" (Edmund Sawyer, ed., *Memorials of Affairs of State in the Reigns of Q. Elizabeth and K. James I* [London, 1725], II, 155). When Prince Charles went on his courting expedition to Madrid, "so large a troop of the flower of the young nobility and gentry hastened to offer their attendance to the heir apparent and the favorite [Buckingham], that within a few days the hotel of the earl of Bristol assumed the appearance of an English court" (Lucy Aikin, *Memoirs of the Court of King James the First* [London, 1823], II, 353).

9. *A Declaration Against Spain,* ed. Thomas Ollive Mabbott and J. Milton French, in *The Works of John Milton* (New York, 1937), XIII, 513, 515.

10. Quoted by Godfrey Davies, *The Early Stuarts* (Oxford, 1945), p. 203.

nal date of the present study, Admiral Robert Blake destroyed the Spanish fleet.

English Interest in Spanish

A ddiction" to Spaniards obviously cannot be equated with a knowledge of Spanish, nor can a brief summary of major political encounters do more than suggest the countless minor, personal contacts of people whose lot it was to be involved but not remembered. Yet all these subjects are intertwined. Englishmen never learned Spanish as widely as they did French or, of course, Latin, but when Henry VIII married Catherine of Aragon, and later, when their son-in-law Prince Philip brought three thousand grandees to England in his train, it behooved at least some Englishmen to learn the tongue.[11]

The earliest comment that I recall having seen on the language itself was penned by Andrew Borde in a book dedicated to Princess Mary on May 3, 1542. Borde had made a Grand Tour which included "Catalony," "Andalosye," and "Castell," and when he returned he wrote one of the first guidebooks to Europe. In it he observes that English "is a base speche to other noble speches, as Italion Castylion and Frenche. . . ."[12] He even introduces a brief list of Spanish words and expressions, saying that for those who would "learne to speake some castilion[,] englishe and castilion doth folowe." And at this point he gives the earliest printed Spanish lesson that I have encountered: "vna dos tros quarter sinco sisse saeto ocho nowe diece. . . ."[13]

Although some early Tudor Englishmen were compelled to learn Spanish for diplomatic and commercial reasons, relatively little interest seems to have attached to the language until the closing years of the sixteenth century. Then, in 1591, we find James Lea addressing some informative verses to fellow "practitioners in the Spanish," and, in the process, giving several hints

---

11. Among those who learned the tongue was a certain John Bradford, who was placed in the service of one of Philip's advisers. Bradford writes: "My frendes putte me to learne their [the Spaniards'] language and compelled me to liue amongest them, because I myghte knowe perfectlye, whether their nature were so vyle, as men reported, or not. And I assure your lord shipes, and all my frendes, that the vileste reporte, that euer I heard Englishmen speake, by the worste of all Spaniardes, is nothinge to the vilenes which remaineth amongest the best of that nacion, except the kĩgs maiestie" (*The Copye of a Letter . . . Declaring the Nature of Spaniardes* [*ca.* 1555], Aviii⁵—Biʳ).

See *Appendix A* for a fuller note on those who learned Spanish.

12. *The Fyrst Boke of the Introduction of Knowledge* (1548?) Biiʳ.

13. *Fyrst Boke,* Liiʳ.

concerning Spanish studies in those years just after the defeat of the first Armada, when the exploits of Antonio Pérez, the threat of a second armada, and the battle of the *Revenge* continued to draw English eyes toward Spain. Lea writes:

> Though Spanish speech lay long aside within our Brittish Ile,
> (Our Courtiers liking nought saue French, or *Tuscane* stately stile)
> Yet now at length, (I know not how) steps *Castile* language in,
> And craues for credit with the first, though latest she begin:
> Who lists not yeeld to neither both, of those rehearst before,
> But iumpe as stately and as sweete, or rather stately more:
> As full of prety prouerbs, and most dainty priuie quips,
> Of graue aduices, bitter taunts, and passing gawling nips.
> Though learned pens in Italy and France do florish more,
> And in our happy Britaine, where are learned men such store:
> Yet Spanish speech lists giue no ground. . . .[14]

Lea's doggerel is partly friendly drumming for Richard Perceval, in whose *Bibliotheca hispanica* it appears,[15] but it nevertheless serves to record the comparatively late rise of the "Castile language" in England, and to acknowledge certain virtues of the tongue. Also of interest is Lea's opinion that while Spanish is a worthy language, the "learned pens" of Spain do not really rank with those of Italy, France, or Britain.

Additional acclaim for Spanish was offered in the same year by William Stepney. In an "Epistle to the Reader" written for his *Spanish Schoole-Master,* Stepney says, "I doubt not but that in future age the Spanish tongue will be as well esteemed as the French or the Italian tongues, and in my simple judgement, it is farre more necessary for our countrey-men then the Italian tongue is. . . ."[16] In a word, Spanish was important by the close of the sixteenth century.

In the seventeenth century, Englishmen as a whole were still a long way from being "Hispaniliz'd," but it was simply common sense that some should try to know the language of their enemy—or their erstwhile friend. For a time during the reign of James the number of Spanish textbooks increased rather considerably, as we shall see; yet in the long run Spanish was bound to

---

14. *Bibliotheca hispanica*, A4^r.

15. Perceval himself, incidentally, refers to Spanish as *"the toonge with which by reason of the troublesome times, thou arte like to haue most acquaintance . . ."* (A3^r).

16. Quoted by Caroline B. Bourland, *"The Spanish Schoole-Master* and the Polyglot Derivatives of Noel de Berlaimont's *Vocabulare," RH,* Pt. I of LXXXI (1933), 288.

give most of the "ground" it had gained to French. In 1606 Thomas Palmer believed that for English travelers "the Latine, the French, and the Spanish tongues are most necessary, and like to hold."[17] But in 1656 Francis Osborne remarked in his *Advice to a Son* that *"Languages* are the richest lading of a Traveller; among which *French* is most usefull; *Italian* and *Spanish* not being so fruitfull in Learning (except for the Mathematicks and Romances) Their other Bookes being gelt by the Fathers of the Inquisition."[18]

A Sketch of Some Means of Learning Spanish

Then as now, Spanish was learned in various ways. For instance, a student could engage in outside study at the universities. On the one hand, official academic approval came late: the earliest known professor of Spanish in England was Antonio Alcalá Galiano, who was not elected to his post at the University of London until 1828.[19] On the other hand, extra-statutory instruction in Spanish was available at the universities at a much earlier date. As Mark Curtis points out,

Sometimes the colleges, individually or collectively, provided funds to pay lecturers in special fields. Certain tutors and scholars formed informal groups to pursue their avocations in a more or less systematic manner. Frequently a group of students might hire a man who could give them the instruction they wanted even though he might not be a member of the university. On occasion, some

17. *An Essay of the Meanes How to Make Our Travailes into Forraine Countries, the More Profitable and Honourable,* p. 59.

18. (Oxford), pp. 75–76.

19. E. Allison Peers, "The First English Professor of Spanish: Antonio Alcalá Galiano," in *Estudios hispánicos: Homenaje a Archer M. Huntington* (Wellesley, Mass., 1952), pp. 491–497. Not until 1858 was a "teachership" in Spanish established at Oxford (*Historical Register of the University of Oxford . . . to . . . 1900* [Oxford, 1900], p. 89).

The reader may wonder about language study in the schools. After completing a thorough study, Foster Watson concluded: "The teaching of French, Italian, Spanish, was by individual private teachers, and I know of no instance in which these [languages] were taught in schools in the period of which I am speaking" ("The Curriculum and Text-Books of English Schools in the First Half of the Seventeenth Century," *Transactions of the Bibliographical Society,* VI [London, 1903], 175). Ungerer, however (pp. 158–159), indicates that William Stepney (whose *Spanish Schoole-Master* is cited just above) taught Spanish at St. Paul's School; and the *Janua linguarum* promises good linguistic results, both in Spanish and other languages, for those who wish to *"repaire the defect of not going to publicke Schooles"* (1617), A5ᵛ. Suggestions for schools which would have included Spanish in their curricula were formulated by Sir Francis Kynaston, Sir Balthazar Gerbier, and Sir Humphrey Gilbert, but these seem to have come to nothing.

student with a strong bent to a particular field voluntarily lectured to men with similar but more casual or less developed interests. By these means the university men fostered expansion of the education available to scholars, particularly to young gentlemen.[20]

Among the teachers who came to Oxford was the Sevillian Antonio de Corro.[21] At first the pastor of the Spanish Protestant flock in London, Corro later lectured on divinity at Oxford (1578–1586), lived as a student in Christ Church, Oxford (1579), and held the post of censor theologian at the latter (1581–1585), finally receiving the prebend of Harleston in St. Paul's, London (1586). That Corro had specifically linguistic interests is suggested most clearly by his *Reglas gramaticales* (Oxford, 1586), which in 1590 was translated into English by Gabriel Harvey's Flemish friend John Thorius, a student at Christ Church. Another teacher of Spanish at Oxford was Pierre Bense. A native Parisian, Bense "went by virtue of Letters commendatory to *Oxon,* where being kindly received and entertained, [he] became a Sojourner there, was entred into the public Library, and taught for several Years the *French, Italian,* and *Spanish* Tongues. . . ."[22] And at Magdalen the author of *An Entrance to the Spanish Tongue* (1611), John Sanford, tutored students in the same three languages, in addition to serving as chaplain of the college. It is not astonishing, then, to learn that James Mabbe, the greatest translator of Spanish in the Renaissance, was first a student and later an administrator at Oxford. More specifically, he was of Magdalen, a college which seems to have shown particular Hispanic interest.

Study was also possible at the Inns of Court, where an interest in Spanish may have been heightened by the nearby residence of foreign language teachers, notably John Minsheu. (Minsheu dedicated his *Spanish Grammar* to the students of Gray's Inn and those *"affected to languages there."*)[23] Although the evidence concerning private language schools is rather scarce,[24] the *Constitutions* (1607) of the Bury St. Edmunds Town Council contains a

---

20. *Oxford and Cambridge in Transition, 1558–1642* (Oxford, 1959), p. 130.

21. The general subject is treated by Foster Watson, "Notes and Materials on Religious Refugees in Their Relation to Education in England before . . . 1685," *Huguenot Society Proceedings,* IX (1909–1911), 299–475. See also R. C. Simonini, Jr., "The Genesis of Modern Foreign Language Teaching," *MLJ,* XXXV (1951), 179–186.

22. Anthony à Wood, *Athenae Oxonienses* (London, 1721), I, 613–614.

23. (1599), i2ʳ (leaf following title page).

24. Watson, a major student of the subject, has even concluded that Minsheu's is the "only institution in which we can infer that Spanish was taught" (*The Beginnings of the Teaching of Modern Subjects in England* [London, 1909], p. 482).

provision for the registration of all persons "that do keep any school for the teaching of youth to write, read, or understand the English, Latin, French, Italian and Spanish Tongues. . . ."[25] Buck, in *The Third Universitie of England* (1619), refers unmistakably to Spanish teachers in London.[26] The immigrant Juan de Luna, composer of the better sequel to *Lazarillo de Tormes,* alludes to *"MAny of my schollers"* and suggests with no great subtlety that his readers should learn from one who teaches his native tongue.[27] And Thomas Scott (whose anti-Spanish bias doubtless makes him exaggerate) depicts Gondomar, the Spanish ambassador, as reporting thus of his English experiences: "My Lords, you would hardly haue forborne laughter, to haue heard how I haue beene enquired after for Maisters for the Spanish tongue, (that I may say nothing of so many bills set vp in euery corner of the City by Professors). . . ."[28]

As for private tutors, it is tempting to include Thomas Shelton, the translator of *Don Quixote,* who may have taught the language to Lord Walden, the dedicatee of his famous book. In a letter still extant, at any rate, Shelton does express the hope of supporting himself in Paris by teaching Spanish to English tourists.[29] Perhaps James Mabbe may also be included. P. E. Russell believes that Mabbe served as tutor to young Lewis Dyves when the boy's stepfather, John Digby, Earl of Bristol, was sent to Spain as England's ambassador.[30] One is on firmer ground, however, in referring to the tutor engaged by Bishop John Williams. In his *Scrinia reserata* (1693), John Hacket reports that

When the eyes of all our Kingdom were set upon the Infanta of *Spain,* he took into his House . . . a Spaniard by Birth, and a Scholar, *John Taxeda* [*sic*], by whose Conversation he grew expert in the Spanish Grammar, in the Castilian

25. Quoted by Kathleen Lambley, *The Teaching and Cultivation of the French Language in England During Tudor and Stuart Times* (Manchester, 1920), pp. 170–171.

26. Noted by Lambley, p. 169.

27. *A Short and Compendious Art for to Learne . . . the Spanish Tongue* (1623), A5ʳ. Lambley also notes that in Antwerp one Gabriel Meurier had many English students whom he instructed in French, Flemish, and Italian, as well as Spanish (pp. 244–245).

28. *The Second Part of Vox Populi* (1620), p. 10.

29. J. George, "Thomas Shelton, Translator, in 1612–14," *BHS,* XXXV (1958), 161–162.

30. "A Stuart Hispanist: James Mabbe," *BHS,* XXX (1953), 77. It was this Digby who translated two comedies by Calderón and based his own *Elvira* on a third.

Pronunciation, and in the Knowledge of those Authors that in Ten Weeks he could not only understand the most difficult Writers of that Nation, but was able to Entreet with the Ambassadors without an Interpreter.[31]

And James Howell, the Welsh *Johannes fac totum,* turns up at one period as tutor of Spanish to the Marchioness of Winchester.[32]

Of course the boldest method of learning Spanish was by traveling, for Spain was long regarded not only as a place of danger and discomfort, but also as a sink of Romish iniquity. Even in the eighteenth century Dr. Johnson declared that there was "no country . . . less known to the rest of Europe. . . ."[33] On the other hand, ever since Andrew Borde (the author of that early guidebook) had made much ado about noting his impressions of the peninsula, an intermittent trickle of Englishmen had continued to filter down beyond the Pyrenees. "For hard sure it is to know England," wrote Philip Sidney to his brother, "without you know it by comparing it with some other country. . . . France is above all other most needful for us to mark . . . ; next is Spain and the Low Countries. . . ."[34] Despite threats and warnings and considerable inconvenience, men like Barnabe Googe and Lewis Lewkenor made their way into Spain.[35] Bartholomew Yong modestly reports that Edward Paston, author of the fragmentary but "worthiest to be embraced"

31. Cited by William M. Jones, "Foreign Teachers in Sixteenth Century England," *Historian,* XXI (1959), 173.

32. Antonio Pastor guesses that Howell spoke Spanish better than any other Englishman of the seventeenth century ("Breve historia del hispanismo inglés," *Arbor,* IX [Madrid, 1948], 555), although we learn elsewhere that he was afflicted with a speech impediment (William Harvey Vann, *Notes on the Writings of James Howell* [Waco, Texas, 1924], p. 11). See also E. H. Mensel, "James Howell as a Practical Linguist," *JEGP,* XXV (1926), 531–539.

33. Boswell's *Life of Samuel Johnson* (London, 1791), I, 198.

34. *The Correspondence of Philip Sidney and Hubert Languet,* ed. William A. Bradley (Boston, 1912), pp. 214, 216.

35. Among interesting seventeenth-century sources on this topic are James Cleland, *The Institution of a Young Noble Man* (1607); John Sanford, a letter of 1610 reprinted in Godfrey Goodman, *The Court of King James the First,* ed. John S. Brewer (London, 1839), II, 132–135; Henry Peacham, *The Compleat Gentleman* (1622); *The Mirrour of Mindes, or, [John] Barclay's Icon Animorum* (1631), tr. Thomas May; William Lithgow, *The Totall Discourse* (1632); and James Howell, *Instructions for Forreine Travell* (1642) and *Epistolae Ho-Elianae,* collected in 1650 and cited below. Valuable modern sources include E. S. Bates, *Touring in 1600* (Boston, 1911); Clare Howard, *English Travellers of the Renaissance* (London, 1914); and John Walter Stoye, *English Travellers Abroad, 1604–1667* (London, 1952).

English *Diana,* was able to translate as a result of "his trauell in that Countrey, and great knowledge in that language. . . ."[36] Robert Ashley, who translated his *Almansor* from Miguel de Luna, traveled to Madrid, Segovia, and
Valladolid, not only satisfying his appetite for the exotic, but polishing his
Spanish as well.[37] And in the *Memoirs* of Ann Fanshawe we learn that that
lady's husband (who translated from both Spanish and Portuguese) "travelled
to Madrid in Spain, there to learn that language." She adds: "At the same time
for that purpose [italics mine] went the late Earl of Carnarvon and my Lord
of Bedford, and Lord John Berkeley, and several other gentlemen."[38] James
Howell, in fact, in his *Instructions for Forreine Travell,* goes so far as to
say that the first thing a youth arriving in Madrid must fall to is language,
even though "by the helpe of his *Governour* he hath made an introduction
into the *Spanish* tongue before hee left *France*. . . ."[39] Spain was never so
popular a tourist attraction as France or Italy, and yet some of the best-
known translators we shall consider—Berners, Yong, Shelton, Digges, and
Mabbe—all managed to tour or even live there for a while.

Grammars and Dictionaries

One of the most important methods of learning Spanish—and the last to
be mentioned here—is the one which, by its nature, we know most
about. According to his own testimony, Lord Herbert of Cherbury "did, without any master or teacher, attain the knowledge of the French, Italian, and
Spanish languages, by the help of some books in Latin or English translated
into those idioms, and the dictionaries of those several languages. . . ."[40]

---

36. *Diana* (1598), a3ᵛ.
37. Virgil B. Heltzel, "Robert Ashley: Elizabethan Man of Letters," *HLQ,* X
(1946–1947), 354. Heltzel offers additional remarks on Ashley in his edition of
Ashley's *Of Honour* (San Marino, Calif., 1947).
38. *The Memoirs of Ann Lady Fanshawe,* ed. Herbert Charles Fanshawe (London, 1907), p. 28.
39. Edward Arber, ed. (Westminster, 1903), p. 39.
40. *Autobiography,* ed. Sidney Lee (London, 1906), p. 23. Despite conservative
opposition, translations such as Herbert mentions were occasionally used as a means
of learning. Long before Herbert's time, little Edward VI was jotting notes which
show that he often improved his Spanish by reading Spanish versions of the Latin
and Greek books he was studying (T. W. Baldwin, *William Shakspere's Small
Latine & Lesse Greeke* [Urbana, Ill., 1944], I, 218). One of the best foreign lexical
aids after 1611 was Sebastián de Covarrubias y Horozco's *Tesoro de la lengua española.*

Though the "black lord" was sometimes extravagant in his claims, it is certain that grammars and dictionaries did play a major part in helping Englishmen learn Spanish. One may readily count more than twenty texts which could have been useful to translators writing between about 1535 and 1662.[41] Using the same dates as limits and including separate editions as well as titles, one finds the figure swollen considerably. And, of course, if one adds to these the books which made it possible to learn or polish one's Spanish through the convenient intermediaries of French or Latin, the number of titles is greatly multiplied.[42]

It is customary and correct to point to the cluster of linguistic works appearing in the 1590's. These include the books by Corro, Stepney, Perceval, and Minsheu which we have already mentioned. Of these the most famous is Minsheu's multiplagiarism, which was avowedly based on Perceval but actually derived from a variety of sources. It was published in three sections, each with its own title page: *A Spanish Grammar, A Dictionarie in Spanish and English,* and *Pleasant and Delightfull Dialogues in Spanish* (1599). In the grammar section, interestingly enough, one finds numerous quotations from recent editions of Spanish masterpieces, including excerpts from some of the fiction we shall soon be considering—the *Celestina, Lazarillo,* and *Diana.* For early translators, such language aids as these were invaluable tools;

41. The earliest such work I have recorded is the *Sex linguarum dictionarius* (Augsburg, *ca.* 1535), which, admittedly, was not on every English bookshelf.

42. Among the earlier studies which contain information on the Spanish teaching aids available to Renaissance Englishmen are William Knapp, *A Concise Bibliography of Spanish Grammars and Dictionaries from the Earliest Period to the Definitive Edition of the Academy's Dictionary, 1490–1780* (Boston, 1884), and Leo Wiener, "Spanish Studies in England, in the Sixteenth and Seventeenth Centuries," *Modern Quarterly of Language and Literature,* II (1899), 3–10. More recent are Luís Cardim, *Gramaticas anglo-castelhanas e castelhano-anglicas* (Coimbra, 1931); Louis B. Wright, "Language Helps for the Elizabethan Tradesman," *JEGP,* XXX (1931), 335–347; Dámaso Alonso, "Una distinción temprana de 'B' y 'D' fricativas," *RFE,* XVIII (1931), 15–23; DeWitt Talmage Starnes, "Bilingual Dictionaries of Shakespeare's Day," *PMLA,* LII (1937), 1005–1018; William F. J. De Jongh, *Western Language Manuals of the Renaissance* (Albuquerque, N. M., 1949); Cyril Jones, "El estudio del español en Inglaterra," *La Torre* (Puerto Rico), Año 2, Núm. 7 (1954), 163–174; and Otto Funke, "Spanische Sprachbücher im elisabethanischen England," *Studies in English Language and Literature Presented to Professor Dr. Karl Brunner,* ed. Siegfried Korninger (Vienna, 1957), i.e., *Wiener Beiträge zur englischen Philologie,* LXV, 43–57. Most inclusive of the recent works I have seen is Amado Alonso's *De la pronunciación medieval a la moderna en español* (Madrid, 1955). Particularly useful is Marcel Gauthier's reprinting of Stepney, Minsheu, and Luna in "Diálogos de antaño," *RH,* XLV (1919), 34–238.

for us, they are impressive evidence of England's interest in Spanish during the final decade of the sixteenth century.

The early years of the next century saw *The Key of the Spanish Tongue* (1605), "begotten in *Spaine,* and brought foorth in great *Brittaine"* by one Lewis Owen.[43] Some six years afterward the Reverend John Sanford, who was sent to Madrid as chaplain for the English embassy, published his *Entrance to the Spanish Tongue,* noted earlier. Third, and far more impressive than either of these books, was the popular and now frequently overlooked *Janua linguarum.* Apparently composed originally in Spanish and Latin by William Bathe, sometime rector of the Irish college at Salamanca, this work later became—with the addition of English—a text specifically adapted for teaching Spanish to Englishmen.[44] Still other texts were produced by the prolific Minsheu. In 1617 Minsheu published not only his imposing lexicon in twelve languages, *The Guide into Tongues,* but also his *Vocabularium Hispanico-Latinum et Anglicum . . . A Most Copious Spanish Dictionarie, with Latine and English.*

In the productive ten years between 1617 and 1626 there were no less than fifteen editions of language aids by Minsheu, Bathe, Stepney, Oudin, and Luna. Certainly these seem sufficient to indicate the considerable importance of Spanish study during that crucial period when James was dickering for the Spanish infanta, Gondomar was dancing a diplomatic galliard, and "Baby Charles" and Buckingham were jaunting down to Madrid in false beards.

As time slipped by, however, and Queen Henrietta Maria turned England's eyes toward France, there were fewer and fewer Spanish language texts until, reaching 1640, we look out over a long, dry gap that stretches almost to the Restoration. At last, in 1659, we find James Howell's *Particular Vocabulary;* in the following year, his *Lexicon tetraglotton;* and in 1662, *A New English Grammar . . . : Also Another Grammar of the Spanish or Castilian Toung.* The latter was dedicated to Charles II's queen, Catherine of Braganza, princess of the royal house of Portugal. Obviously it was too late to be useful to translators of our period, and yet it tempts one to muse over the fact that a century and a half after another Catherine was led to the incestuous sheets of her brother-in-law, this latter-day queen

43. A2ᵛ. Owen was later a British spy.
44. I have used the London edition of 1617, which Jean Barbier dedicated to Prince Charles. It contains a number of comments relevant to language study at the time.

fanned again the fading interest of England in the peninsula, and again drew forth the tributes of men of letters.

After all the necessary qualifications have been made, and all the reservations clarified, there is reason enough to say that Englishmen showed considerable if inconstant interest in the Spanish language during the century and a half which separated their two Spanish-speaking queens. It was only natural that such an interest would be manifested in translations. It was only natural that some Englishmen would be attracted to the storied tapestries of Spain.

Chapter III

Trouchemen of a
Straungers Tongue

*A Glance at Translators
and Translation*

O ne would like to have heard that conversation held in the winter of
1618 in which one Renaissance Hispanophile observed to another
that John Minsheu was a rogue. Unfortunately, however, Drummond of Hawthornden gives us only this single scrap of Ben Jonson's opinion concerning the lexicographer.[1] Not until many years later did Edward
Phillips, another Hispanophile, offer the oblique but apparently contradictory statement that "Mr. *Minshaw* that spent his life and estate in scru-
tinizing into Languages, still remains obnoxious to the misconstructions of
many."[2]

More important to us than Minsheu's roguery, of course, is the familiarity
of his name among translators. They not only knew of him and talked of
him; they made use of his work. Unfortunately again, however, such knowledge as we have of our translators' practices is very limited. By chance we
know that Mabbe and Thomas Stanley used Covarrubias' *Tesoro de la
lengua española* (1611),[3] but for the most part evidence must be sought in
the fiction itself and in random comments scattered in prefaces and dedications. Granting that it would be unfair to present such remarks as representing fully developed theories of art, it may be of value to consider briefly the
expressed purposes of these men. Then we may the more fairly move on to
their works.

1. *Notes of Ben Jonson's Conversations with William Drummond of Hawthornden,* ed. David Laing (London, 1842), p. 4.
2. *The New World of English Words* (1658), A4ʳ.
3. Noted by E. G. Mathews, "Studies in Spanish-English Cultural and Literary
Relations, 1598–1700," unpublished Ph.D. dissertation (Harvard, 1938), p. 93.

Motives for Translating

Beginning with motivation, one might assume at the outset that hope of financial reward inspired many translators.[4] Sometimes, doubtless, it did. In dedicating the second part of Shelton's *Don Quixote* to Buckingham, Edward Blount listed several reasons why writers in general, not only translators, might come forth in print: *"Some, for the meere ambition of Great names; Others, for the desire, or need of Protection; Many, to win Friends, and so fauour, and opinion; but Most, for the more sordid respect, Gaine."*[5] Nevertheless, Thomas Fortescue, writing in 1571, had entreated his readers to pity the plight of those who translated for a living. Rest assured, he said,

that none in any sorte, do better deserue of their countrie, . . . that none swincke, or sweate with like paine, and anguishe, that none in like sorte hassarde, or aduenture their credite, that none desire lesse stipende, or salarie for their trauaile, that none in fine, are worse in this age recompensed.[6]

Specific data on the subject are scarce, but most clues lead to the same conclusion. In a little-known essay called "Of Translation of Authors," written at the end of our period, Richard Flecknoe echoes the sentiments of Fortescue. He refers to translators as men

Whose office though by the abuse of Times, it be none of the most honourable and splendious, it being accounted by Writers but only *Journey-worke*, as copying is by Painters; yet certainly of all men who Print, they are the most to be commended, for making a sincere profession of the Trade. . . .[7]

A prolific professional such as John Davies of Kidwelly might make a financial success of translation, but for the most part, as Dryden later observed, the booksellers were "very parsimonious" in rewarding the translators in their employ.[8] Some booksellers gave no money at all, hoping that

4. Arthur J. Tieje, by the way, in analyzing the purposes expressed by various early writers (not translators) of fiction, lists amusement, instruction, and edification (social, religious, and moral) as being the three most important ones, their lesser aims being to represent life and, rarely, to arouse sympathetic emotion ("The Critical Heritage of Fiction in 1579," *Englische Studien*, XLVII [1913–1914], 415–448).

5. *Don Quixote* (1620), II, A2.

6. "To the Gentle Reader," *The Foreste*, bi[r], translated from a French version of an Italian translation of Pedro Mexía's *Silva de varia lección*.

7. In *Miscellania* (1653), pp. 116–117.

8. *Life of Lucian* in *The Works of John Dryden*, ed. Sir Walter Scott, rev. George Saintsbury (London, 1893), XVIII, 82. In his preface to *Ovid's Epistles*

their "wretched scribblers" would be satisfied merely to receive a certain number of copies which they might peddle. Moreover, whether one sweated for a patron or a bookseller does not seem to have made any great pecuniary difference, at least as far as the average writer was concerned.[9] Hence we are better prepared to accept as convincing the translators' claims to such other motives as improving their knowledge of a foreign tongue, pleasing their friends, enriching the English language, edifying the reader, and even entertaining.

Bartholomew Yong writes in the dedication of his *Diana* that after he had returned to England from Spain some nineteen years before, his remembrance of Spanish had begun to fade. At the suggestion of his friend Edward Bannister, he therefore determined to make Montemayor's shepherds speak English, and by this means regain his proficiency in Spanish.[10] We are also told that Sir Lewis Lewkenor converted Antonio de Torquemada's *Jardín de flores curiosas* "for his exercise in the Spanish tongue."[11] And toward the end of our period Thomas Stanley, who imported two

---

(1680), a4ʳ, Dryden speaks of the *"Talents which are requisite for Translation"* and laments *"that there is so little praise and so small Encouragement for so considerable a part of Learning."*

9. Phoebe Sheavyn, *The Literary Profession in the Elizabethan Age* (Manchester, 1909), pp. 73, 100, and 101; H. B. Lathrop, *Translations from the Classics into English from Caxton to Chapman* (Madison, Wis., 1933), p. 232; and Edwin Haviland Miller, *The Professional Writer in Elizabethan England* (Cambridge, Mass., 1959), pp. 94–136.

The statement that "translators were highly regarded" (Lewis Einstein, *The Italian Renaissance in England* [New York, 1907], p. 355) nonetheless needs qualification rather than suppression. Perhaps it is most true when applied to the sixteenth century. Even then, however, James VI (not yet James I of England) wrote that *"Inuention* is ane of the cheif vertewis in a Poete. . . ."* Hence "it is best that ye inuent your awin subiect your self, and not to compose of sene subiectis. Especially translating any thing out of vther language, quhilk doing, ye not onely essay not your awin ingyne of *Inuention,* bot be the same meanes ye are bound, as to a staik, to follow that buikis phrasis quhilk ye translate" ("Ane Schort Treatise . . . ," in *Elizabethan Critical Essays,* ed. G. Gregory Smith [Oxford, 1904], I, 221). Then again, we should recall that even original writers, aside from popular dramatists, did not fare very well. Milton, writing after the Restoration, got £10 for *Paradise Lost.*

10. *Diana,* a3ʳ. In 1596, while traveling in Italy and Germany, Thomas Wilson translated the same work, but in his case it was "to keepe my English" (Henry Thomas, "Diana de Monte Mayor, Done out of Spanish by Thomas Wilson," *RH,* L [1920], 372).

11. *The Spanish Mandevile of Miracles* (1600), A3ʳ.

novelas by Pérez de Montalván, took care to indicate that he undertook the task "with no other Intention, then as an exercize of both Languages. . . ."[12]

If the comments in dedications and prefaces are to be trusted at all, however—and certainly some of them are mere crafty cogging—translation for self-improvement was less common than translation to please one's patrons and friends.[13] Very early in our period, in or before 1533, San Pedro's *Cárcel de amor* was translated by John Bourchier, Lord Berners, at the request of Lady Elizabeth Carew. Margaret Tiler produced *The First Part of the Mirrour of Princely Deedes and Knighthood* (1578) because, as she puts it, "The earnestnesse of my friends perswaded me that it was conuenient to laie foorth my talent for increase"[14]—which may also mean, of course, that her friends wished to be pleased by her financial gain. And at a later period, Shelton's *Don Quixote* was Englished "through the importunitie of a very deare friend, that was desirous to vnderstand the subiect. . . ."[15]

A third and lesser motive might be called the "patriotic." In 1641, toward the end of our period, we find Edward Messervy dedicating a work by Quevedo to Henry Jermyn, master of the horse to the queen, avowing that he has "clad this Spanish Knight, after this Countrey fashion, at the request of my friends, and for the Publike good. . . ."[16] Translating "for the Publike good" was almost a necessity in the early years (and of course such a comment, like many others in this section, reaches far beyond translations from the Spanish). England was so short of original compositions that publishers long after Caxton were obliged to continue Caxton's practice of printing English versions of foreign works. Fortunately, despite the protests of obscurantists, a growing portion of the public realized that the nation might be improved by a familiarity with books from other lands. But the scarcity of affirmative evidence suggests that patriotic motives were no great spur to translators of Spanish fiction. As one might expect, patriotic

---

12. *Aurora, & The Prince* (1647), A2ʳ.

13. When one was writing for a patron, obviously, pleasing might merge with gain as a motive.

14. *Mirrour of Princely Deedes,* Aiiʳ, from Diego Ortúñez de Calahorra's *Espejo de príncipes y caballeros.*

15. *Don Quixote,* I, ¶2ʳ.

16. *Hell Reformed* (1641), A7ᵛ.

motives were more clearly evinced in translations of more indubitably practical works.[17]

Ancillary to patriotism as a motive was the desire to improve the English language. At the beginning of our period English prose was rough and unstandardized, gangling in structure and weak in vocabulary. J. L. Moore reports that before 1561 most commentators on the vernacular were perceptive enough to complain about it, whereas those writing between 1561 and the end of the century mingled praise with blame, and those in the seventeenth century showed increasing respect.[18] The main criticism seems to have been lack of "copiousness," a dearth of words to express shades of meaning. A possible remedy was the revival of old-fashioned words. Another was indicated by Richard Carew, who declared about 1595 that "wee seeke to make our good of our late Spanish enymye, and feare as little the hurt of his tongue as the dinte of his sworde."[19] Perhaps partly as a consequence of such thinking, the Spanish translators—especially Mabbe—introduced a few Spanish terms in their writing, sometimes for seasoning, doubtless, but apparently sometimes with the hope of naturalizing them. In any case we find words like *picaro, regalos, albricias,* and *alguazil* merged in with the flow of English.

Generally, however, Spanish translators and their friends seem to have been more impressed by the capabilities of English than by any need for improving it. Edward Burton, referring to Mabbe's *Rogue,* says that "The *Spanish,* was too small a Mapp; But this/ Drawes him at large; and shewes him as hee is."[20] Burton is quite extravagant on the subject:

17. Explaining his reasons for turning Corro's Spanish grammar into English, Thorius writes thus: "In so much that I beeing requested by diuers, but especially mooued with loue and affection toward my country men (beeing most ready at all times to vndertake any labour to procure their ease, and imploy my dearest time to do them pleasure) haue in such sort translated & altered this booke, that any English man may vse it to his profite" ("The Epistle to the Reader," *The Spanish Grammer* [1590], leaf following title page).

18. "Tudor-Stuart Views on the Growth Status and Destiny of the English Language," *Studien zur englischen Philologie,* XLI (Halle, 1910), 15. In the early seventeenth century, says Albert C. Baugh, there "still existed a considerable variety of use—alternative forms in the grammar, experiments with new words, variations in pronunciation and spelling" (*A History of the English Language* [New York, 1957], p. 303).

19. "The Excellency of the English Tongue," in *Elizabethan Critical Essays,* ed. G. Gregory Smith, II, 290.

20. *Rogue* (1623), II, **7ᵛ. The work was rendered from Mateo Alemán's *Guzmán de Alfarache.*

> . . . Loe, what Art hath done.
> Here the *Reflection's* brighter then the *Sunne*.
> One Language is too narrow to containe
> The boundlesse-rascall-froath of *Guzmans* braine.
> It cry'd for more. This Author, hearing it,
> Imployes his Pensill, drawes it to the quick
> In English colours. . . .[21]

And W. Browne (perhaps the author of *Britannia's Pastorals*) lauds the same book with these words: "By what you giue vs here, you . . . vindicate our Tongue."[22] Mabbe, of course, was a good man to praise. Although destined to be overshadowed by more original authors in all of the general literary histories, he was one of the liveliest and most dexterous prose writers of his day.

By the end of the period, English prose was well on its way to maturity. A change had begun to take place at least as early as the time of John Rastell, the man who issued the shortened early version of the *Celestina*. In fact, Rastell himself expressed pleasure that "our vulgare Englysh tong [has been] maruellously amended and augmentyd by reason that dyuers famous clerkis and lerned men had translate[d]. . . ."[23] The process continued down through the time of Richard Flecknoe, who in 1653 enumerated the several virtues of modern English, then concluded: "To all which perfections, our Language is arriv'd chiefly by *Travell*, & *Translation*. . . ."[24] In 1658 the translator Edward Phillips went so far as to say in his *New World of English Words* that English would not give place to any other modern language in Europe. Without undue reticence, he even maintained that he himself had "illustrated and refined it, instated it in its proper majesty, rendred it admirably useful for all persons on all occasions, worthy of the greatest masteries of Rhetoricians and the tongues of our Vernaculous Oratours. . . ."[25]

The improvement of English must certainly be considered among the motives of Renaissance translators, but it would be necessary to look at the evidence through a multiplying-glass to conclude that translators of Spanish

---

21. *Rogue*, II, **7[r].
22. *Rogue*, II, **7[v].
23. Quoted by Richard F. Jones, *The Triumph of the English Language* (Stanford, Calif., 1953), p. 88.
24. "A Discourse of Languages," *Miscellania*, p. 103.
25. *New World*, a4[v]. Phillips, by the way, included some one hundred and thirty-five words connected with Spain.

fiction express this aim to any great degree. Far more important, both to them and most other writers, were those age-old chameleon motives, each of which masqueraded as the other, delight and edification. As Owen Felltham put it, "that is the best worke, where the *Graces* and the *Muses* meet."[26] On the one hand there was an attempt to bait hooks, to coat pills with sugar, to get the rhubarb down with a bit of candy. In fiction, besides the lure of exciting matter—most notably love and adventure— there was also the lure of art. (Leonard Digges, for example, assured readers that they would find delight in the *"weauing and contexture"* of his translation of *Gerardo*.[27]) On the other hand, the bait, the sugar, and the candy were seldom offered alone. Even Boccaccio's *Decameron*, translated in 1620, appeared with a warrant of moral utility.[28]

With regard to these two motives, *dulce* and *utile,* translators from Spanish differed little from their fellows. Even though Rastell's version of Rojas' *Celestina* contained a few obscenities and introduced to England the most famous bawd in western literature, the little interlude came equipped with a non-Spanish "morall cõclusion & exhortacyon to vertew."[29] A hundred years later, Mabbe's version of the same work was presented under the blunt title of *The Spanish Bawd* (1631), but the title page went on immediately to indicate the book's "many Philosophicall Sentences, and profitable Instructions necessary for the younger sort. . . ." In fact, much like Chaucer's Pardoner, who bade only the virtuous come forward for his wares, Mabbe asserted in his dedication that "the reading of *Celestina,* to those that are prophane, is as poyson to their hearts; but to the chaste, and honest minde, a preseruatiue against such inconueniences as occurre in the world."[30] Assurance of moral utility was also provided with *A Paire of Turtle Doves, Persiles and Sigismunda, Gerardo,* and *The Sonne of the Rogue.* In short, after we have surveyed the evidence offered by various translators of Spanish fiction, we are better prepared to understand Arthur J. Tieje's observation concerning narratives in general: "Nowhere in Europe could one write prose fiction before 1740 without a mild blush of shame."[31]

26. *Resolves* (1628–1629), p. 355.

27. *Gerardo,* A3^r.

28. If Renaissance fancy could bolt bran and think it flour, a probable reason was the deeply ingrained habit of scriptural interpretation. A willingness to find good in almost everything is revealed in such places as Thomas Wilson's *Arte of Rhetorique* (1553) and Philip Sidney's *Defence of Poesie* (1595).

29. *A New Cõmodye* . . . , Malone Society Reprints (London, 1908), A1^r.

30. *Spanish Bawd* (1631), A4^r.

31. "The Expressed Aim of the Long Prose Fiction from 1579 to 1740," *JEGP*, XI (1912), 406.

Times were already changing, though. When Mabbe came to publish his version of Cervantes' *Novelas ejemplares* in 1640, he wrote thus: *"I will not promise any great profit you shall reape by reading them: but I promise they will be pleasing andd elightful [sic]. . . ."*[32] Furthermore, although Cervantes' stories were first sold in England under the correctly translated title of *Exemplarie Novells,* they reappeared fourteen years later as *Delight in Severall Shapes.*

Before setting aside such an important topic as the interrelation of sweetness and enlightenment in early fiction, a topic which will repeatedly force its way into the following pages, we should acknowledge the modern temptation to be skeptical about Renaissance claims of utility. When the lamp was rubbed, admittedly, it was often the genie Morality that was invoked, and Mirth, Sentiment, or Rhetoric which appeared; but judging from what readers of fiction were offered, it is fair to assume that what they wanted most and liked best was mirth, sentiment, or rhetoric trailing clouds of morality. We should also acknowledge that, as a slap at vice or simply as a means of civilizing, fiction always has been and always will be of use. And finally, if one chooses to distinguish between moral and cognitive usefulness, even the most frivolous fiction (witness the *novelas* of Pérez de Montalván) may sometimes prove a source of insight.[33]

Methods of Translating

As we turn from motives to methods we again find variety. During our century and a half, some translators naturally made discoveries about their art. Fairly early Sir Thomas North wrote that a good translator is responsible not only for conveying his author's meaning, but for *"resembling*

32. *Exemplarie Novells,* A3ᵛ. As James Routh observes, "the conception of moral, social, or political truth masquerading as art gradually disintegrated, while the conception of art for the spontaneous joy of it grew" ("The Purpose of Art as Conceived in English Literary Criticism of the Sixteenth and Seventeenth Centuries," *Englische Studien,* XLVIII [1914], 141).

33. See Helen M. Condon, "The Ethical Element in Literary Criticism of the English Renaissance," unpublished Ph.D. dissertation (Stanford, 1953), and Sidney Zink's excellent article, "The Moral Effect of Art," *Ethics,* LX (1949–1950), 261–274.

To the varied motives for translation considered here, or to some combination of them, we may perhaps add one that is left unexpressed. No translator that I recall admits to writing for the sake of self-satisfaction. It would seem, however, that the man endowed with a low-powered "ingyne of *Inuention*" and a strong desire to write might have found translation a pleasurable outlet, especially in an age when originality was only beginning to matter.

and shadovving out of the forme of his style. . . ."[34] Throughout the succeeding years, nonetheless, we find translators who forgot or never learned
these requisites. The simple fact is that most Renaissance translators, whether
rendering Spanish fiction or something else, neither cared much for the
theories of their predecessors nor for making theories of their own. Since
they had little or nothing to guide them (the ancients were of little
help on the subject), it is easy to see how some might confuse theft with
translation, or translation with imitation, and produce a mongrel like the
first English version of the *Celestina*.

It was not until the Restoration that any serious attempt was made to
analyze the types of translation possible. Then, in his preface to *Ovid's
Epistles*, Dryden distinguished the following: (1) Metaphrase, *"turning an
Authour word by word, and Line by Line,"* as in Jonson's translation of
Horace; (2) Paraphrase, *"Translation with Latitude, where the Authour
is kept in view by the Translator, so as never to be lost, but his words
are not so strictly follow'd as his sense, and that too is admitted to be amply-
fied, but not alter'd,"* as in Waller's *Aeneid;* and (3) Imitation, *"where the
Translator (if now he has not lost that Name) assumes the liberty not only
to vary from the words and sence, but to forsake them both as he sees occasion: and taking only some general hints from the Original, to run division
on the ground-work, as he pleases,"* as in Cowley's *Odes*.[35] By his own at-

34. From North's translation of Amyot's Plutarch (1579), *vii[r]. North comes
within view by virtue of his translation of Antonio de Guevara's *Reloj de príncipes*,
called in English *The Diall of Princes* (1557).

35. Preface to *Ovid's Epistles*, A8. See also his "Dedication of the Aeneis" and
"Preface to Silvae"; and William Frost, *Dryden and the Art of Translation* (New
Haven, Conn., 1955). Another important work devoted to translation before the
nineteenth century was Alexander F. Tytler's *Principles of Translation* (London,
1791). More recent studies of the subject are innumerable. Among those not cited
elsewhere in this chapter are Charles Whibley, "Translators," *CHEL* (New York,
1910), IV, 1–28; O. L. Hatcher, "Aims and Methods of Elizabethan Translators,"
Englische Studien, XLIV (1912), 174–192; Flora Ross Amos, *Early Theories of
Translation* (New York, 1920); F. O. Matthiessen, *Translation: An Elizabethan Art*
(Cambridge, Mass., 1931); Louis B. Wright, "The Pathway to Foreign Learning and
Languages," *Middle-Class Culture in Elizabethan England* (Chapel Hill, N. C.,
1935), pp. 339–372; William C. Atkinson, "Translation from Spanish," in *A
Handbook to the Study and Teaching of Spanish*, ed. E. Allison Peers (London,
1938), pp. 88–101; Paul Ervin Hadley, "Principles of English Literary Transla-
tion," unpublished Ph.D. dissertation (Univ. of Southern California, 1955); and
Robert L. Politzer, "A Brief Classification of the Limits of Translatability," *MLJ*,
XL (1956), 319–322. Recently, of course, the field has been explored more than
ever before. See *On Translation*, ed. Reuben A. Brower (Cambridge, Mass., 1959),
esp. "A Critical Bibliography of Works on Translation," pp. 269–293.

tempts to aim between metaphrase and paraphrase, Dryden acknowledged his belief that faithfulness to intention is more to be desired than strained and ragged exactness. As he put it, "*'Tis almost impossible to Translate verbally, and well, at the same time.*" And this is in keeping with both the old and the modern view that a work should be rendered word for word when possible, but most often sense by sense—*and git of and giete*—so that thoughts and emotions may be most accurately conveyed. Speaking of metaphrase and championing paraphrase, Chapman had earlier exclaimed in his edition of Homer,

> *how pedanticall and absurd an affectation it is, in the interpretation of any Author . . . to turn him word for word; when (according to* Horace *and other best lawgiuers to translators) it is the part of euery knowing and iudiciall interpreter, not to follow the number and order of words, but the materiall things themselues. . . .*[36]

Throughout our entire period the problems of translation were legion, as they still are, but the Renaissance translators of Spanish fiction generally displayed either unconcern or at best a rather unsystematic awareness. For a better understanding of their views, let us consider the words of Clerc and Mabbe, Digges and Davies.

The words of John Clerc are of particular interest because he seems to have been the first Englishman to publish his own version of a Spanish narrative. In 1543 he fumblingly rendered Diego de San Pedro's *Arnalte y Lucenda* from the French, adorning his fractured prose with a generous supply of Gallicisms, and dedicating the result to Henry Howard, Earl of Surrey. In his preface he first calls Surrey's attention to "the wytty deuyse of the thynge, the maner of Locucyons, the wyse sentences and the subtyll and dyscret answeres made on bothe parties. . . ."[37] Then, with more acumen than he demonstrates in the work itself, he goes on to say that he has not

estemyd the order of the wordes in yᵉ other tonges,[38] as it is seen some haue done ĩ sõdry places of theyr trãslacions, wherby it is not only thought they publysshe theyr owne folye, but also vndoubtedly certayne that they by the same in the place of lybertie submyt themselfes to seruytude without hauyng respecte to thobseruacyon of that thyng whiche in this case is moste specyally requisit, wherby the sence of the Aucthour is oftẽ depraued, and the grace ne perfection

36. (*ca.* 1616), A4ʳ.
37. *A Certayn Treatye Moste Wyttely Deuysed* . . . , A1ᵛ.
38. Use of the plural implies Clerc's acquaintance with more than one version.

of thone ne other tonge dewly expressed, but vnderstandynge that euery tonge hath his [pro?]perties, maner of Locucyons[,] perticuler vehemēcies, dignyties, and rychesses, I haue arrested my self onely vpon the sentēces & maiesties therof so curyously as I fyrmely trust thintenciõ of thauthor is truely expressed. . . .[39]

In other words: Clerc does not translate literally, as some have mistakenly done; he believes in the primacy of matter over manner; he sees that different tongues have different capabilities; and he implies that the original author's purposes may be most faithfully fulfilled if the translator endeavors to express his meaning with the "grace" peculiar to English. It is not to be expected that Clerc would regard style as the surface of meaning—as it assuredly is in the work that he renders. It is enough, in view of his shortcomings as a writer, that he seems to be groping toward the concept expressed more clearly (and later, to be sure) by Flecknoe, namely that the translator is so to

put on *the person of the* Author, as to imagine himself him, and that he rather writes the Book then translates it: so he is not to think, nor reflect on the Language he translates out of, but how the Author would best express himself in that he translates into.[40]

Perhaps it is no coincidence that one of the best remembered of the translators of Spanish fiction was also the one who wrote most on the subject. In the preface to his version of Fr. Cristóbal de Fonseca's *Discursos,* James Mabbe writes thus:

Some peraduenture may dislike it [his version of Fonseca], because it was first composed by a Spaniard; as if *Eliah* should haue refused his meat, because it was brought him by a Rauen. . . . Shal not the rose be pluckt because it grows on a Brier? And yet let me tell thee, to hearten thy aduenture against all needlesse & imaginarie fears, The captiue here hath her head shorn, and may well be admitted for a true Israelite. Thou shalt not cry out, *Mors in olla, Death is in the pot;* that little lease of *Coloquintida* which was in it, is taken out, and the children of the Prophets may tast of the broth without danger.[41]

Even if one is sufficiently literal-minded to overlook the irony in Mabbe's words, one can hardly mistake that because of England's hatred for Spain Mabbe feels it necessary to censor some of Fonseca's ideas. More important, however, Mabbe does not hesitate to make excisions. By removing the needles, he turns the cactus into provender.

39. A1ᵛ-A2ʳ. A turned "n" has been righted.
40. "Of Translation of Authors," p. 114.
41. *Devout Contemplations* (1629). These remarks appear on two unsigned leaves preceding A1.

If one may judge from this and from his performance elsewhere, Mabbe was truly interested in conveying the basic spirit of his sources, however far he sometimes strayed. He says in the dedication of his *Spanish Bawd:*

so differing is the Idiome of the Spainish from the English, that I may imitate, it but not come neere it. Yet haue I made it as naturall, as our language will giue leaue, and haue more beaten my braines about it in some places, then a man would beate a Flint to get fire. . . .[42]

He has tried hard, then, at least "in some places," to translate exactly, though the nature of idiomatic expression has made his task very difficult.[43] Mabbe seems to imply that it is only when he is most lucky that he becomes a "poore Parret, who accents but other folkes words. . . ."[44] A similar view is inherent in some remarks he addresses to Sir John Strangwayes in the dedication of *The Rogue.* Here Mabbe, writing in Spanish, says that he who would turn words and concepts from one language into another should have faithfulness, discretion, and wisdom, together with an equal knowledge of both tongues; and he makes explicit his belief that allusive and metaphorical passages are rendered best when altered.[45]

Mabbe's friend Digges expresses a similar willingness to alter his source. In his *Gerardo* he says first that *"a Translator hath no commission to better (suffice to come neere), his Originall."*[46] But with the very next dip of his pen he goes on to confess that

Some of the Verses in the Spanish Copie, I haue purposely left out, as being (in my iudgement) vnworthy to bee ranked with the Prose; others I haue altered, to make them more sutable to an English Reader. One by-discourse I haue left wholly out, as superstitiously smelling of Papisticall Miracles; in which I haue no beleefe.[47]

And yet he has no commission to better his original! Of course Digges might have been so ingenuous as to suppose that by leaving out those artistic and religious elements which offended him, he did not really change his story. Then again, he was deemed a master of English, a "perfect under-

42. *Spanish Bawd,* A5ʳ.
43. In other places in the same work he makes intentional modifications, largely of a religious nature. See Ch. VII of the present study and Helen Phipps Houck, "Mabbe's Paganization of the *Celestina,*" *PMLA,* LIV (1939), 422–431.
44. *Spanish Bawd,* A5ʳ.
45. *Rogue* (1622), I, *3ʳ. He also writes, "Muchos vierten; y las mas vezes, peruierten."
46. *Gerardo,* A3ʳ.
47. *Gerardo,* A3.

stander" of Spanish, "a good Poet and no mean Orator."[48] Perhaps, believing with Roscommon that " 'tis much safer to leave out than *Add*,"[49] he
means merely to say that such changes as he has made do not affect the main
action and lesson of his story. The important point here, however, is that he
expresses a willingness to alter his source in accordance with both his taste
and his emotion.

At the end of our period we encounter John Davies of Kidwelly. One of
the more sprightly and entertaining of the later translators, Davies confesses
on the title page of *La Picara, or The Triumphs of Female Subtilty* (1665)
that his work has been "Render'd into English, with some *Alterations* and
Additions." And in his dedication to Sir John Berkenhead he enlarges on
this statement by saying that he has translated *"with a freedome of alteration and addition, as my fancy led me, to make it the most divertive I could
in ours* [our tongue], *which is the onely recommendation of all things of
this nature."*[50] Actually Davies' additions are neither many nor great. On the
whole he did less "adapting to the English taste" than a considerable number of his colleagues. But like most translators of his time, he felt few obliga-
tions to his source.

French Intermediaries

To throw more light on this last statement we need merely add that
Davies gives no evidence of knowing Spanish. Indeed, we shall have the
fun of including Quevedo's *Buscón* (see below, Chapter VII) only because
Davies made "it his livelihood to translate Books from *French* into *English*. . . ."[51] Quevedo's Spanish *Buscón* concludes with the hero, Pablo, as-
sisting in a couple of drunken murders and setting sail for the Indies; but
the English *Buscon* (which uses the word *buscón*—thief or cheat—as if it
were a proper name) follows the French translation by La Geneste, and
hence concludes with the marriage of the hero in Spain.[52]

A more worrisome example of a book which was translated through the
French is the Caroline version of San Pedro's *Arnalte y Lucenda*. In 1639

48. Anthony à Wood, *Athenae Oxonienses* (London, 1721), I, 600.

49. "An Essay on Translated Verse" (1684), in *Critical Essays of the Seventeenth
Century*, ed. J. E. Spingarn (Oxford, 1908), II, 303.

50. *La Picara*, A3ʳ. Based on Castillo Solórzano's *La garduña de Sevilla*.

51. Wood, II, 902. See also Joseph E. Tucker, "John Davies of Kidwelly
(1627?–1693), Translator from the French," *PBSA*, XLIV (1950), 119–152.

52. See Henry Thomas, "The English Translations of Quevedo's *La vida del
buscón*," *RH*, Pt. 2 of LXXXI (1933), 282–299.

Leonard Lawrence brought out a versified form which he called *A Small Treatise Betwixt Arnalte and Lucenda Entituled the Evill-intreated Lover, or the Melancholy Knight.* The title page continues: *Originally Written in the Greeke Tongue* [N.B.], *by an Unknowne Author. Afterwards Translated into Spanish; after That, for the Excellency Thereof, into the French Tongue by N. H. Next by B. M. into the Thuscan, and Now Turn'd into English Verse by L. L.* As we have already noted, this story was first translated into English from the French by John Clerc. Its next appearance in English was at the hands of Claudius Hollyband, a Huguenot refugee who had set up shop as a language teacher in London. Hollyband (whose real name was Claude de Sainliens) had made a synoptic Italian-English version of the work, adding to it "certen Rules and Dialogues set foorth for the learner of th'Italian tong."[53] In making his own translation, therefore, Lawrence might have turned to a number of sources: the original Spanish of San Pedro (1491), the French of Nicolas Herberay des Essarts (1539), the English by Clerc (1543), the Italian by Bartolommeo Maraffi (1570), or the Italian-English by Hollyband (1575). Since it is evident from Lawrence's work that he was less interested in translating than in finding a field where he might frolic among flowers of rhetoric, it would be easy to imagine him turning to a version already in English. But there is some to-do in his introductory matter about the little work being rendered from a foreign tongue. Lawrence even refers to himself as "The Translator," thus leaving little doubt that his source was not in English. Because his version is actually more of an adaptation (or "imitation," as Dryden would term it) than a true translation, the source-puzzle might prove difficult to solve if an answer were not available in the words of R. Knowles, a friend of the writer:

> *Thou shew'st us* Arnalt, *yes, and thy Translation*
> *Sheweth thy* Genius, *and thy* Education:
> *And we that can no* French, *are bound to thee. . . .*[54]

Thus we learn of Lawrence's probable source.

It will come as no surprise to students of Renaissance literature that France was an important dispatcher for Spain. From the time of Caxton through that of Davies, Englishmen were quite likely to turn to French go-betweens for aid. And that included Englishmen interested in fiction. All too few were the men like Bartholomew Yong, who refers to the French

---

53. *The Pretie and Wittie Historie of Arnalt & Lucenda* (1575), title page.
54. *Arnalte,* a4.

translators of the *Diana* as "blind guides,"[55] or Thomas Stanley, who asserts
in the preface to one of his works that "the Licentiousnesse of the French
Translation brings hither no assistance. . . ."[56] On the contrary, we find
two important reasons for dependence on France. First, Englishmen were
more likely to know French than any other contemporary foreign language;
and second, France was interested in Spain. Even a cursory study of French
translations of Spanish fiction, to say nothing of the Spanish language
manuals which abounded in France, will make this interest manifest.[57]

As Gide has observed, wherever there is a relationship, there is the possibility of an influence.[58] With regard to our present subject this is a matter which would require considerable investigation before a final evaluation could be offered, and yet, even with our limited glance at the problem, we shall see that in some cases the use of a French intermediary left
discernible marks on an English translation, and, in others, threw an English translator completely off the track. It is all the more amazing, then,
that a work like *Buscon*, despite the liberties which La Geneste and
Davies took, sometimes seems nearly as Spanish as if it had sailed directly
from Cadiz up the Thames.

Characteristics of the Translations

C an any conclusions be drawn when we compare the translations with
the theories and practices of the translators? We shall gather more evidence as we go along, but maybe it is not too early to observe that the anonymous *Pilgrime of Casteele* and Lawrence's *Arnalte and Lucenda* are both

55. *Diana*, a3ʳ.
56. *Aurora, & The Prince*, A2ʳ.
57. In seventeenth-century France, Spanish even acquired some of the characteristics of a national tongue (José Francisco Pastor, *Las apologías de la lengua castellana
en el siglo de oro* [Madrid, 1929], p. xxvii). Much has been written on the Franco-
Spanish relationship. See, e.g., Gustave Lanson, "Études sur les rapports de la littérature française et de la littérature espagnole au XVIIᵉ siècle (1600–1660),"
Revue d'Histoire Littéraire de la France, 3ᵉ *Année* (1896), 45–70, 321–331; 4ᵉ
Année (1897), 61–73, 180–194; Alfred Morel-Fatio, *Ambrosio de Salazar et
l'étude de l'espagnol en France sous Louis XIII* (Paris, 1900); J. Mathorez, "Notes
sur les espagnols en France," *BH*, XVI (1914), 337–371; Paul Patrick Rogers,
"Spanish Influence on the Literature of France," *Hispania*, IX (1926), 205–235;
and Lois Strong [Gaudin], *Bibliography of Franco-Spanish Literary Relations* (New
York, 1930). R. Foulché-Delbosc's "Bibliographie hispano-française" in *Bibliographie Hispanique* (New York, 1912 and 1913) is invaluable.
58. *The Journals of André Gide*, tr. and ed. Justin O'Brien (New York, 1956),
I, 25.

very different from the Spanish works on which they are based. Rather near to their sources are stories such as Stanley's *Aurora* and Style's *Axa and the Prince*. And in between these extremes lie Shelton's *Don Quixote* and Digges's *Gerardo.* In brief, the body of literature we are concerned with is sufficiently great to furnish samples of a wide range of translating methods, omitting only, perhaps, Dryden's first category, the metaphrase. Moreover, even within the work of a single man, there are divergent tendencies, a fact which indicates as strongly as anything could that variations were sometimes wilful, not the result of an incomplete grasp of Spanish. We may safely conclude that for translators of Spanish as well as for Renaissance translators in general, the job at hand often seemed to offer a chance to step higher and wider in an already-trodden path.

Just how satisfactory, then, was the average translation? The answer depends on whether the work is to be judged according to its literal accuracy or its literary merit. That there is a vital distinction here is shown most clearly, perhaps, by the fact that we, like a good many of our ancestors, tend to read the greatest of the Tudor and Stuart translations, when we read them at all, as original works of literature. Shelton's *Don Quixote* stands on its own merit just as surely as North's Plutarch and Chapman's Homer, yet none of these works is noted for accuracy.

Quite as well as we, the translators of the Renaissance knew that no matter how hard they tried for accuracy, a translation is never really like its source. Perhaps in a book on navigation they might hope to avoid some of the colors of connotation, some of the pitfalls of pattern; but the form of a literary work is a part of its meaning, and whatever their varying degrees of awareness of this fact, the translators could not avoid the problems it implies. Even if they tried to insert no stitches of their own —and this was seldom the case—"*TRanslations* (as sayes a witty *Spaniard*) are, in respect of their Originals, like the knottie wrong-side of Arras-Hangings. . . ."[59]

James Howell, an Hispanophile and translator (though not of Spanish fiction), repeats the old weaving figure. It is in his *Epistolae Ho-Elianae* that one encounters these words:

I must confess, my Genius hath often prompted me that I was never cut out for a Translator, there being a kind of servility therein: For it must needs be somewhat tedious to one that hath any free-born thoughts within him, and genuine conceptions of his own (whereof I have some, tho' shallow ones) to

59. Digges, *Gerardo*, A2ʳ.

enchain himself to a verbal servitude, and the sense of another. Moreover, *Translations* are but as turn-coated things at best, 'specially among Languages that have Advantages one of the other, as the *Italian* hath of the *English.* . . . Or I may say, *Translations* are like the wrong side of a *Turkey* Carpet, which useth to be full of thrums and knots, and nothing so even as the right side. . . .

Moreover, touching Translations, it is to be observ'd, that every Language hath certain Idioms, Proverbs, and peculiar Expressions of its own, which are not rendible in any other, but paraphrastically; therefore he overacts the office of an Interpreter who doth enslave himself too strictly to Words or Phrases. . . . The greatest fidelity that can be expected in a Translator, is to keep still a-foot and entire the true genuine sense of the Author, with the main design he drives at. . . .[60]

In rather brief compass Howell furnishes here an epitome of several important ideas: even at the close of England's greatest age of translation, a translator is not regarded as highly as an original writer, for he has sacrificed the freedom to be himself; the English language is to be appraised and compared with the tongues of other lands, not always to its advantage; and, most important, a translation can never be wholly accurate because the art of the translator is the art of compromise, compromise by means of paraphrase. Thus we have seen Clerc, Mabbe, and Howell—our first translator, our best translator, and an informed observer—all take note of the impossibility of complete translation.

For a fuller awareness of what was happening, we may turn to the translations themselves.

60. Joseph Jacobs, ed. (London, 1890), pp. 544–545.

Chapter IV

The Road to
La Mancha

Don Quixote *and Its Precursors*

The history of Spain's greatness may be said to date from 1469, when Isabella of Castile married Ferdinand of Aragon. Nearly everything this royal pair did was intended to unify the peninsula and strengthen the crown, and Spain, seemingly guided for the first time by sure hands, half unwittingly arrived at that *annus mirabilis* 1492: Granada was conquered, the riches of America were laid bare, and Antonio de Nebrija published the first grammar ever composed for a modern tongue. In a sense our investigation might be said to begin here, too, because it was in 1491 that San Pedro's *Tractado de amores de Arnalte y Lucenda* was first printed for Isabella and her ladies, and it was half a century later, in 1543, that this same story became the first translated Spanish fiction to be printed in England.[1]

The labeling of John Clerc's translation as "first" is to some extent arbitrary. Before taking a look at it, therefore, it seems only fair to glance briefly at some other early contenders for the title.

Some Predecessors of Clerc's *Arnalte*

Because William Caxton felt that England had a real need for translations, one might be inclined to wonder if he ever turned to Spanish fiction. As it happens, a bit of Catalan fiction did appear in the opening passages of his *Book of the Ordre of Chyvalry* (1484). This was a work "translated oute of Frensshe in to Englyssche,"[2] but based ultimately on the

---

1. N.B. "printed." Lord Berners' translation of San Pedro's *Cárcel de amor*, discussed below, remained unpublished until *ca.* 1548, but it cannot have been translated after 1533, the year of Berners' death. Berners' book is thus another kind of "first."

2. *Ordre of Chyvalry*, glʳ. See Carlos Clavería, "Sobre la traduccion inglesa del 'Libre del orde de cavalleria' de Ramon Lull," *Analecta Sacra Tarraconensia*, XV (1942), 65–74.

Libre del orde de cavayleria (*ca.* 1275) by the prolific and famous philosopher Ramón Lull. Dedicated to Richard III, Caxton's version was a belated attempt to arouse visions of the glories of chivalry in a courtly community that had newer ideas on its mind. For the most part the book is a squire's guide to knighthood, but its beginning, both in the Caxton version and the Lull original, contains a bit of unmistakable narration. An old "wyse knyght" and a young and ready-to-be-enlightened squire are introduced, and their situation is established. But then, surprisingly enough, the book proceeds without them. Until a fictional introduction is felt to be sufficient cause for doing otherwise, the *Ordre of Chyvalry* will continue to be omitted from studies of early fiction.

Before we set it aside, however, its historical position commands another word. In addition to Caxton's version and a Scottish translation in 1494 by one Adam Loutfut, there has also been brought to light a still earlier version by Sir Gilbert Haye, a poet-priest who at one time was chamberlain to Charles VII of France. Called the *Buke of the Ordre of Knychthede* and dating back almost to the middle of the fifteenth century (1456), this work is among the earliest extant bits of Scottish prose "which is not either a legal document, a law, or a letter."[3] Thus in the North (if not in England) the beginnings of Catalan (if not Castilian) fiction may be traced as far back as the Wars of the Roses.

Perhaps it was the truncated *Celestina* (*ca.* 1530) that came northward next. Based on the late fifteenth-century masterpiece by Fernando de Rojas, the English version was published by John Rastell as *A New Cõmodye in Englysh in Maner of an Enterlude Ryght Elygant & Full of Craft of Rethoryk Wherein Is Shewd & Dyscrybyd as Well the Bewte & Good Propertes of Women as Theyr Vycys & Euyll Cõdiciõs*. Rastell, besides being a printer and lawyer, was also a dramatist of sorts. The latter point is of some importance. Although the Spanish *Celestina* is a work *sui generis,* one that has been described as a novel in dialogue form, the truncated English translation is best regarded as a play. Since Rastell is remembered primarily as a writer of interludes; since this particular work bears the labels of "Cõmodye" *and* "Enterlude" and is shortened to the extent that it certainly is actable (Gustav Ungerer suggests that it was performed in 1529 during the marriage festivities for Sir Thomas More's son);[4] and since scholars usually regard it as a play, we may, I think, con-

---

3. J. H. Stevenson, ed., *Gilbert of the Haye's Prose Manuscript* (*A.D. 1456*) (Edinburgh, 1901), I, lv.

4. *Anglo-Spanish Relations in Tudor Literature* (Berne, 1956), p. 26.

clude that the *Celestina* in its first English form belongs to the history of the drama.[5] The translation is of considerable importance and interest. It is especially significant because the translator—possibly Rastell himself—worked directly from the Spanish.[6] But it simply is not fiction.

About five years later, in 1535, John Bourchier, Lord Berners, brought out the famous *Golden Boke,* based on Antonio de Guevara's *Libro áureo* (1527). This somniferous work contains endless letters purporting to come from the pen of Marcus Aurelius. It is chock-full of actual and manufactured data about the flawless Roman and the life and customs of the ancients. But is the result to be regarded as fiction? Since Henry Thomas refers to it as *"a romantic novel of a moralizing character with a pseudo-classical background,"* one cannot altogether ignore it in a study of English translations of Spanish narratives.[7] One cannot deny that the garrulous Guevara was working with the raw materials of fiction, that he invented both characters and episodes; and yet he took so very little advantage of them that I have decided not to swell my final count of translations with his *Golden Boke.*

Having brought up Guevara's first work, it is tempting to mention his later ones. At the height of the *Golden Boke's* glory, in 1557, Sir Thomas North published his version of another and similar Guevara effort, the *Reloj de príncipes,* in which was incorporated *El muy famoso libro de Marco Aurelio* (1529), called in English *The Diall of Princes with the Famous Booke of Marcus Aurelius.* James Fitzmaurice-Kelly says that "Perhaps no prose work of fiction [and note his label] has made more immediate noise in the world. . . ."[8] It was, to be sure, very well received. Hardin Craig writes that "The Sixteenth Century knew no more popular books than *The Golden Boke* . . . and the *Diall of Princes. . . ."*[9] And Casaubon is quoted as saying that no book but the Bible circulated

5. E.g., Charles Mills Gayley, *Representative English Comedies* (New York, 1903), I, lxviii, calls it "the earliest romantic play of intrigue in our language."

6. Apparently with help from the French version of 1527 (Ungerer, p. 180).

7. Thomas's reference appears in his introductory remarks to Henry Vaughan's translation from Guevara called *The Praise and Happinesse of the Countrie-life* (Newtown, Wales, 1938), p. vii. Thomas is also the author of a helpful article called "The English Translations of Guevara's Works," which appears in *Estudios eruditos in memoriam de Adolfo Bonilla y San Martín* (Madrid, 1930), II, 565–582. Also helpful, though more general, is María Rosa Lida's "Fray Antonio de Guevara," *RFH,* VII (1945), 346–388.

8. "Some Correlations of Spanish Literature," *RH,* XV (1906), 77.

9. "A Contribution to the Theory of the English Renaissance," *PQ,* VII (1928), 328.

as widely in its time as *Marco Aurelio.*[10] Guevara is also accountable for the *Familiar Epistles* (translated by Edward Hellowes, 1574) and the *Golden Epistles* (translated by Geoffrey Fenton, 1575), which together eventually helped to expand the Spanish bishop's total number of English editions to over thirty. To all this one may add that no other author is to be credited with a more impeccable example of the influence of English translations from Spanish. I do not refer to the old and now-retired notion that Guevara inspired euphuism, but to the little-known fact that his writing moved a certain John Felton to nothing less than purchase of a ten-penny knife and assassination of King James's beloved "Steenie," the Duke of Buckingham.[11] Still, Guevara's books are not fiction. That is, they are not sustained imaginative narratives. They are not even epistolary fiction. The episode of *El villano del Danubio,* which depicts a German peasant's protest to Rome (a thinly veiled comment on contemporary Spaniards in America), is known to have circulated independently,[12] and hence constitutes the strongest reason available for including Guevara's life of Marcus Aurelius in a list of fiction. But *The Diall* itself, I submit, is not fiction.[13] Fortunately it is unnecessary to try to determine here exactly what

10. Cited by Adolfo de Castro, *Obras escogidas de filósofos* in *Biblioteca de autores españoles* (Madrid, 1929), LXV, 154.

11. Pinned to the lining of Felton's hat was this encouraging sentence from Guevara: "That man is cowardly and base and deserveth not the name of a gentleman or soldier that is not willing to sacrifice his life for the honour of his God, his king, and his country" (quoted by S. L. Lee, *DNB* [London, 1889], XVIII, 307).

12. Américo Castro, introd., *El villano del Danubio y otros fragmentos* (Princeton, 1945), p. xv.

13. The only exception I make to my rule of omitting intercalated stories is *Axa and the Prince,* which was inserted by a Spanish writer in an Italian book. See Ch. VI.

William Painter, *Palace of Pleasure* (1567), II, **i[v]-**ii[r], lists each of his own borrowings from Guevara's *Epístolas* as a "Nouel," including some spurious letters of Plutarch and Trajan. (See Douglas Bush, "The Classical Tales in Painter's *Palace of Pleasure*," *JEGP*, XXIII [1924], 331–341.) In our own time Sterg O'Dell has listed Guevara's *Golden Boke* and *Diall* in several places in his *Chronological List of Prose Fiction in English Printed in England and Other Countries 1475–1640* (Cambridge, Mass., 1954), and Elaine Kimmelman, in "A Forerunner of Euphuism," *Boston Public Library Quarterly,* II (1950), 189, calls the *Golden Boke* a "didactic novel." The phrase "didactic novel" is also applied to Guevara's *Diall* by Maxim Newmark, *Dictionary of Spanish Literature* (New York, 1956), p. 150, and even by the *Encyclopaedia Britannica* (Chicago, 1961), X, 953. It is not a new phrase, however. In 1919 K. N. Colvile, in his edition of North's translation of *The Diall* (p. xxiv), pointed out that "It is ridiculous and suggestive of a complete lack of first-hand acquaintance with the text [of *The Diall*] to call it, as some writers do, a 'didactic novel.' " Perhaps the words of Menéndez Pelayo are the best on the subit is—whether a didactic treatise, pseudo-history, or something else. Here it suffices to say that Guevara's over-all contribution is more to the history of fiction than to fiction itself, and perhaps even more to social history.

Glancing as they do at a handful of early translations, the preceding paragraphs will have served their chief purpose if they suggest how the problem of defining fiction is involved in the problem of naming the first English narrative translated from Spanish. If one arbitrarily rejects (as I think best) the partly fictional Lull work, the dramatic Rojas work, and the somewhat dubious, proto-fictional Guevara work, one next approaches the translation by Clerc of San Pedro's *Arnalte*. From here on, the ground is more firm.[14]

The subject matter of the present chapter—which extends from *Arnalte* to *Don Quixote*—reaches well into Spain's cultural and political Golden Age. It extends from the reign of the great Castilian Isabella until after the death of that *otra Isabella enemiga,* as James I is said to have called her, the great English queen who did her best to weaken Spain.[15] Most important here, it includes the introduction into England of the Spanish *novela sentimental,* the Spanish chivalric romance, the picaresque anti-romance, the pastoral romance, the Moorish *novela,* and what is sometimes called the world's first novel, *Don Quixote.*[16]

The *Novela Sentimental*

The first three narratives to come from Spain to England were all of a single genre. *Arnalte y Lucenda* and the *Cárcel de amor,* both by San Pedro, and the *Grisel y Mirabella* by Juan de Flores are usually described as *novelas sentimentales.* Each presents a stylized, ritualistic, aristocratic world, and each is dominated by rhetoric and focused on love. The form is said to derive in part from Boccaccio's fourteenth-century *Il Filocolo* and

ject. In his *Orígenes de la novela,* II, ed. Enrique Sánchez Reyes, in the *Edición nacional de las obras completas de Menéndez Pelayo* (Santander, 1943), XIV, 109, he lists *Marco Aurelio* as a *novela histórico-política,* but then goes ahead to say that he hesitates to do this because even though the greater part of it is invented, the work lacks true novelistic action. The didactic intention predominates, and the form is oratorical, not narrative.

14. See below, *Appendix D,* for additional marginal works.

15. William B. Rye, *England as Seen by Foreigners* (London, 1865), p. 121, quoting Juan Fernández de Velasco, Constable of Castile, at the time of the 1604 proclamation of peace.

16. Obviously some of these forms were not entirely new or entirely Spanish.

La Fiammetta (Flores even wrote a sequel to the latter); from Æneas Sylvius' *De duobus amantibus* (a love story written in Latin in 1444 and renounced by its author when he became Pius II); from the difficult-to-date but originally medieval *Amadís de Gaula* (which paved the way also for the numerous chivalric romances that followed it); and even from the humanistic *tractado* that developed in the reign of Juan II (1406–1454).[17] Perhaps Juan Rodríguez de la Cámara, in his mid-fifteenth-century *Siervo libre de amor,* was the first to weave together the sentimental, chivalric, and rhetorical strands provided by these various works, but it was Diego de San Pedro who first gave the genre fame.

San Pedro's *Arnalte y Lucenda* is a sort of preliminary cartoon for the *Cárcel.* Basically it is the story of a knight who ceaselessly importunes a "Belle Dame Sans Mercy." After long being spurned, the knight finally decides to solve his problems by challenging the lady's husband—his own former friend—to a duel. The husband is slain, the wife enters a convent, and the frustrated lover, wedded only to his woes, retires to a mansion in the midst of a wilderness. (The latter is a sort of lovers' hell, a reflection, it would seem, of the Spanish genius for misery.) Less important than external action, however, is style. It is style which elaborately graphs what might be termed the inner action—the emotional adventures of the hero. Arnalte's story is conveyed almost entirely by means of formal letters and speeches which are thickly studded with comparisons, conditions, apostrophes, and exclamations.[18]

As we have seen, Clerc's version, called *A Certayn Treatye Moste Wyttely Devysed,* came through the French of Herberay. As we have also seen, the result is disappointing. Although Clerc was enough of a linguist to venture forth as author of the first Italian grammar in England, his knowledge of French was shaky, his skill with English slight, and his translation of *Arnalte* satisfactory only in the simplest passages.[19]

17. The final suggestion here is made by Anna Krause, "El 'tractado' novelístico de Diego de San Pedro," *BH,* LIV (1952), 245–275. See also Rudolph Schevill, "Ovid and the Renascence in Spain," *UCPMP,* IV (1913), 1–268; Charles E. Kany, "The Beginnings of the Epistolary Novel in France, Italy, and Spain," *UCPMP,* XXI (1944), i–x and 1–158; and Gustave Reynier, *Le roman sentimental avant L'Astrée* (Paris, 1908).

18. William G. Crane's chapter called "The Sentimental Novel and the Romance," in *Wit and Rhetoric in the Renaissance* (New York, 1937), pp. 169–178, is helpful on the matter of style.

19. See A. Koszul, "La première traduction d'*Arnalte et Lucenda* et les débuts de la nouvelle sentimentale en Angleterre," Publications de la Faculté des Lettres de l'Université de Strasbourg, Fasc. 105, Mélanges 1945, *Études Littéraires,* II (Paris,

As the earliest specimen of its kind in English, however, his book deserves to speak for itself. After the passage in which it depicts Arnalte's dispatching of Lucenda's husband, it has him offer himself to Lucenda with these consolatory words:

LUcenda yf in the tyme of so great warre I demaunde the peace, I pray ye take it not in yll parte seynge that whiche I do, is for more testeme thy vertue great, than ye fault that I haue cõmytted towardes the, as to the myschaunce come in ye parsone of thy deed husbãde, the vsurpateur of my moste great riches, thonly god hath knowledge of the dyspleasure that I haue therof, howbeit yf he haue dyspleased me by his occasyõ he hath pleased me for thyne, for that yf I had not offended thee, thou had dest not knowen to manyfest ye vertue to pardon that is in the, the whiche amõge all is worthy of prayse. Than to thende that in pardonynge me the same vertue may be apparaunt to all others, gouerne ye dyspleasure by dyscretion. For yf thou do otherwise thy reputacyon shall dyminysshe therby, and shall remayne blamed, wyll not than to deney me the benefyte that I requyre y^e to satysfye vs bothe, doinge mercy to hym of whom thou sholdest demaunde pardone.[20]

Neither "the grace ne perfection of thone ne other tongue" comes through (to turn back to Clerc's own phrase), and it would seem that the fault is not altogether dependent on what Rastell called "our vulgare Englysh tong."

The next version of the story was that by Claudius Hollyband, who, as we noted earlier, rendered it in 1575 for a textbook designed to aid students of Italian. Since this second *Arnalte* enters English literature in the guise of a schoolbook, Hollyband, at worst, would deserve no more rigorous criticism than Clerc. He might bear it better, however. Though it was probably not his purpose to stray far from a literal rendering, his "Historie" is both reasonably fluent and readable. If the old story itself is no longer *"a Pearle amongst the best,"* as he claimed,[21] the book as a whole was nevertheless sufficiently popular to warrant later printings in 1597 and 1608, and as late as 1638, men were still concerned about property rights to it.[22]

In 1639, roughly a century after its introduction in England, the lugubri-

---

1946), 151–167; and Sergio Baldi, "The Secretary of the Duke of Norfolk and the First Italian Grammar in England," *Studies in English Language and Literature Presented to Professor Dr. Karl Brunner*, ed. Siegfried Korninger (Vienna, 1957), i.e., *Wiener Beiträge zur englischen Philologie*, LXV, 1–16.

20. *A Certayn Treatye*, Ri.

21. *The Pretie and Wittie Historie of Arnalt & Lucenda*, verso of title page.

22. *A Transcript of the Registers of the Company of Stationers of London*, ed. Edward Arber (London, 1877), IV, 444. Useful on the subject of Hollyband are A. W. Pollard, "Claudius Hollyband," *Transactions of the Bibliographical Society*, XIII (London, 1916), 253–272; and R. C. Simonini, Jr., "The Italian Pedagogy of Claudius Hollyband," *SP*, XLIX (1952), 144–154.

ous San Pedro story was translated still a third time. Ostensibly published at the request of well-wishing friends, this is the versified version by Leonard Lawrence which we had occasion to glance at in the preceding chapter. Fortunately it is Lawrence's first and only literary fruit, for he was a young man accustomed more to *"trade, and trafficke"* than the garden of the muses.[23] The following passage appears at that point where the heroine's husband tells Arnalte how they shall arm for their combat:

> . . . I select and chuse
> The proper Armes that men at Armes use;
> We will be arm'd as men at Armes be,
> *A cap, a pe,* compleat in each degree:
> Onely our right Armes they shall be excepted,
> For they shall naked be, and quite detected.
>
> . . . .
> NOw since the Armes were denoted, I
> Did straight-wayes goe to the Kings Majesty,
> Informing him exactly of what had
> Past betwixt *Yerso* and my selfe, (most sad)
> So that he hearing th' infidelity
> Of my past friend, then growne my enemy,
> It seem'd so strange to him that he did yeeld
> At my request to grant us both the field.
> Then on the day assign'd, *Yerso* and I,
> We did appeare before his Majesty,
> He having caus'd a Scaffold for to be
> Built and erected, that he there might see
> Who should be Master of the field, and gaine
> A glorious conquest, to maintaine his fame. . . .[24]

As Louis B. Wright has observed, skill in the use of language was "often believed to be the mark of the fine gentleman"; hence "the aspiring tradesman was eager to improve his language,"[25] and, one might add, to display it, once improved. Granted an English poet, granted a Marlowe, a verse translation of San Pedro's story might have risen to poetry. As it is, contorted into meter, it is more painful than pedestrian prose.

Because our terminal date is 1657, we need not concern ourselves here with a still later work called *Arnaldo, or, The Injur'd Lover,* though it will do no harm to add that in 1660 a work with this title appeared, and that

23. *A Small Treatise Betwixt Arnalte and Lucenda,* B1^r.
24. *A Small Treatise,* p. 91.
25. *Middle-Class Culture in Elizabethan England* (Chapel Hill, N. C., 1935), p. 371.

it was a new translation based on a much expanded and *"Ornify'd"* Italian version by Girolamo Brusoni. Diego de San Pedro, who is designated casually as *"some* Spaniard," is regarded as no more than one in a series of translators.[26]

After Clerc's 1543 *Arnalte,* the next Spanish fiction to be translated was the *Cárcel de amor.* Despite the differences which might be pointed out between these two books, the *Cárcel* was so much like the *Arnalte* in tone, treatment, and plot that San Pedro apologized to his dedicatee for repetitiousness. Rendered into English by Lord Berners (the *Golden Boke* translator, who died in 1533), it was apparently not printed until about 1548, when it appeared as *The Castell of Love.* It appeared again about 1552, and, still again, about 1560.[27]

Berners had doubtless learned some Spanish as King Henry's envoy to Spain in 1518–1519. His final years were spent as deputy of Calais, however, and when he took up literature about the age of sixty, his current French environment probably made it easier for him to turn to René Bertaut's translation than to San Pedro's original. At any rate, he worked from the French, which, in turn, had come through the Italian. To complicate matters still further, Berners included in his own version the continuation of the *Cárcel* by Nicolás Núñez, which had first been published in 1496. Since the latter was apparently available in no French version of Berners' time, the English translator must have worked here, at least, with a Spanish text.

As the *Castell* begins, a chained knight named Lereano (in Spanish, "Leriano") is being led through the wilds of the Sierra Morena by a fearful allegorical figure "Coueryde all in here lyke a sauage creature."[28] This suggestively hirsute guide, we are told, is Desire. For some reason the narrator is moved to follow the captor and his captive on their way to the castle—in the original it was a prison—of Love. Prison or castle, it is really another lovers' hell, and Lereano proceeds to suffer impressively. After a good deal of rhetoric, the narrator finally makes a visit to the

26. See "A Brief Accompt of the Book and Author," two leaves preceding the text.

27. Dating the editions of this translation is difficult. I follow here the notes made by William A. Jackson for the revised *STC.* But see William G. Crane, "Lord Berners's Translation of Diego de San Pedro's *Cárcel de amor,*" *PMLA,* XLIX (1934), 1032–1035.

28. *The Castell of Loue,* fac. ed., introd. William G. Crane (Gainesville, Fla., 1950), Aiii^v.

Princess Laureola on Lereano's behalf, and thereafter serves as go-between. When at last Lereano himself goes to see his beloved, whose sense of honor prompts the most excessive reticence, he is falsely maligned by the dastard Persio (who in both name and function resembles the villain Yerso in *Arnalte*). Naturally Lereano fights with and conquers Persio, but after he has freed Laureola (who has been imprisoned by her royal father because of Persio's lies), the girl still refuses to deal with her worshipper. In fact, informed of his impending martyrdom for love of her, she tells him to give up hope, even "though thou shuldest dye as thou sayst."[29] Lereano's friend Teseo thereupon begins to inveigh against women. This has the bad effect of inspiring Lereano to allege ".xv. poyntes agaynste all them that erreth in spekynge euell of women, and .xx. other reasones . . . wherby we are bound to say well of all women, with dyuerce other samples of theyr bountie & goodnes."[30] This done, he has only to die. Hating to leave Laureola's correspondence behind, "he callyd for a cup of water, and then brake the lettres in to small peces, and so sette vp in his bed, and dranke vp the water with the peces of the letters. . . ."[31] Thus he expires in communion with the subject of his worship. The Núñez continuation brings allegory back into the story (it is set aside much of the time) and manages to give Laureola her first and only speech to Lereano; and fortunately for the original Laureola's delicate sense of honor, this final confrontation takes place in the comparative safety of a dream which comes to the narrator.

San Pedro's original and Núñez's continuation are both presented in an English style which delivers the facts but shows evidence of syntactical growing pains. For instance, a letter from Lereano to Laureola reads in part as follows:

When a man hathe any busynes with a greate personage: thynkyng to attayn to haue grace: fyrste he must wynne the good wylles of the seruauntes, wherby a man lightely shall come to his entent. But as for me I can fynde no remedye. I haue done my deuour to serche for ayde whome I haue found alwayes ferme & stable for all they haue requyred you to haue mercy vpon me: ye sowle bycause he sufferet, hand [suffereth, and] the lyfe bycause it susteyneth, the harte bycause it endureth, the vnderstandynge bycause it feleth. And syn ye wyll gyue no reward for all these, in that they desyre, and by reasone haue deseruyd, I ame the moste vnfortunat of all other vnhappy. The water refressheth the yerth: but my

29. *Castell*, Kiii^v.
30. Kvii^v.
31. Mvii^r.

wepynges can not molefye your endurat hardnes. The water gyueth liquor to the feldes, herbys, and trees, but my wepynge can not entre in to your harte.[32]

C. S. Lewis writes that "no prose writer of that period has deserved nearly so well of posterity as Sir John Bourchier, Lord Berners. . . . All of his work that is still read with delight shows him as the last of the great medieval translators."[33] Here is high praise, indeed. Perhaps it is better suited, however, to the translator of Froissart than of San Pedro.

After the first printing of the *Castell*, eight lean years passed by. Then in Antwerp, 1556, there appeared the anonymous *Histoire de Aurelio et Isabelle . . . Nyeuley Translatede in Foure Langagies, Frenche, Italien, Spanish, and Inglishe.* As its title page indicates, this work was a language textbook. Interestingly enough, its Spanish original, Juan de Flores' *Grisel y Mirabella,* had also been didactic, but in rather a different way; it had figured on the affirmative side in the heated feminist debate that flourished in fifteenth-century Spain.[34] Although its style was relatively simple to begin with, the narrative became more florid upon passing into the Italian (during which process the characters were renamed), and when the English version was evolved from the Italian, floridity was compounded with awkwardness.[35]

The plot is the same in all four languages. It concerns a Scottish princess who is such a paragon *"that neuer no body might prayse hir so muche, that he might come to the ende of the laudes, that she deserued."*[36] So many swains die for love of the young lady, in fact, that the king must have her conveyed to a secret place so as to reduce the mortality rate. Among the last competitors hoping to win her there are finally left but two, the hero Aurelio and one of his friends. Aurelio kills his rival, and, in less time than it takes to imagine, is welcomed to Isabel's bed. Subsequently he is surprised in it, and the two of them are whisked away to prison. Now, since

32. Ki^v–Kii^r. Two turned "u's" have been righted.

33. *English Literature in the Sixteenth Century Excluding Drama* (Oxford, 1954), p. 149.

34. The oldest Spanish version known was printed in 1495 but composed earlier, perhaps in the 1480's. The work was to prove quite popular. Before Cervantes' time it attained at least fifty-six editions in several languages. The definitive Flores study is that by Barbara Matulka, *The Novels of Juan de Flores and Their European Diffusion* (New York, 1931).

35. The Italian version, from the hand of one Lelio Aletiphilo, appeared first in 1521. "Aletiphilo" was probably the pen name of Lelio Manfredi.

36. The foliation is erratic, but this appears on the first page of the English text. A turned "u" has been righted.

Scottish law presumably decrees that in such cases the lover who is most guilty must be executed, each altruistically tries to maintain his own guilt. To settle matters, the king finds a gentlewoman and a knight who are *"moste experimentede in batailles of loue"* so that they may hold a debate, the outcome of the trial to depend on the outcome of the debate. After Affranio and Hortensia, the two champions, have talked at great length, the judges (dressed in black and carrying bloody swords) decree that it is Isabel who must die. At the time of execution, however, Aurelio leaps into the flames intended for his sweetheart, and although the princess is thereupon pardoned, she manages to jump from a window into a courtyard full of hungry Scottish lions. After this point, the story must get along without its titular lovers. At first the forensic victor, Affranio, falls in love with his opponent, Hortensia, but finally she, the queen, and a number of other distinguished ladies tie him to a pillar, strip him, torture him at leisure, and cast him into a fire so that each may have a sample of his ashes as a "realycke" to wear in a locket about her neck. The Scottish ladies, it might be thought, are credited with that very cruelty which many a northern writer would have deemed most suited to the Spanish temperament. Still more striking, the character of their victim seems to have been based on an historical figure, Pedro Torrellas, a fifteenth-century poet. Notorious as an anti-feminist, Torrellas is even reputed to have died at the hands of irate ladies.[37]

When the unknown translator of the English *Aurelio* is baffled by vocabulary or grammar, he makes invention do for knowledge. The most that can be said for him is that he probably did not have a speaking knowledge of English, that he was writing a text, not attempting belles-lettres, and that he had a certain reckless courage. His book was issued a second time in 1556, perhaps reappeared in 1586 and 1588, and came out in two variant forms in 1608.

In 1606 the old Spanish story appeared in a new English guise. This was an anonymous version entitled *A Paire of Turtle Doves*. To suggest how the piece differs from its original, one need say only that it has sometimes been thought to be the work of the dramatist-romancer Robert Greene. Miss Matulka concludes that, by Greene or not, it is a sloppy affair, tossed together with haste.[38] Charles Mish, on the other hand, thinks

37. Matulka, pp. 159–160.

38. Writes Miss Matulka: "Although it is based on the *Aurelio e Isabella* [i. e., the Italian version], and follows its plot incident by incident, it had been transposed into a different setting, and had been so completely changed and reworded, that it

it shows "a proficient skill in graceful writing."[39] Granted that *A Paire of Turtle Doves* has passed beyond the limits of Dryden's first two categories, traveling well on into the realm of imitation, and granted some sympathy for its type, it is certainly not unreadable. The problem of its authorship, however, remains to be solved.[40]

Taken together, the three *novelas sentimentales* considered here—two by San Pedro and one by Flores—are of interest on several counts. The first is their equivocal position between medieval and modern. Although vestiges of their sentimental anatomizing may seem discernible in the art of Samuel Richardson and even later, they themselves look backward toward medieval allegory, fine talk, and chivalry. In the *Castell,* for instance, allegory is baldly explicit and unsustained, traits more typical of the Middle Ages than the Renaissance; the word-duel of Affranio and Hortensia is a reflection of the game of debating a question, carried over into the Renaissance but perhaps more characteristic of earlier times; and there are even knightly combats and tournaments.

Second, and dominating over all, is the subject of love. Of course love figures in some way in most of the world's fiction, but in the *novelas sentimentales* it is so primary and pervasive as to require special mention. In these stories it is a latter-day manifestation of courtly love, worthy of being elevated to the greatest of heights, even sanctified (as in Donne) by the language of religion. In *Arnalte* we read of the hero's "martirdome," suffered for love in testimony of his faith.[41] In San Pedro's second story we find that the Castle (or Prison) of Love is built on the rock of the lover's faith, and supported by his understanding, reason, memory, and will. As in

---

resulted very different in tonality from the Spanish work which it reproduced" (p. 212). She also reminds us that Greene died in 1592, some fourteen years before the *Turtle Doves* appeared.

39. Charles C. Mish, "English Prose Fiction, 1600–1642: A Survey," unpublished Ph.D. dissertation (University of Pennsylvania, 1951), p. 178. Mish also remarks that the book is lacking in Greene's customary allusions to natural history and legend.

40. Perhaps it is worth noting that the book is listed among Greene's works by Samuel A. Tannenbaum, *Robert Greene: A Concise Bibliography* (New York, 1939), p. 16. Some version of the story also proved useful in the composition of Beaumont and Fletcher's *The Woman Hater* (1607) and Fletcher's *Women Pleased* (revised [?] 1619–1623).

41. Hollyband, *The Pretie and Wittie Historie of Arnalt & Lucenda*, p. 299. See Denis de Rougemont, *Love in the Western World*, tr. Montgomery Belgion (New York, 1956), esp. pp. 159–160; Bruce Wardropper, "El mundo sentimental de la 'Carcel [*sic*] de Amor," *RFE*, XXXVII (1953), 168–193; and Samuel Gili y Gaya's introd. in San Pedro's *Obras* (Madrid, 1950).

the writings of the great Spanish mystics, we find declarations of the hero's dying of not being able to die. We find masochistic complaints of pains valued more than every conceivable good. In fact, for its treatment of love, the *Cárcel* was denounced by the Spanish moralists and banned by the Inquisition. Conveyed as love is in the *novelas sentimentales,* however, expressed as it is in a formal, rhetorical complex of words which somehow act as substitutes rather than vehicles for emotion, these stories are apt to strike the modern reader as little relevant to life.

Third, and inseparable from the foregoing, is the archaic stiffness which informs the genre. One might wonder if this stiffness is traceable in part to the fact that Spanish dignity, restraint, and decorum are not conducive to a display of personal feeling; yet, in comparison with that found in other writing of its time, the emotional content of the genre is considerable. It simply seems that stylized, generic sentiment and superficial verbal complexity are better resistors than transmitters. Like certain other kinds of Renaissance literature, the *novelas sentimentales* may well remind one of those early pictures whose painters have ignored "the natural tridimensional expansion of the lines and the illumination rather than permit it to disturb their closely knit surface patterns."[42] I would say of these stories as Hagen says of such painting—and reservations are always necessary when comparing one art with another: the result is "a paraphrase of reality into the artificial language of tapestry design." In the world of these narratives, life seems to have been arrested, dehydrated, and clad in patterned brocades. Despite the fact that they are stories of passion and mental strife, everything they present seems categorized, circumscribed, and partitioned. (The narrative itself in the *Castell* is conveyed in discrete segments bearing labels such as "The letter of Laureola to the kynge," "The Auctor," and "Lereano to his company.") And here we come upon an important feature of much early Spanish fiction, namely, that characters constantly say they feel, and eventually they act, but they do not really seem to think. They only recite the words dictated by their social situation.

Renaissance Englishmen, of course, were in a somewhat better position than we to be appreciative. One thinks of the popularity of George Pettie's *Petite Pallace* (1576). Pettie's lack of concern for narration (at least as moderns conceive it), his long speeches and letters, and his copious style are all reminiscent of the *novelas sentimentales,* which of course would

42. Oskar Hagen, *Patterns and Principles of Spanish Art* (Madison, Wis., 1943), p. 59.

have been available to him. One thinks of Lyly, too. Like *Arnalte,* Lyly's *Euphues* takes place at a Grecian court and concerns the unfortunate love of two men for one woman. Like San Pedro, Lyly takes time to eulogize his queen. Even more to the point, Lyly is a rhetorical stylist weaving an intricate web of words on a sentimental narrative frame which is all but hidden from view. Whether or not Lyly read these Spanish stories, there is less reason to call *Euphues* a novel than an English *novela sentimental.*[43]

The Chivalric Romance

Springing also from medieval sources was the next genre to come northward. The flower of chivalry drooped rather low in England as the sixteenth century drew to a close, and yet the knightly heroes of literature never really lost their appeal. In fact a rather important revival occurred in the 1580's and 1590's, thanks in part to the newly imported Spanish romances of chivalry, works such as *The Myrror of Knighthood, Palmerin d'Oliva, Palladine of England,* and *Palmendos.* Although these stories lie by the side of our main path, it may be useful to make a few observations on their belated success in England.

Contrary to what one might think, they were not spontaneous outgrowths of Spanish taste. Although they certainly became acclimated in the Iberian Peninsula fairly early, they were exotics there, with Greco-Oriental, Carolingian, Breton, and other strains.[44] Briefly, they relate the stories of

43. One should also be aware of the view that "The narrative form developed by Pettie, Lyly, and Greene was primarily the result of fitting euphuism to the Italian novella" (John Weld, "Studies in the Euphuistic Novel [1576–1640]," unpublished Ph.D. dissertation [Harvard, 1940], p. 1). George B. Parks, "Before *Euphues,*" in *Joseph Quincy Adams Memorial Studies,* ed. James G. McManaway, Giles E. Dawson, and Edwin E. Willoughby (Washington, D. C., 1948), pp. 475–493, considers *Euphues* as a psychological novel and discusses its relation to various earlier works, including those of San Pedro.

44. Among many discussions available are the following: Menéndez Pelayo, *Orígenes . . . ,* Vol. I, Ch. 4; Henry Thomas's "The Romance of Amadís of Gaul," *Transactions of the Bibliographical Society,* XI (1912), 251–297, and *Spanish and Portuguese Romances of Chivalry* (Cambridge, Eng., 1920); María Rosa Lida de Malkiel, "Arthurian Literature in Spain and Portugal," *Arthurian Literature in the Middle Ages,* ed. Roger Sherman Loomis (Oxford, 1959), pp. 406–418; and Edwin B. Place's "Fictional Evolution: The Old French Romances and the Primitive *Amadís* Reworked by Montalvo," *PMLA,* LXXI (1956), 521–529, and his introd., *Amadís de Gaula,* Vol. I (Madrid, 1959).

doughty heroes who, according to their most famous admirer, Don Quixote, spend their time in the "cleauing of *Gyants,* beheading of Serpents, killing of Monsters, ouerthrowing of Armies, putting Nauies to flight, and finishing [undoing] of Inchantments"[45]—largely, it should be added, for the sake of ladies. Unblessed and unbound by probability of incident, unity of action, or depth of character, these works were written primarily to depict the eye-popping prowess of armored supermen. Remembrance of Don Quixote's devotion to the green-eyed Dulcinea is enough to remind us that they also furnished examples of elegant love-making. Sometimes, for instance in the *Amadís de Gaula,* love is as idealistically, almost religiously, chaste as in *The Castell of Love;* but sometimes, too, it is designed for more terrestrial tastes.

The earliest versions of the *Amadís*—which is the best and most famous of its kind—were apparently composed somewhere on the peninsula during the thirteenth or fourteenth century.[46] It is still uncertain whether "Gaula" was meant to be Wales or Gaul, but two points do seem clear: the background of the *Amadís* is definitely Arthurian,[47] and for Garci Rodríguez de Montalvo, author of the earliest extant text (Saragossa, 1508), "Gaula" was a small feudal realm in Brittany.[48] Like other successful narratives in Spain, the *Amadís* was followed by sequels and imitations. And in all, as Fitzmaurice-Kelly lamented, it seems that "the giants grow taller, the monsters fiercer, the lakes deeper, the torments sharper."[49]

Fully as characteristic as exaggeration is repetition. Although the early parts of the *Amadís* are much less monotonous than are most works of its kind, Oskar Hagen has compared its later development with the multiplication of similar cells. Rodríguez de Montalvo took on the task of rework-

45. *Don Quixote* (1620), I, 231. In this chapter and elsewhere, all *Quixote* quotations are from this edition unless otherwise specified.

46. Aubrey F. G. Bell considers the *Amadís* in his study called *Portuguese Literature* (Oxford, 1922), and Henry Thomas includes it in his discussion of "English Translations of Portuguese Books before 1640," in *Miscelánea de estudos em honra de D. Carolina Michaëlis de Vasconcellos* (Coimbra, 1930), pp. 1–22. The oldest manuscript fragments of the *Amadís,* however, dating from about 1420, are in Castilian. See Antonio Rodríguez-Moñino, "El primer manuscrito del 'Amadís de Gaula,'" and Rafael Lapesa, "El lenguaje del 'Amadís' manuscrito," both in *Boletín de la Real Academia Española,* XXXVI (1956), 199–216 and 219–225.

47. William J. Entwistle, *The Arthurian Legend in the Literatures of the Spanish Peninsula* (London, 1925), pp. 213–224.

48. Edwin B. Place, *"Amadis of Gaul, Wales or What?"* HR, XXIII (1955), 99–107.

49. *A History of Spanish Literature* (New York, 1898), p. 124.

ing the four books of an earlier version of the romance, and then, as Hagen says, he

very appropriately called his fifth book *sergas* (derived from *serica,* "tapestry"). The subsequent increase of the five books to an ultimate twelve was indeed like the weaving of additional square feet to a carpet already covered with similar motifs. . . . [In the various parts of the *Amadís*] the subject of the "tapestry" and the design of its pattern . . . remained exactly the same—the sons, the grandsons, and the great-grandsons of the hero experiencing virtually the same adventures as had their ancestors.[50]

Why was repetitiousness not a deterrent to popularity? One can only suggest that when read in many instalments—by ladies in a castle closet or to country folk at an inn—each incident would be regarded on its own merit. Repetition in a long work is most apparent when considered in a scholar's study.[51]

The first known English translation of a Spanish romance of chivalry was a partial version of the *Amadís*. In 1571, at the request of his mother, a fifteen-year-old lad named Charles Stewart translated the first one and a half chapters from the French. Son of the regent of Scotland, brother of Lord Darnley, uncle of King James, and later the father of Arabella Stewart, Charles was no average schoolboy. But his position *per se* is scarcely more significant to us than the fact that his training involved translation, and that his tutor was David Rowland of Anglesey, the translator of *Lazarillo de Tormes*. Stewart's writing, however, never reached print.[52]

Equally tentative was the first printed translation from the *Amadís*. Thomas Paynell, a friar who had been chaplain to Henry VIII, brought out *The Treasurie of Amadis of Fraunce* in about 1572. Based on the popular *Tresor de livres d'Amadis de Gaule,* Paynell's book was really no more than a sugar-coated primer of rhetoric, consisting of model letters and speeches, and hardly to be considered fiction.

It was not until about eighteen years later, in fact, when Spain was

50. Hagen, p. 40. The meaning of *sergas* (usually "exploits" or "achievements") is problematical; but see R. Foulché-Delbosc, "Sergas," *RH,* XXIII (1910), 591–593.

51. After a typical romance is imported thence, the very most that can be said is that its art "depends more on simple manipulation of a highly stylized body of conventions than on thoughtful adaptation of literary means to new narrative ends" (Donald Marcus Beach, "Studies in the Art of Elizabethan Prose Narrative," unpublished Ph.D. dissertation [Cornell, 1959], p. 13).

52. See H. L. D. Ward, *Catalogue of Romances in the Department of Manuscripts in the British Museum* (London, 1883), I, 787–788.

much in men's thoughts, that Anthony Munday, a prolific translator and minor lyrist, finally made the story of Amadís available to the English public. About 1590, he produced Part I, *Discoursing the Adventures and Love of Many Knights and Ladies.*[53]

Meanwhile our only known woman translator, Margaret Tiler, had introduced *The Mirrour of Princely Deedes and Knighthood* (1578).[54] But even Mistress Margaret was a little late to score a coup. To be sure, romances had had distinguished readers, among them St. Teresa and St. Ignatius, Charles V (an avid fan of Don Belianis) and Francis I (a devoted Amadisiac). Later in the sixteenth century there were some among the English intelligentsia— Sidney and Spenser, for example—who continued to find the romances appealing and even useful. But by the turn of the seventeenth century such books seemed pretty old-fashioned, their appeal being greatest among the middle or lower classes. In 1621 Robert Burton made scathing reference to "such inamoratoes as read nothing but play-books, idle poems, jests, Amadis de Gaul, the Knight of the Sun, the Seven Champions,

53. In a preface which Munday wrote in 1588 he makes a grave show of telling his readers that "in translating, men are bound to their Writers words" (*The Famous . . . Historie of Palladine of England,* *iv^r). In actual practice, however, Munday gave his public only the gist of his originals, abridging ad libitum, adding where it suited his whim or plan, substituting songs of his own for songs of the original, and in some cases even farming out parts of his work to helpers. Gerald R. Hayes's verdict is that Munday's "translations show passages sometimes correctly rendered but badly expressed; in other places a perfectly wrong translation is well expressed; while at times passages are simply a meaningless assembly of words" ("Anthony Munday's Romances of Chivalry," *The Library,* ser. 4, VI [1926], 74; see also [Julia] Celeste Turner [Wright], *Anthony Mundy: An Elizabethan Man of Letters* [Berkeley, Calif., 1928]). Munday worked not only on the *Amadis* and *Palladine,* but on several parts of the *Palmerin* cycle—*Palmendos, Palmerin d'Oliva, Palmerin of England,* and *Primaleon of Greece.*

54. Translated from Diego Ortúñez de Calahorra's *Espejo de príncipes y caballeros.* In 1905 Joseph D. Perott pointed to *The Mirrour* as the source of *The Tempest* ("The Probable Source of the Plot of Shakespeare's *Tempest,*" *Publications of the Clark University Library,* I, 209–216). Although my purpose is not to trace influences, it seems advisable here to note that Shakespeare has sometimes been credited with considerable borrowing from Spanish fiction. A list of commentaries printed on the subject between 1904 and 1940 is given by Selma Guttman, *The Foreign Sources of Shakespeare's Works* (New York, 1947). See also Homero Serís, *Manual de bibliografía de la literatura española* (Syracuse, N. Y., 1948– 1954), I, 57–59. Nevertheless Geoffrey Bullough's *Narrative and Dramatic Sources of Shakespeare* (New York, 1957———) will not prove a happy hunting ground for Hispanists. Two conservative correctives for overenthusiastic claims are given in Henry Thomas's *Shakespeare and Spain* (Oxford, 1922) and "Shakespeare y España," *Homenaje ofrecido a Menéndez Pidal* (Madrid, 1925), I, 225–253.

Palmerin de Oliva, Huon of Bordeaux, etc. Such many times prove in the end as mad as Don Quixote."[55] And yet chivalric romances continued to be read. They were imitated by such men as Emanuel Forde, Richard Johnson, and Henry Roberts, and later on, in the 1660's, they even enjoyed something of a revival.[56]

The Picaresque Story

Five years after Charles Stewart translated part of the *Amadís,* his tutor published a translation of the first of the Spanish picaresque stories, the anonymous *Lazarillo de Tormes.*[57] David Rowland's *Lazarillo* really enters the history of English fiction several years before, however. As early as 1568–1569 a translation of it was registered with the Stationers' Company by Thomas Colwell. So far as is known, Colwell never published it, but in 1573 sold his rights to Henry Bynneman.[58] Once again, so far as is known,

55. *The Anatomy of Melancholy* (London, 1932), II, 93.

56. The various chivalric romances that were translated into English are listed below, *Appendix C.*

It is pleasant to be able to append to the present brief treatment the remarks of a scholar who has had the stamina to read a number of these books. Mary Patchell, in *The Palmerin Romances in Elizabethan Prose Fiction* (New York, 1947), p. xii, writes thus:

> In addition to their inaccessibility, other factors which have deterred scholars from studying them are the monotony and absurdity of the subject matter, the very poor typography of the books, which makes reading them a real physical labor, and their excessive length. The complete cycle of four [*Palmerin*] romances is contained in five quarto volumes of some 3,075 pages printed in black letter.
>
> The intrinsic merit of these works is so slight that they deserve the oblivion into which they have fallen. . . .

57. Although the work was formerly attributed to Diego Hurtado de Mendoza, current opinion on authorship is divided. The earliest known editions appeared in Burgos, Alcalá, and Antwerp in 1554. Restitution of a hypothetical *editio princeps* has been attempted, however, by R. Foulché-Delbosc, and this, in turn, has been translated by Louis How (New York, 1917) and J. Gerald Markley (New York, 1954).

Some students would reserve the label of "first picaresque novel" for Francisco Delicado's *Retrato de la loçana andaluza,* written in dialogue form and published in Venice, 1528. The problem of primacy is further complicated if one believes *Lazarillo* goes back to 1525 or 1526. (For a discussion of dating see Manuel J. Asensio, "El *Lazarillo de Tormes:* Problemas, crítica y valoración," unpublished Ph.D. dissertation [University of Pennsylvania, 1955], pp. 393–404.)

58. Arber (London, 1875), I, 378.

no edition was actually printed. Not until 1576 did the English public have their first look at *The Pleasaunt Historie of Lazarillo de Tormes.*[59]

With the addition of this work the subject of Spanish fiction in England begins to attain a breadth and stature such as never could have derived from the *novelas sentimentales* and chivalric romances. *Lazarillo* is, as Fonger de Haan observes, "one of the most curious, entertaining and important works in the Spanish language."[60] And David Rowland did it justice.

Rowland was a Welshman and linguist. Although little is known of him, Wood says that he was educated at Oxford, "partly in Grammar and partly in Logic . . . , particularly as it seems in St. *Mary's*-hall. . . ."[61] Doubtless it was after leaving Oxford that he became tutor to the son of the Earl of Lennox. His *Comfortable Ayde for Scholers* (1568), a perfunctory textbook translated from the Italian *Specchio de la lingua latina,* is dedicated to *"my singular good* Lorde and Maister, the Earle of Lennox . . . *as a token of my true and affectionate seruice,"* and put forth as *"the first fruites of my trauell,"* which have been *"chiefly done in the fauour of your Lordshippes noble and towarde Sonne,"* in order that the boy might continue his linguistic progress.[62] Apparently Rowland had done some traveling, and then, back in England, become "a profess'd Tutor as it seems of the *Gr.* and *Lat.* Tongue," a man who "wrote for the use of his Pupills."[63]

In the second edition of his *Lazarillo* (1586), the oldest now extant, Rowland relates that "WHEN I had read ouer this litle treatise . . . finding it for the nūber of strãge and mery reports, very recreatiue & pleasant. [*sic*] I thought it no labor euill bestowed, to occupie my selfe in the translation thereof."[64] We need not be shocked, by the way, that the chief ostensible subject of the book, the near-starvation of a child, struck Rowland as a good subject for mirth. It was an era, after all, when "the deformitie of a

59. No copy of a 1576 edition is known to be extant, though Frank W. Chandler reports that it was described by Bagford (*Romances of Roguery* [New York, 1899], p. 211).

60. *An Outline of the History of the Novela Picaresca in Spain* (The Hague, 1903), p. 14.

61. *Athenae Oxonienses* (London, 1721), I, 230.

62. *Comfortable Ayde,* Aii^r–Aiii^v.

63. Wood, I, 230. Rowland dedicated *Lazarillo* to Sir Thomas Gresham, but I know of no evidence for Martin Hume's statement that Rowland was one of Gresham's clerks or that *Lazarillo* was already *well* known to educated Englishmen in 1576 ("Some Spanish Influences in Elizabethan Literature," *Transactions of the Royal Society of Literature,* Ser. 2, XXIX [1909], 9).

64. *Lazarillo,* Aii^r.

mans bodye" gave "matter enoughe to be ryght merye. . . ."[65] On the other hand, mere amusement, as we have seen, was seldom a sufficient excuse for fiction. Rowland goes on to add that "besides much mirth, here is also a true discription of the nature & disposition of sundrie Spaniards. So that by reading hereof, such as haue not trauailed Spaine, may as well discerne much of the maners & customs of that countrey, as those that haue there long time continued."[66]

The translation itself is good evidence that an honest tale speeds best being plainly told. It is easily the most recreative bit of prose brought out of Spanish up to that time. The fact remains, however, that despite its similarity to the wry, dry Spanish version, Rowland's translation leans heavily on the French one by the mysterious J. G. de L.[67] The latter had changed some references to the church, omitted a couple of literary allusions, and added the opening chapter of the spurious 1555 continuation, all of which changes Rowland incorporated. As J. E. V. Crofts observes, "even the marginal notes explaining Spanish customs are in more than a dozen cases derived from the same source."[68] It is not that the Welsh translator ignored the Spanish text; he simply depended more on the French.

The story which Rowland rendered is the pseudo-autobiographical narrative of young Lazaro, a boy who was born in a mill out in the river Tormes, near Salamanca. Although some would claim, rather strangely, that it is not truly picaresque because its hero is motivated by the will to live rather than by roguery, the book nevertheless set the pattern for that type of fiction in which a boy or youth wanders about having adventures with a series of masters, enabling the writer to satirize various aspects of society.[69] Lazarillo's chief masters are a blind man, a priest, and a squire,

65. Thomas Wilson, *The Arte of Rhetorique* (1553), 78ᵛ.
66. *Lazarillo*, Aii.
67. I take these initials from Jean Antoine Rigoley de Juvigny's *Les bibliothéques françoises . . .* (Paris, 1772), I, 588, which suggests that Jean Garnier de Laval is the translator, and indicates why the work is usually ascribed to Jean Saugrain.
68. Introd. to his edition of Rowland's translation (Oxford, 1924), p. viii.
69. Some students would distinguish between two sorts of *picaro:* (1) the underdog who barely manages to survive the buffets of life, and (2) the crafty rogue who prospers from his tricks, yet is finally discovered (see, e.g., E. M. W. Tillyard, *The Epic Strain in the English Novel* [London, 1958], p. 14). Discussions of the word are given in A. R. Nykl, *"Pícaro," RH,* LXXVII (1929), 172–186; Angel Valbuena Prat's introd., *La novela picaresca española* (Madrid, 1943), pp. v–xxvii; and Alberto del Monte's *Itinerario del romanzo picaresco spagnolo* (Flor-

and the chief lesson he learns is that in order to survive he must have "one tricke more than the diuel him self."[70] Finally he is settled in marriage with the mistress of an archdeacon of Toledo, at which time, he observes, "I was in my prosperitie, and in my chiefest time of good aduenture."[71]

In analyzing the sources of this modest little story, scholars have turned to traditional tales, the literature of various ages, and the life of the times, all of which, taken together, are insufficient to negate the author's originality. Studies of *Lazarillo* are filled with references to such varied works as the *Satyricon, The Golden Ass,* the *Aethiopica,* the *Roman de Renart, Till Eulenspiegel,* the *Morgante,* the *Celestina,* the *Liber vagatorum,* and even the Arabic *Maqamat.* But if one feels the urge to seek a literary point of departure for the book, one might equally well turn—and the idea is not new—to the chivalric romances. Crammed as they are with impossible perfections, these stories must soon have satiated at least some readers' taste for such things. Conceivably the *Lazarillo* author was one such reader. Conceivably he felt that a scrawny, barefoot rogue like his ten-year-old hero (who has broken teeth, patches of bare scalp, and sundry bruises) was a fitting, even a necessary antidote for the less credible Amadís. Certainly Lazarillo's struggle with hunger was more relevant to the times than was any chivalric struggle with dragons and giants—or any quixotic attack upon windmills. In contrast to the chivalric romances, *Lazarillo* was a basically sober, down-to-earth fiction. Not only was it perfectly congenial to the austere Castilian temperament, but it was sharpened by satire in such a way that it was capable of implying a standard of values more honestly "idealistic" than anything to be found in the romances.

Fully as important as *Lazarillo's* literary background, as this implies, was its social milieu. The reign of that "thunderbolt of war," Charles V, was in some ways both the beginning and end of Spanish grandeur, a dazzling millenium which was blighted from the start, a prime example for those

---

ence, 1957), pp. 3–5. See also the numerous studies listed by Homero Serís, *Manual,* I, 325–326, 842–843.

Chandler, p. 30, observes that "neglected children, joining in bands for juvenile depredation, were feeders for companies of elder rogues. So great a scandal had they become, indeed, that in 1552 the Cortes was brought to consider them in a petition requesting the appointment of special officers to have charge of collecting and providing with work the little rascals, who were running wild." In 1608 Cristóbal Pérez de Herrera estimated that there were 150,000 vagabonds in Spain.

70. *Lazarillo,* Aviii[v].

71. Hv[r]. Rowland then goes on to translate five pages of the spurious sequel.

who believe that the best of epochs carry the germs of their own decay.[72] With admirable economy the *Lazarillo* author pointed out some of the real and potential ills that he could see lying beneath the bold, bright surface of his time, especially in mendicancy, the church, and the squirearchy. In the blind man, priest, and squire he showed the nature of craftiness, corruption, and pride; and in Lazarillo himself he created an unforgettable protest against the general decadence of a society which had produced the real-life *pícaro*. The people who believed that God created Spain to rule the world needed to be told that honest toil was neither useless nor base, and the writer of *Lazarillo* did all that he could to enlighten them, perhaps most deftly of all when he depicted the boy's third master, a down-at-heels gentleman who delicately picks his teeth with a bit of straw when he has had nothing to eat and when, in fact, there is even a shortage of straw.[73]

The initial three episodes of the book—those of the blind man, priest, and squire—are masterfully conceived and executed. Then the writer's first fine rapture falters. The fourth episode, an account of a pardoner's clever cozening, is well told and interesting, but shifts the entire narrative onto a new plane.[74] Lazarillo is nearly forgotten. He becomes an observer rather than the chief participant. And succeeding episodes in his story are so quickly and cursorily presented that one cannot help thinking that the author simply tired of his task. Because at its early best *Lazarillo* is characterized by a remarkable inventiveness and spontaneity, one is tempted to wish that its author had somehow sustained the quality of his beginning.[75] Even as it is,

72. About the same time that Charles V became emperor, Cortez provided him with the kingdom of the Montezumas, and, somewhat later, Pizarro served up Peru. Charles's son and successor, Philip II, was even depicted as "sitting on horsebacke vpon a *monde* or world, the horse prauncing forward with his forelegges as if he would leape of, with this inscription, *Non sufficit orbis,* meaning . . . that one whole world could not content him" (cited from George Puttenham in *Elizabethan Critical Essays,* ed. G. Gregory Smith [Oxford, 1904], II, 109). When he died, however, Philip II left Philip III with a debt of some hundred million ducats. Spain certainly did not fall in a day. In fact the empire of Philip III seemed supreme in Europe. But those "who looked below the surface saw . . . an exhausted, depopulated country, riddled by corruption from top to bottom, swarming with beggars and hangers-on of the court, of the nobles and of the monasteries . . ." (R. Trevor Davis, *The Golden Century of Spain* [London, 1937], p. 260).

73. The toothpick was a sign of gentility.

74. Lazarillo's fourth master, a friar, is disposed of in a breath. The pardoner is really Master No. 5.

75. It seems needless to maintain that "The four final *tratados* are suspiciously short and betray the hand of the pruner" (George T. Northup, *An Introduction to Spanish Literature* [Chicago, 1936], p. 176), or that, "Although short and concise,

however, the book is superior to practically any other fiction of the time. Still more important, it introduced a valuable genre which has yet to run its course.

That *Lazarillo* now seems superior may be explained in various ways. One of these concerns its use of the first-person narrator. San Pedro had spoken through a persona in both *Arnalte* and the *Castell,* yet the stories he told and his narrators themselves are almost totally lacking in recognizable human traits. The author of *Lazarillo,* in contrast, has created a narrator who not only has some personality of his own, but one who tells of subjects that are lastingly relevant to life. Like San Pedro, the writer of *Lazarillo* places his narrator in his picture rather than merely in front of it, but his success is the greater because he goes on to try some other important things: he specifies the setting of his story (a technique which fortifies the individuation of character), and he attempts a more extensive mimesis of sense data. Furthermore, his representation of the sensuous world, instead of being chiefly decorative, is a means of giving the reader a broader basis for understanding and evaluating the subject and theme of the book. This is not to say that *Lazarillo* conveys "reality." (In the first place, it is impossible to put reality on paper. In the second, *Lazarillo* does not even represent a serious effort to transmit life unmodified.)[76] It is to say that beneath its surface details and exaggerations—and there is no denying that these have more lasting appeal than their counterparts in the *novelas sentimentales*—there lie matters of enduring significance.

For an illustration of the writer's approach, let us glance at the narrator's

---

this [Ch. 4] is an adequate picture of the restless friar" (F. Courtney Tarr, "Literary and Artistic Unity in *Lazarillo,*" *PMLA,* XLII [1927], 413). Better is Raymond S. Willis's suggestion (in "Lazarillo and the Pardoner: The Artistic Necessity of the Fifth *Tractado,*" *HR,* XXVII [1959], 267–279) that the author's acceleration of time and the "disengagement of the protagonist from our closely sympathetic attention" are good means of preparing us for Lazarillo's culminating cynicism. Since the story is said to be that of Lazarillo—i. e., *little* Lázaro—it might be expected that the mature Lázaro would be dealt with somewhat briefly; what is appealing about a ten-year-old rascal may fade as he becomes a bearded sharper. I think it unnecessary, however, to try to explain away the shortcomings of the work. It is superb in spite of its flaws.

76. To the extent that its focus is on the meanest levels of life, *Lazarillo* is quite as one-sided as the *novelas sentimentales* and chivalric romances. At the same time, the author's handful of nature is better than an armful of empty rhetoric, better than a cartload of sentimentality. For a discussion of some of the ways in which *Lazarillo* is unrealistic see Angel González Palencia, *Del "Lazarillo" a Quevedo* (Madrid, 1946).

initiation into the way of the world. It occurs just after he has left home and become the blind man's boy.

So wee departed out of Salamanka, and came on our way as farre as the bridge, at the entrance whereof standeth a beast of Stone, fashioned much like a bul: as sone as we came nere it, y⁰ blindmā willed me to approche, saying *Lazaro*, put thine eare to this Bull, and thou shalt heare a terrible noise within it: as soone as he had said y⁰ worde, I was ready like a foole to bowe down my head, to do as he had cōmāded, thinking that his wordes had bene most true: but the traiterous blind man suspecting how neare it my head was, thrusteth forth his arme vpon a sodaine, with such force, that my sore head tooke suche a blowe against the diuelish Bull, that for the space of three dayes my head felte the paines of his hornes, wherefore he was right glad & saide: Consider nowe what thou art thou foolish calfe, thou must vnderstand, that the blind mans boy ought to knowe one tricke more than the diuel him self. It semed then immediatly that I awaked out of simplicitie, wherein I had of long time slept (like a child,) & I said to my self, my blind master hath good reason, it is ful time for me to open mine eyes, yea & to prouide & seeke mine owne aduantage, cōsidering y⁰ I am alone with out any helpe.[77]

Here the setting is not only a specific city, Salamanca, but an identifiable Roman bridge. Against such a background, Lazarillo-the-narrator depicts Lazarillo-the-boy, and, furthermore, depicts his character in the very process of developing. "I awaked out of simplicitie," says Lazarillo.

It is luckily impossible to prove the nature of the author's purpose or even (shades of the intentional fallacy!) that it extends beyond simple diversion. Surely most readers will agree, however, that *Lazarillo* is intended as a comic satire. Whether or not its author was an Erasmian, as has sometimes been thought, his book has a depth which is quite unlike anything to be found in the other works discussed so far. Successfully combining an objective social purpose with a deceptively simple subjective approach, he had no need to preach directly on such topics as the folly of being tied by pride to a social position requiring wealth beyond one's means. Why should he make a direct attack on the standards of the threadbare gentry? He could achieve his purpose simply by having his narrator record the famished squire's request that the little beggar, Lazarillo, let no one know "that thou dost dwell with me, nor that I am thy maister: For that touched mine

77. *Lazarillo,* Aviii. Marcel Bataillon, *El sentido del Lazarillo de Tormes* (Paris, 1954), p. 16, speaks of this episode as a sort of initiation rite. Pursuing the matter slightly further, one might remark the appropriateness of the bull as a symbol of masculine maturity. (See Jack Randolph Conrad, *The Horn and the Sword* [New York, 1957].)

honor. . . ."[78] To reveal the standards of the squire—or the blind man, priest, or pardoner—was to condemn them.

We are not explicitly told how the author would have the squires of our world change. We are simply shown that the age of Amadís and Hotspur has become the age of Falstaff. ("What is honor?" asks Falstaff. And he answers himself: "A word.") Whether it be in the secular or religious realm —and *Lazarillo* is devastatingly clear in its depiction of clerical corruption[79] —the victim of false standards is a subject for mirth. He is the cause for compassionate humor in the case of the squire, and for hard jocularity in the case of the priest, pardoner, and archpriest. In the case of the hero himself, the fact that Lazarillo is a persona and not an alter ego may be demonstrated in no way more clearly than by indicating the humor in the conflict between his standards and those of his creator. Toward the close of the book, having risen from urchin to water carrier, Lazarillo buys himself "an old black fustian dublet, and a coate threede bare with gathered sleeues and whol before, and a cloake that had bene of felpado, and a sworde of the olde making. . . ."[80] In other words, equipped with second-hand finery and an old-fashioned sword, he is as ready as the next man to succumb to false standards, to blur reality with appearance.

It is just as well, however, not to limit the book's meaning. It seems best to recognize that, like the author of the *Canterbury Tales,* the author of *Lazarillo* has created characters and situations which are unmistakably satiric, but enigmatically and intriguingly so. One cannot say finally whether Chaucer's Prioress and Pardoner are intended to satirize the church, decay of the church, or something else. With Chaucer as with the author of *Lazarillo,* it is enough that he has given us an entertaining work that makes us think.

Like San Pedro's *Castell* and the chivalric romances, the first of the picaresque narratives received the compliment of sequels. The better one, that composed by Juan de Luna, did not appear even in Spanish until 1620, and will be discussed as a separate work in a later chapter. The weaker one, however, anonymous like its model, was published in Spain as early as 1555. This one tells how Lazarillo meets some Germans in Toledo,

---

78. Evii[v].

79. When applied to religious depravity, the author's attitude of seemingly calm acceptance becomes almost Swiftian. In 1559 the book was placed on the *Catalogus librorum qui prohibentur.*

80. Hii[r].

accompanies them to sea, is shipwrecked, and subsequently becomes a fish. Disregarding the original work's balance between reality and hyperbole, the unknown author has Lazarillo train an army of fish and even marry a fish. Admittedly this is not first-rate stuff. But neither is it as bad as the condemnation of scholars might suggest. In the first place, the idea of a man–fish did not seem as absurd four hundred years ago as now. Not only was it a staple of folklore, but it was seriously discussed by Pedro Mexía, royal chronicler to Charles V, in his *Silva de varia lección* (1540).[81] In the second place, although the book may be attacked on other grounds, it seems unfair to condemn its use of the very metamorphic device for which *The Golden Ass* is commended. Third and possibly most important, the author chose the bottom of the sea as his setting because his purpose was satirical. In William Phiston's translation of 1596 we read of such timeless incidents as killing off the undesirables. The original writer was conceivably thinking of Spain's trouble with the Moors, but the book's treatment of the subject is ambiguous enough to be relevant at any time: "Heere I haue set downe for a perpetuall memorie, the crueltie of these Fishes, and howe farre differente the state of man is, from this of theirs."[82] When given a chance to choose a council, Lazarillo the "Tonnie" fish selects the richest, not the wisest, because that is how he has seen it done on land. He notes that to show respect, the tunnies kiss the tails of their betters. He advises the king of the tunnies that governing may be made more profitable by taxing fish for calling themselves "Don" when they have no lineage. Such a procedure would be impossible on land, of course, because the situation is different there; but "the pride of the fishes is so great, that both good and bad, riche & poore, all are Dons. . . ."[83] And when Lazarillo goes to Salamanca, once again in man's form, his clothes

---

81. Ludwig Pfandl, *Historia de la literatura nacional española en la Edad de Oro,* tr. Jorge Rubió Balaguer (Barcelona, 1952), p. 101, relates Mexía's usage to Juan de Luna's continuation, but makes no mention of the sequel at hand. In some remarks to the reader in his own sequel to *Lazarillo* Luna observes that "Pliny, Ælian, Aristotle, Albertus Magnus . . . *affirme, That there are certaine Fishes in the Sea, the males they call* Titons [*sic*] & *the Females* Nereids, *and all of them Seamen, who from the Girdle vpward haue the shape of perfect Men, and from thence downeward of Fishes*" ([1622], A7). Rudolph Schevill, in "Some Forms of the Riddle Question and the Exercise of the Wits in Popular Fiction and Formal Literature," *UCPMP,* II (1910–1912), 183–237, is one of the few to speak well of this sequel. Although his chief point is that the riddle episode belongs to a well-established tradition, he defends the man–fish concept and reminds us of Caliban.

82. *The Most Pleasaunt and Delectable Historie of Lazarillo de Tormes . . . The Second Part,* D2ʳ.

83. G3ᵛ.

alone win him the respect of the learned. Were it not for his finery, he says, "those long gowned fellowes would haue made no more account of mee, than I did of the Tonnyes in the sea. . . ."[84] Such ideas were old in 1555, to be sure, even older in 1596, but they are never out of date.[85]

Although Phiston's translation of the *Segunda parte* seems to have had no subsequent edition, Rowland's translation of the original made what was at least a third appearance in 1596, and in 1624 was brought out again by Thomas Walkley. In 1639 there came still another edition (erroneously labeled the third), and fourteen years later, in 1653, James Blakeston brought out what he claimed to be a new and more accurate version. In his introductory matter Blakeston makes the following ungrateful and twisted statement:

THis little History of a Spaniards Life, (for those will mistake it who imagine it a Fiction) hath travail'd all France and Italy, and lately return'd into Spain, where it was born; for there the Originall receiv'd some mutilation by lopping off such Passages as grated too hard upon the honour of that Nation. I saw it take so well in other Languages; endeavour'd (at my late aboade in Toledo) to get a sight of the entyre originall which had not suffered the Inquisitors hand; and such clauses as I found wanting in other Copies, I transcrib'd out of that. I knew it was done in English before; but by comparing the Translation I found so many Lapses (especially in the former Part) that I resolved to help Lazaro out of worse hands than any of his seven Masters.[86]

Blakeston's was not a new translation, however. As a matter of fact the so-called castigated copies of the *Lazarillo* had had very little influence on Rowland's work, as Blakeston probably knew. Perhaps he really did reside for a while in Toledo. Biographical data are lacking. But his version varies scarcely at all from that of Rowland.

Long before, even before the first appearance of Rowland's *Lazarillo,* native English writers had attempted the theme of roguery. Among the earliest vagabonds in modern English were those in Robert Copland's *Hye Way to*

84. I4ʳ. Robert H. Williams suggests that Ch. XV of the *Segunda parte* seems truncated because originally it may have contained anticlerical satire that was suppressed. He further suggests reasons for thinking the author was Cristóbal de Villalón ("Notes on the Anonymous Continuation of Lazarillo de Tormes," *RR,* XVI [1925], 223–235).

85. Little is known of Phiston, the translator, beyond the facts that he was a resident of London, had a knowledge of Latin, French, Italian, and Spanish, and produced a number of fairly unimportant works, e.g. *The Welspring of Wittie Conceits* and a revised version of Caxton's famed *Recuyell.*

86. (1653), A3ʳ–A4ʳ.

the Spyttel House (1535), a dialogue between Copland and a porter of St. Bartholomew's Hospital. About thirty years later, John Awdeley, author of *Fraternitye of Vacabondes,* came forth with detailed descriptions of various types of low-life characters; and a couple of years later still, Thomas Harman gave definitions expanded with anecdotes in his *Caveat or Warening for Common Cursetors.* Perhaps, however, the *Geystes of Skoggon* (ca. 1565) was the first English book to be based on the exploits of a single knave-hero.[87] Here we find even a rough sort of continuity between some of the episodes, a point of particular interest if, as is sometimes said, Andrew Borde was the author of the book, for Borde, as we saw in glancing at his *Introduction of Knowledge,* had traveled in Spain and might have known of *Lazarillo.*

Coming toward the end of the century was Robert Greene's *Blacke Bookes Messenger* (1592). This is a work which may remind one of some of the later Spanish rogue stories (for example, Alemán's *Guzmán*), though its conny-catching hero, Ned Browne, has little resemblance to Lazarillo.[88]

Then, two years later, Thomas Nashe produced his *Unfortunate Traveller.* Because this is one of the more enjoyable pieces of English fiction in the period, scholars have naturally been much attracted by it. Furthermore, though its hero is not a *pícaro* of the Lazarillian stamp, they have frequently been tempted to say that it is indebted to the Spanish work. Eighteen-year-old Jack Wilton, nevertheless, with his perfect complexion, handsome frame, and elegant attire, has sufficient appeal to attract the pope's own mistress, which is another way of saying that no matter what characteristics he shares with Lazarillo, some of his differences are so great as to make contrast more convenient than comparison. If one grant a Spanish influence on Nashe, one must hasten to add that it was transformed in his writing beyond the point of demonstrable proof.[89]

87. The work apparently survives only in subsequent editions.

88. Martin Hume (p. 11) describes Greene's various pamphlets as "so many short rogue tales inspired by the similar experiences of the Spanish picaroon, Lazarillo," but what really inspired Greene would be difficult to prove. Despite his own avowal of having learned some of his wickedness while traveling in Spain, Greene's writing seems less closely connected with Spanish than English rogues.

89. One may find authority for every shade of opinion on the subject. E. A. Baker, in *The History of the English Novel* (London, 1929), II, 161, writes that "There is no evidence, . . . in his novel or elsewhere, that he had ever read it [*Lazarillo*], or had any appreciation of the distinctive method and design of picaresque fiction," but Fredson T. Bowers, in "Thomas Nashe and the Picaresque Novel," *Humanistic Studies in Honor of John Calvin Metcalf* (Charlottesville, Va., 1941), p. 26, ex-

Since our concern is translations, not their influence, suffice it to say that authors with an English heritage could find plenty of rogue materials in native writing and life. Equally important, whatever they borrowed from the Spanish was so modified and thoroughly melded with other elements that the results could often pass as English inventions. The same was true in other lands. Wherever the Spanish *pícaro* went, says Chandler, "his exploits and the tales devoted to them were modified, more or less, by the genius of the nation as well as by the talent of transcribers."[90] When Englishmen wanted to read about rogues of Spanish stripe, therefore, they turned perforce to translations of Spanish books. And for a long time, the only one to turn to was *Lazarillo de Tormes.*[91]

The Pastoral Romance

Though terseness and simplicity make the Spanish language an ideal vehicle for *Lazarillo,* some have acclaimed Spanish as the language best for declaring love. Probably not even Margaret of Navarre, however, who made such a claim,[92] could have guessed what melting strains were to be drawn from the tongue by the sentimental genre which gained favor shortly after she wrote.

---

presses the belief that Nashe was "consciously modifying and developing the Spanish novel according to the English temper and his own inclinations."

With all the concern for *The Unfortunate Traveller,* little attention has been given Henry Chettle's *Piers Plainness* (1595). Baker suggested long ago, however, that *Piers* "opens as a pastoral novelette and then turns into a picaresque tale with an unmistakable likeness to *Lazarillo de Tormes.* . . . This is the first English story in which direct imitation of Spanish picaresque fiction is evident" (II, 122). Probably *Piers* does reflect the influence of *Lazarillo,* but one should be careful not to magnify the likeness.

90. *Romances of Roguery,* p. 1.

91. In *Blurt, Master-Constable* (1602) one finds Lazarillo degenerated to a prancing fool who tries to show a house of whores "all the tricks and garbs of Spanish dames," only to be badly scratched by the "puss-cats" for his pains (*Works of Thomas Middleton,* ed. A. H. Bullen [London, 1885], I, 48–49, 80). Another Lazarillo appears in *The Woman Hater* (mentioned earlier in connection with Juan de Flores). *The English Rogue* (1665–1671), by Francis Kirkman and Richard Head, seems to be one of the few English works which borrows directly from the Spanish, but it steals promiscuously from everywhere. The third part of *The Pleasant Adventures of the Witty Spaniard Lazarillo de Tormes* (1688) concerns the son of Lazarillo and is stolen from various places, including, ironically, *The English Rogue* (see E. R. Sims, "Four Seventeenth Century Translations of *Lazarillo de Tormes,*" HR, V [1937], 316–332).

92. *L'Heptaméron,* nouvelle 24, ed. Michel François (Paris, 1950), p. 198.

The Spanish pastoral romance has a long and complicated pedigree.[93] Pastoralism in various forms had of course figured in the writing of such men as Theocritus, Vergil, and Longus, of Petrarch and Boccaccio; but Jacopo Sannazaro, a Neapolitan of Spanish origin, is probably the most significant writer in the early history of modern bucolics. Sannazaro's *Arcadia* (1502) was translated into Castilian in the 1540's, and perhaps first imitated on the peninsula—though not closely—by a Portuguese, Bernardim Ribeiro, in his *Menina e moça* (1554). However, it was another Portuguese, Jorge de Montemayor, who composed the first pastoral romance in Spanish. Montemayor's *Diana,* written for the most part in Castilian, appeared in 1559 and soon commanded a place among the most popular and influential books of its day, inspiring no less than fifteen Spanish imitations, to say nothing of two sequels that are relevant here, one by the Valencian poet Gaspar Gil Polo (1564), and another (also 1564) by Alonso Pérez, a physician of Salamanca.

Left unfinished at the time of his death, the *Diana* is in part the story of Montemayor's own life. The shepherd Sireno ("Syrenus" in English), who must leave Diana to go to a faraway land, seems to represent the author, and the woman thought to be the model for Diana herself was visited by Philip III and his queen as late as 1603. Since Sireno was away on a trip when his beloved married another man, it is of interest that Montemayor seems to have come to England when Prince Philip came to wed the English queen. In other words it just might be that a trip to England helped to bring forth his book. But speculation is dangerous. Actually we know relatively little of Montemayor except that he was a court musician, a distinguished lyric poet, and the victim of a violent death for obscure but amorous reasons.

His *Diana* is a generally placid work, a reflection of man's eternal dream of escape. Perhaps it is also a reaction against the particular kind of escape afforded in the chivalric romances. At any rate it manages to avoid some aspects of real life, and it transfigures others, making use of shepherds'

---

93. Among helpful studies are the following: Hugo Rennert, *The Spanish Pastoral Romances* (Baltimore, 1892; revised ed., Philadelphia, 1912); Menéndez Pelayo, Vol. XIV, Ch. VIII; Walter W. Greg, *Pastoral Poetry & Pastoral Drama* (London, 1906); Frederick Morris Warren, *A History of the Novel Previous to the Seventeenth Century* (New York, 1895); Hector Genouy, *L' "Arcadia" de Sidney dans ses rapports avec l' "Arcadia" de Sannazaro et la "Diana" de Montemayor* (Paris, 1928); Mia Irene Gerhardt, *La pastorale: Essai d'analyse littéraire* (Assen, Netherlands, 1950); and Juan Bautista Avalle-Arce, *La novela pastoril española* (Madrid, 1959).

crooks instead of swords, and emphasizing sentimentality rather than chivalry. According to Américo Castro, Montemayor's reason for seeking refuge in pastoral daydreams is involved with the stigma of his Jewish heritage,[94] but whether or not Castro is correct, the *Diana* does tell of well-bred shepherds who are insulated from many of life's problems, hence may sigh away their days carving poems on trees and pleasing themselves with music and leisurely discussions of love. Like *Arnalte,* the *Castell of Love,* and *Aurelio,* the *Diana* is a sort of anatomy of love.

Fairly early in the work there appears a passage which may be helpful in clarifying its subject and dominant tone. In the following paragraph, taken from Bartholomew Yong's edition of 1598, we find references to at least six significant matters: travel, inserted stories, songs, sentimental love, and the bucolic setting, all of which are compounded in the book so as to produce a stylized and rather plaintive vision of life.

When *Seluagia* had made an end of her sorrowfull tale, she began to weepe so bitterly, that both the Shepherdes (being a kinde of friendly dutie, wherein they had no small experience) began also to helpe her with their teares, and after hauing spent a little time in this sort, *Syrenus* saide vnto her. Great is thy greefe (faire *Seluagia*) and yet I iudge thy patience and discretion greater. Take example by other mens harmes, looke into their paines, consider their woes, if thou wilt the better support thine owne: And bicause it growes now towardes night, let vs be iogging towardes our towne, and to morrow passe away the heate of the day neere to this cleere fountaine, where we will all three meete. Let it be as thou saiest (said *Seluagia*) but bicause betweene this and the towne there is a pretie way, let euery one of vs (to passe it away with some thing) sing a song befitting the condition and qualitie of his loue. The Shepherdes answered, if she would begin, they would follow, which *Seluagia* did, all three going on softly towardes the towne.[95]

One might first remark this "going on softly towardes the towne." Surely a reader looking back on the *Diana* tends to remember the work as being rather static. It lacks the restless motion of both the real-life *conquistadores* and the stories where fictional knights-errant and *picaros* go knocking about the countryside, but, like all of these, it is finally dependent on travel. The *Diana* and its sequels are built on the folklore motif of a journey undertaken by several people with the aim of solving their problems.

94. *The Structure of Spanish History,* tr. Edmund L. King (Princeton, 1954), pp. 564, 570.

95. *Diana,* p. 28. So far as I know, the only large segment of Yong's translation to be reprinted is in *Diana enamorada* (1564) *Together with the English Translation* (1598), ed. Raymond L. and Mildred B. Grismer (Minneapolis, 1959).

Second and equally important, much of the action occurs in inserted stories, such as the one concluded here by Selvagia. (Another intercalation is the famous tale of Felix and Felismena, borrowed from Bandello.)[96] While the *Diana* and its sequels are basically pastoral, in other words, long parenthetical flights allow their authors to utilize a variety of settings, for example a Portuguese village and a Spanish court. Noting this, Juan Bautista Avalle-Arce concludes that Montemayor "has tried to integrate the pastoral world with other spheres of life."[97] To the extent that this is true, we have one of the reasons why the *Diana* may be called a precursor of *Don Quixote*. But how complete is the integration that Avalle-Arce refers to? Certainly the resolution of the inserted stories is dependent on the journey of the main characters. More particularly, Montemayor makes the resolution dependent on the magic of the allegorical Lady Felicia, who presides over affairs at the journey's destination. In this way, true enough, the stem- and branch-stories are connected. But the result has been variously appraised. Bruce Wardropper feels that the structure of Montemayor's *Diana* resembles "the interweaving of various themes in a tapestry. As the eye roves over the surface, now one theme, now another attracts attention. If the eye could take in the whole surface an organized unity would be apparent."[98] Robert Southey re-

96. Reprinted in J. B. Trend's *Spanish Short Stories of the Sixteenth Century* (London, 1928).

97. "The *Diana* of Montemayor: Tradition and Innovation," *PMLA*, LXXIV (1959), 5.

98. "The *Diana* of Montemayor: Revaluation and Interpretation," *SP*, XLVIII (1951), 132. Wardropper's analysis (pp. 133–134) may also serve as a synopsis:

> The seven books of the *Diana* are perfectly symmetrical. Books I–III pose a number of love problems. Book IV is the pivot on which they turn: the possibility of a solution to these problems is revealed. In the final three books the problems are solved.
>
> In Books I–III we meet a gradually increasing group of shepherds and shepherdesses journeying to the saga [*sic*] Felicia in the Temple of Diana in search of a remedy to love's malady. Each book is constructed in the same way. First, the author describes a natural scene: he constructs the setting for the growing group of love-sick shepherds to pass through. Then (except in Book III) new characters are introduced to swell the group (Silvano, the three nymphs). Then a distressed shepherdess appears (Selvagia, Felismena, Belisa). Finally this shepherdess tells the cause of her distress: the story of her failure in love. In Book I Selvagia's story is one of pastoral love; Felismena's (Book II) is of city love; Belisa's (Book III) is of village love. These tales, far from being episodic, are an integral part of pastoral life.
>
> In the central, pivotal book the themes of Books I–III are transposed to a new key. The scenic description is replaced by a description of the

garded the result less enthusiastically. To him the *Diana* seemed "a multitude of stories hooked and eyed together clumsily." To him it was no more artfully structured than the chivalric romances.[99] Avalle-Arce, who takes a middle stand, goes so far as to say that Montemayor's *Diana* represents "a striving for the harmonious combination of history and poetry, the two antithetic thematic poles of Neo-Aristotelian poetics, by the use of the traditional device of the intercalated stories, which are here the vehicles for the introduction of nonpastoral matter." But the striving fails, he says (and here concurs with Southey) because the stories are "largely hermetic unto themselves."[100] The shepherds remain observers of other ways of life, he believes. Reality and fiction remain unblended. I would add that the difference between reality and fiction, tentative in the original, is blurred beyond recognition when the tapestry is turned. In Yong's version the Portuguese shepherds speak the same sort of English as the Spanish ones, and all seem quite as elegantly sensitive and articulate as their courtly companions.

Most interesting of the intercalations in the *Diana* is its celebrated Moorish tale, which concerns a famous family of Granadan Moors named Abencerraje. Added to the work after Montemayor's death, the anonymous *Abencerraje o Historia de Abindarráez y Jarifa* is the first, best, and most popular example of the so-called *novela morisca,* a minor genre whose semi- or pseudo-historical background is the colorful and heroic conflict between the Spanish Christians and the Moors.[101] This particular tale relates how a noble

---

Temple of Diana; the natural background is replaced by a supernatural one. At the point where the distressed shepherdess is expected to appear, Montemayor introduces Felicia, the priestess of Diana. Felicia, instead of telling a love story, holds forth on love and its problems in abstract terms.

The pattern of Books V–VII is different. They are the books of reconciliation, on both the magical and the natural planes. The several love problems are solved parallelly. The communal search for the remedy—all the shepherds journeying in a group—is replaced by an individual search for salvation. The shepherds separate, and each sets out alone to seek a reconciliation with his destiny.

The threads of the pattern now intertwine, disappear, and reappear in an intricate manner. We follow Sireno, lose him, and find him again at the end. In his absence we follow the adventures of his erstwhile companions.

99. *Southey's Common-place Book,* ed. John Wood Warter (New York, 1850), II, 163.

100. "The *Diana* of Montemayor . . . ," p. 5.

101. Barbara Matulka believes that "the original version of the Abindarráez story occurred in a chronicle now lost, and that between 1550–1565 it became a rather wide-spread and favorite tale . . ." ("On the European Diffusion of the

Moor ("Abyndaraez" in English) is conquered and captured by a band of Spanish gentlemen while he is on his way to woo the lady of his soul, "Xarifa." His chief captor, it turns out, is an historical figure, Rodrigo de Narváez, who graciously allows the Moor to join his sweetheart, provided only that he will surrender himself at the end of three days. When Abyndaraez fulfils his hard bargain, Narváez is moved to reward both him and his bride with freedom.

To Spanish readers the fifteenth-century Moorish background was still quite relevant. After the Mohammedan invasion of the peninsula in A.D. 711, Spain had embarked on a great political and religious crusade that dragged on for nearly eight hundred years, presumably ending with the conquest of Granada in 1492. During this time, the contributions of the Moors became an integral part of Spanish culture; and afterwards, during the sixteenth century, and even after 1609 when they were officially purged, the Moors continued to be a major cause of Spanish and Catholic concern. It is only natural, then, that the Moorish theme is to be found running like a dark thread through many of the Spanish translations—not only the *Diana*, but *Lazarillo, Don Quixote, The Rogue, Gerardo, The Pilgrime of Casteele*, and *Don Fenise*.

A third and pervasive feature of the *Diana* and its sequels is lyricism. Pastoral characters seem in constant need of bagpipes, flutes, and rebecks in order to "sing a song befitting the condition and qualitie" of their current mood. After all, Montemayor was both a musician and lyrist, and Gil Polo was a poet of note. For both men, therefore, the narrative form of the pastoral romance must surely have had the special attraction of giving lyric poems a dramatic character. At any rate, both authors present a world in which "there is no greefe that is not with musicke relented and passed away, and no sorrow, which is not with the same againe increased."[102] In the continuation of Alonso Pérez we even encounter a giant who simultaneously sings and plays a hundred bagpipes.

'Last of the Abencerrajes' Story in the Sixteenth Century," *Hispania*, XVI [1933], 375). See also H. A. Deferrari, *The Sentimental Moor in Spanish Literature before 1600*, University of Pennsylvania Publications of the Series in Romanic Languages and Literature, No. 17 (Philadelphia, 1927); Enrique Moreno Báez, "El tema del Abencerraje en la literatura española," *Archivum* [Oviedo], IV (1954), 310–329; María Soledad Carrasco Urgoiti, *El moro de Granada en la literatura* (Madrid, 1956); and Francisco López Estrada, introd., *El Abencerraje y la hermosa Jarifa* (Madrid, 1957). Trend reprints the translation under discussion in his *Spanish Short Stories*.

102. *Diana*, p. 12.

Which brings us to a fourth point: versification and singing are especially important in the *Diana* because of their appropriateness in treating the theme of sentimental love. Whether conveyed by verse or prose, love is the constant subject of the book. Selvagia's "sorrowfull tale," referred to in the excerpt at hand, is both typically and thoroughly amorous. In brief, we are told that the "onely exercise" of Lady Felicia, the *dea ex machina* of the three-part romance, "is to cure and remedie the passions of loue."[103] In realistic fiction it would have been impossible to depict chaste young Spanish ladies wandering through idyllic glades having amours.[104] It would have been impossible to dissociate the world of the lover from the world of social man. But in a work like the *Diana* one need not wonder if the lover is also a soldier, a student, or something else. The singing Arsileus, who keeps time with his tears and observes rests with his sighs, happens to be a student at Salamanca. But it does not matter. The important thing about him is that he loves.

Although passion as it is depicted in the *Diana* is less angular and more lyric than that in the *novelas sentimentales,* here, too, it is rhetorical and code-bound, more mechanical than human. Selvagia says that "If *Ismenia* went by chaunce to the fielde, *Alanius* went after her; if *Montanus* went to his flockes, *Ismenia* after him; if I went to the hils with my sheepe, *Montanus* after me; if I knew that *Alanius* was in the wood, where he was wont to feede his flocks, thither I hied me after him."[105] Yet it would be rash to say that the authors of the pastoral romances give us nothing but poetry and amorous geometry. Avalle-Arce, who has carefully distinguished between the *Diana* and its sequels, concludes that major differences result from their varying presentations of love. In Montemayor, Neo-Platonic love is given absolute primacy; in Pérez, a scholastic approach makes love seem a sickness of the soul; and in Gil Polo, a latter-day stoicism places love in an

103. *Diana,* p. 52.

104. Spanish girls were generally reared behind bars and guarded by duennas. Lady Ann Fanshawe reports that before young ladies marry, "they never stir so much as down stairs—nor marry for no consideration under their quality, which to prevent, if their fortunes will not procure them husbands, they [the parents] make them nuns" (*Memoirs,* ed. Herbert Charles Fanshawe [London, 1907], p. 169). Also see Wardropper, esp. pp. 127–128.

105. *Diana,* p. 23. Vergil had written that "The wild-eyed lioness pursues the wolf; the wolf pursues the kid; the kid herself goes gambolling in search of flowering clover. And I chase you" ("Eclogue II," *The Pastoral Poems,* tr. E. V. Rieu [Aylesbury, Eng., 1954], p. 35).

intermediate position, neither as high as in Montemayor nor as low as in Pérez, but subordinate to reason.[106]

A particularly interesting aspect of the *Diana's* treatment of love is that concerning its wild men. At one point the decorum of Montemayor's romance is shattered by the sudden intrusion of "three monstrous and foule Sauages" who descend from nowhere upon three helpless nymphs.[107] In both continuations of the work we find other savages. In Pérez we read of a fierce and hairy character who wears animal skins and pursues a damsel with a sheep-hook which is "Almost a whole Pine tree, (big enough for the mast of some tall ship)";[108] and in Gil Polo, at the very palace where Felicia presides, we find still other savages, though these are bound with silver chains.

J. D. Williams suggests that the braggadocio savage in Gil Polo's work derives from Sannazaro's "very hairy and extremely rustic man."[109] In one of San Pedro's *novelas sentimentales,* however, we have already met not only a wild man who antedates Sannazaro's, but also a strong hint as to the symbolic meaning of these creatures; in San Pedro we saw the suffering Lereano led to the Castle of Love by a savage named Desire. Where the tradition begins one cannot say. Investigation shows only that such wild men played an "astoundingly persistent, although on the whole subordinate, part in the art and literature of the Middle Ages."[110] They were not, of course, limited to meridional countries. Wild men are mentioned by Geoffrey of Monmouth, the *Gawain* poet, and Malory, to say nothing of later writers such as Munday, Chettle, and Spenser. (Because of Caliban, one might wish to include even Shakespeare.) Long considered a rather gentle figure in English tradition, the wodewose or wild man suddenly evolved in the late sixteenth century as "the brutal and lecherous creature that his name and dress had always

106. *La novela pastoril española*, p. 109. See Wardropper's article and also A. Solé-Leris, "The Theory of Love in the Two *Dianas:* A Contrast," *BHS,* XXXVI (1959), 65–79.

107. *Diana,* p. 49.

108. *Diana,* p. 230. One thinks of the spear assigned to Milton's Satan, "to equal which the tallest pine/ Hewn on Norwegian hills, to be the mast/ Of some great ammiral, were but a wand . . ." (*Paradise Lost,* I, 292–294).

109. "The Savage in Sixteenth Century Spanish Prose Fiction," *KFLQ,* III (1956), 44.

110. Richard Bernheimer, *Wild Men in the Middle Ages* (Cambridge, Mass., 1952), p. 2.

implied that he was."[111] But decorum triumphs in the pastorals. The archeress Felismena rescues the nymphs of Montemayor, and at the close of Gil Polo's work the chained and rose-bedecked savages appear as part of some pleasant allegorical games, an attractive diversion along with the musk balls of red and white wax and the painted eggshells full of orange and rose water.[112]

A fifth matter of importance is related to the "cleere fountaine" that Syrenus refers to. Mary Lascelles thinks that water is the dominant symbol of the refuge afforded by the pastoral setting.[113] In any case, a rural setting is a *sine qua non* of pastoral romance. One of its chief attractions seems to be that sheep do not interfere much with loving and lamenting. Pérez, to be sure, has Lady Felicia remind the lovers of their long-neglected flocks, but by this time the poor things have been forgotten so long that one is struck by her sudden practicality.[114] In actual life there were many Spanish shepherds. The chief raw material of Castile was wool, and twice each year the people of Spain watched millions of sheep go plodding across the land, following ancient sheep-tracks in cultivated regions and spreading over the countryside elsewhere. But real sheep make no appearance in pastoral romance. To sense their decorative quality one need only contrast the chapter in *Don Quixote* where real flocks raise clouds of dust to the passage where the don encounters make-believe shepherds wearing peasant clothes of fine brocade. The counterfeit shepherds even study the eclogues of Garcilaso and Camões.[115]

A sixth and final point, and one related to all the foregoing, concerns the book's rather complex relation to "reality." The *Diana* was presumably based on life, and yet its connection with actuality may be suggested best by the information that Lady Felicia, with "her supernaturall powers," can parcel

111. Robert Hillis Goldsmith, "The Wild Man on the English Stage," *MLR*, LIII (1958), 485.

112. Although he makes no mention of the *Diana enamorada*, Goldsmith spells out some of Gil Polo's symbolism: "The chaining of the wodewose, as represented on tapestries, has definite moral implications. The taming of the wild man by the refining influences of a lady or the spiritualizing power of religion finds expression in many . . . tales, poems and plays" (p. 490). See also Chandler R. Post, *Mediaeval Spanish Allegory* (Cambridge, Mass., 1915).

113. "Shakespeare's Pastoral Comedy," *More Talking of Shakespeare*, ed. John Garrett (New York, 1959), p. 75,

114. *Diana*, p. 161.

115. In the *Coloquio de los perros*, one of his *Novelas ejemplares* (1613), Cervantes contrasts such counterfeit shepherds to real ones who hunt fleas and mend sandals. (Not translated into Renaissance English, this important story is now available in Samuel Putnam's *Three Exemplary Novels* [New York, 1950].)

out valor, power, riches, and wisdom; that with her "cruets of fine cristall" she can make people fall in or out of love;[116] and that in her paradisiacal garden, where trees are made of gold and fountains of beaten silver, Orpheus himself provides the entertainment.[117] In other words, the *Diana*, even more than its sequels, presents an ideal otherworld which quite transcends the world where all men live. It depicts a golden-age realm in which the only real issue is love. Careless that their subject and scene admitted but a fraction of the aesthetically useful materials available to them, and denying "history" at the expense of "poetry," Montemayor and his followers in some ways advanced little beyond San Pedro and Flores. Not that readers complained. After all, the Renaissance believed with Plato and Aristotle that there was "an excess among Limners, call'd too much to the Life, which happens when one aims at Similitude more than Skill. . . ."[118] And the view, within limits, is sound. Its weakness lies in the fact that the pastoral writers could demonstrate considerable skill and yet show little or no awareness of unaccommodated man. Alys of Bath and Shylock, Celestina and Sancho are not really true-to-life, either. But they have a living quality. We hear them talk of things which still concern us, and we see them, as we never hear and see the miscellaneous thwarted lovers in the pastoral romances. The conclusion of Greg seems sound: "Every literature of course wears the livery of its age, but where the body beneath is instinct with human life it can change its dress and pass unchanged itself from one order of things to another; where the livery is all, the form cannot a second time be galvanized into life."[119]

In England the career of the *Diana* is most closely associated with the name of Bartholomew Yong. The latter was the nephew of Dr. John Yong of Cambridge, who was a distinguished professor of divinity, the master of Pembroke Hall, and vice-chancellor in the time of Mary. In 1580 Sir Henry Cobham reported to Walsingham that "Bartholomew Yonge, . . . the nephew of Dr. Yonge imprisoned for papistry, . . . was sent by him into Spain on purpose to have gone into Italy upon the doctor's direction."[120] Bartholomew probably was involved in Anglo-Spanish political affairs, though

116. *Diana*, pp. 123–124.
117. *Diana*, p. 94.
118. James Howell, *Epistolae Ho-Elianae*, ed. Joseph Jacobs (London, 1890). p. 545.
119. *Pastoral Poetry & Pastoral Drama*, p. 421.
120. *Calendar of State Papers, Foreign Series . . . 1579–1580*, XIV, ed. Arthur John Butler (London, 1904), 309.

we cannot be sure in what capacity.[121] We do know that he was in Spain as late as 1580, entered New Inn in May, 1582, completed his *Diana* by the following May, and in October, 1583, was admitted to the Middle Temple.

After dedicating his translation to Sidney's Stella (Lady Rich, who was already familiar with the work), Yong went on to observe that he had "compared the French copies with the Spanish originall" and judged

the first Part to be exquisite; the other two [by Pérez and Gil Polo] corruptly done with a confusion of verse into Prose, and leauing out in many places diuers hard sentences, and some leaues in the end of the third Part, wherefore they are but blind guides by any to be imitated. Well might I haue excused these paines, if onely *Edward Paston* Esquier (who heere and there for his owne pleasure (as I vnderstand) hath aptly turned out of Spanish into English some leaues that liked him best) had also made an absolute and complete translation of all the Parts of *Diana.* . . .[122]

Yong himself was no "blind guide." E. G. Mathews, who has looked more closely than anyone else at the English *Diana,* concludes that "Yong attacked his work in a scientific manner, and with a definite sense of duty to his original. Such care as he professes is evident in his work, and should perhaps be taken as a denial of his intention to keep the work from the press."[123] This does not mean that Yong resists the temptation to amplify occasionally, to sprinkle alliterations here and doublets there. It means that he follows with reasonable care not only Montemayor—who, he says, writes a "hard and strange kinde of Spanish"[124]—but also Pérez and Gil Polo. Pérez's part is the longest, most tangled, and least pastoral of the three.[125] Gil Polo's is somewhat reminiscent of Heliodorus (of whom more later), and yet it is neater in outline and superior in style. In fact Gil Polo's *Diana enamorada* is unusual among sequels for being virtually equal to its model. In the auto-da-fé scene in which Don Quixote's friends condemn most of the don's library to the

121. T. P. Harrison's "Bartholomew Yong, Translator," *MLR,* XXI (1926), 129–139, is valuable.

122. *Diana,* a3ᵛ.

123. "Studies in Spanish-English Cultural and Literary Relations, 1598–1700," unpublished Ph.D. dissertation (Harvard, 1938), p. 294.

124. *Diana,* A3ʳ. He also alludes to the "low and pastorall stile" of the romance, but in both cases he may merely be repeating comments he found in the edition he worked from.

125. Says Mathews (p. 202): "While Pérez was acting in accord with the best critical precepts of the Renaissance in borrowing prolifically from the classics and the best Italians, he so resolutely tangled all his purloined skeins that it is impossible to read him."

flames, the curate says, "since we begin with the *Diana of Montemayor,* I am of opinion that it be not burned, but onely that all that which treats of the wise *Felicia,* and of the inchanted water, be taken away, and also al the longer verses, and let him remaine with his proses, and the honour of being the best of that kinde." As for Pérez's work, he continues, let it "augment the number of the condemned in the yard, and that of *Gil Polo* be kept as charily, as if it were *Apollo* his owne worke. . . ."[126] Whatever the quality of their originals, none of the three parts of Yong's volume belongs in the front rank of English translations. Although his prose is adequate, Yong himself admits that he has never before tried his hand at "making an English verse."[127] Besides this handicap, he sometimes endeavors to be faithful to the extent of preserving both the content and the form of the poems he renders. As a whole, to be sure, his book has a certain narrative interest and a general freedom from stylistic excess, but it seems destined to be read only by students.

Two years before Yong's version reached print, Sir Thomas Wilson also translated the *Diana.*[128] Although Wilson's version was never published,[129] its title and introductory matter are provocative. The former reads as follows: *Diana de Monte Mayor Done out of Spanish by Thomas Wilsõ Esquire, in the Yeare 1596 & Dedicated to the Erle of Southamptõ Who Was Then uppon ye Spanish Voiage wth My Lord of Essex. Wherein under the Names and Vailes of Sheppards and Theire Lovers Are Covertly Discoursed Manie Noble Actions & Affections of the Spanish Nation, as Is of ye English of y^t Admirable & Never Enough Praised Booke of Sr Phil: Sidneyes Arcadia.*[130] The Earl of Southampton, who had received dedications of works before this (*Venus and Adonis* and *The Rape of Lucrece*), was away with Essex on the Cadiz expedition at the time when Wilson was writing, but his apprecia-

126. *Don Quixote,* I, 42.

127. *Diana,* a3^r.

128. This Thomas Wilson, who was later consul in Spain (1604–1605) and the keeper of records at Whitehall (1606–1629), should not be confused with Queen Elizabeth's secretary of state, who bore the same name but died in 1581. Greg, pp. 141–142, notes that Wilson's translation has sometimes mistakenly been ascribed to Thomas Wilcox.

129. D. M. Anderson denounces Wilson's verses as "complete strangers to the graces, let alone the Muses," and cites one passage which is "obviously too bad to deserve extended comment" ("Sir Thomas Wilson's Translation of Montemayor's *Diana,*" *RES,* VII [1956], 176–181).

130. Cited from Henry Thomas, "Diana de Monte Mayor Done out of Spanish by Thomas Wilson," *RH,* L (1920), 372.

tion of the romance may conceivably be reflected in Shakespeare's use of some form of it in *The Two Gentlemen of Verona*.[131] In subsequent remarks Wilson not only goes on to say more about the *Arcadia*, but reveals some of his feelings about translating:

Soe it may bee said of mee that I shewe my vanitie enough in this litle, that after 15 yeares painfully spent in Vniversitie studies, I shold bestow soe many ydle howres, in transplanting vaine amorous conceipts out of an Exotique language. . . . Sʳ, when the rest of these my chyldish exercises can be found [part of the translation was lost during Wilson's travels], yoʳ Honor only, shall haue the vse of them, for that I know yow will well esteeme of them, because that your most noble and never enough honored frend Sʳ Phillipp Siddney did very much affect and imitate the excellent Author there of. . . .[132]

To be sure, Sidney had borrowed from the *Diana*. He even translated a number of verses from it.[133]

The conclusion to which the foregoing facts all point is that the single printing of Yong's rendition is no accurate gauge of England's reception of the Spanish romance. Nearly forty years earlier, in fact, within a year after its appearance in Spain (1559), the book was already available in Spanish in Lord Burghley's circle.[134] Shortly after, Barnabe Googe included translations from it in his *Eglogs, Epytaphes, and Sonnetes* (1563), which is sometimes said to have introduced pastoral verse into England. A decade or two later (*ca.* 1573–1583) the romance was added to the library of James VI.[135]

131. Among others, John Garrett Underhill, in *Spanish Literature in the England of the Tudors* (New York, 1899), p. 363, makes the plausible (though overstated) guess that the source of *The Two Gentlemen of Verona* is "indubitably" the lost *Felix and Felio[s?]mena*, which, in turn, was probably based on the *Diana*. T. P. Harrison, Jr., has written two pertinent articles: "Shakespeare and Montemayor's *Diana*," University of Texas Bulletin, *Studies in English*, No. 6 (1926), 72–120; and "Concerning *Two Gentlemen of Verona* and Montemayor's *Diana*," *MLN*, XLI (1926), 251–252. Selma Guttman, *The Foreign Sources of Shakespeare's Works*, gives references to several other studies of the matter. See also Bullough (1957), I, 225–253.

132. Cited from Thomas, "Diana de Monte Mayor . . . ," p. 373.

133. T. P. Harrison, Jr., "A Source of Sidney's *Arcadia*," University of Texas Bulletin, *Studies in English*, No. 6 (1926), 53–71; and Paul John Cooke, *The Spanish Romances in Sir Philip Sidney's . . . Arcadia* (Urbana, Ill., 1939). Dwight Chambers adduces evidence from primary sources that Sidney knew Spanish ("Deffensa de Poesia: A Spanish Version of Sir Philip Sidney's *Defence of Poesie*," unpublished Ph.D. dissertation [University of Kansas, 1956]).

134. Ungerer, p. 71.

135. José Antonio Muñoz Rojas, "Apuntes para un estudio de las relaciones literarias de Donne con España," *Ensayos hispano-ingleses: Homenaje a Walter Starkie* (Barcelona, 1948), p. 231.

Still later Spenser seems to have found the Pérez sequel of considerable help in writing of Pastorella and Calidore, and of Placidas and Amyas.[136] In 1585 a now-lost play called *The History of Felix and Felio[s?]mena*, probably based on Montemayor, was performed by her majesty's servants. Gabriel Harvey mentions the *Diana* in the marginalia of his copy of Corro's *Grammer* (1590). A portrait of young John Donne, painted in 1591, bears the slogan "Antes muerto que mudado," taken from Montemayor and suggestive of constancy in love.[137] In 1599 John Minsheu used many "Words, Phrases, Sentences and Prouerbes out of DIANA" in order to enhance his *Spanish Grammar*.[138] In 1600 *England's Helicon* appeared with Yong's version of some twenty-four *Diana* poems—more than were furnished by any other source.[139] The *Diana* was even used by William Browne in the writing of *Britannia's Pastorals* (I, 1613–1614; II, 1616; III, in MS until 1852).[140] And about 1633 Henry Reynolds was praising the second part of the *Diana* as "better much then the first."[141] Furthermore, since the *Diana* was imitated in Honoré d'Urfé's *Astrée* (1610), perhaps the most influential work of French fiction in the seventeenth century, Englishmen who turned to French romances—a portion of the *Astrée* appeared in 1620—were still indebted to Spain.

The subject of the book's reception lies so close to that of its influence that one is tempted to mention also an obscure romance called *The Troublesome and Hard Adventures in Love*, an unfinished amalgam which bears some of the marks of pastoral, Heliodoran, and even chivalric fiction. The earliest known reference to this work was recorded in the Stationers' Register on June 15, 1594.[142] At this time, four years before Yong's book was published, there was "Entred for his [Thomas Creed's] copie vnder th[e h]and of master warden Cawood/ a booke intituled *The troublesom and hard adventures in love with many fyne conceyted sonnettes and pretty poemes de-*

---

136. T. P. Harrison, Jr., "*The Faerie Queene* and the *Diana*," *PQ*, IX (1930), 51–56.

137. T. E. Terrill, "A Note on John Donne's Early Reading," *MLN*, XLIII (1928), 318–319.

138. Pp. 75–78. A lesser number of items are also taken from the *Celestina*, *Lazarillo*, *Menosprecio de la corte*, *Marco Aurelio*, *Floresta española*, and *Araucana*.

139. See "Index of Authors," *Englands [sic] Helicon*, ed. Hugh MacDonald (Cambridge, Mass., 1950), pp. 253–254.

140. Greg, pp. 136, 138.

141. See his "Mythomystes," in *Critical Essays of the Seventeenth Century*, ed. Joel Elias Spingarn (Oxford, 1908), I, 146.

142. Arber (London, 1875), II, 654.

lightfull to the reader/ written in Turkey by R C." Although it seems that
such a book actually appeared some time during or shortly after 1594 (a
fragmentary copy has turned up at the British Museum), the only complete
editions now extant were printed about fifty-eight years later, in 1652 (or
perhaps 1651).

In some prefatory remarks to the reader, the printer, Bernard Alsop,
writes that in the romance *"many Histories are recorded; among which,
though some are inserted that have been written by others before, yet were
never seene in English till now."*[143] Despite the fumbled syntax, Alsop's words
imply that *Adventures in Love* was derived from multiple sources. One of
these proves to have been Montemayor's *Diana.* R. C. frankly confesses borrowing the Lady Felicia when he observes that because

Monte Mayor copiouslie setteth foorth the sumptuousnesse and magnificence of
the pallace wherein this Ladie Felicia kept her Court, in the fourth booke of the
first part of his . . . Diana, I thinke it superfluous for me to retaine the Readers
eare with vnnecessary relations of those things that by others haue so exactly
bene performed.[144]

Another of R. C.'s sources was the *Diana enamorada,* Gil Polo's sequel.
Gil Polo seems to have furnished R. C. not only with the names and characters for his Marcelio-Alcida story, but also with general contours and
details of plot. Another example of extended borrowing is the Ismenia-
Lexander story. Although Montemayor indeed invented Ismenia, it was in
Gil Polo's continuation that her tale of love was finally unfolded, and as in
the case of the Marcelio-Alcida story, a comparison of the Spanish and English works reveals many and close similarities.

No one knows who R. C. was.[145] The simple fact is that *The Troublesome*

143. *Adventures in Love* (1652), A4^v.
144. *Adventures in Love* (fragmentary ed.), Q4^r.
145. Since the Stationers' Register entry was made in 1594, R. C. is obviously
not Robert Codrington (1602–1665), the candidate usually named. Although wary
of guesswork, I would suggest the name of Raffe (Ralph) Carr, author of *The
Mahumetane or Turkish Historie* (1600). Carr has the proper initials and was
writing at the right time on an appropriate subject (*Adventures in Love* was "written in Turkey"). In the introductory matter of the *History* we learn of Carr's knowledge of French (the first fragmentary page of the early *Adventures* contains these
scraps: "French Pamphl[et?]" and "I translat[ed?]"); we learn of his "loue sick
Sonets" (N. B. the *"fyne conceyted sonnettes"* in *Adventures*); and we learn of his
"rich discourse, where loue in louing dies." Such evidence is obviously inconclusive,
but so far I have failed to turn up any candidate more likely than Carr. (For a fuller
discussion see my note, *"The Troublesome and Hard Adventures in Love:* An English Addition to the Bibliography of *Diana,"* BHS, XXXVIII [1961], 154–158.)

and Hard Adventures in Love raises several troublesome and hard questions to which no final answers are yet available. Still the book is of interest, if not because of its own literary merit, at least because of the place which it may rightfully assume in the bibliographical history of the *Diana,* first and greatest of the Spanish pastoral romances.

Don Quixote

The elements of the pastoral romance, as well as those of the picaresque story, Moorish tale, and chivalric romance, were absorbed and transmuted in the Spanish narrative which came to England next. First printed in Madrid in 1605 (a second part was added in 1615), it was the masterwork of Spanish literature. In writing it Cervantes had heeded those literary mentors who recommended a web woven of various fair strands, and thereby he proved once and for all that in literature the whole may be infinitely greater than the sum of its parts. Although seams between some of the parts of *Don Quixote* are noted by Cervantes himself, and although the work is riddled with inconsistencies, there is perhaps no other single book that has exerted greater influence on the modern novel. As Lionel Trilling puts it, "all prose fiction is a variation on the theme of *Don Quixote.*"[146] Because of the Cervantean tapestry simile, and because it was an Irishman who enabled the English to read *Don Quixote* in their own language, it is fitting that the only witty baroque tapestries now known are first referred to in an inventory of Kilkenny Castle, and, furthermore, that they depict the adventures of the mad knight of La Mancha.[147]

Few readers need be told that *Don Quixote* is the story of a poor, dried-up hidalgo (literally, "son of somebody") who loses his mind as a result of reading too many romances, including the *Amadís* and the *Diana* and their continuations. Specifically, Don Quixote's madness consists of believing such fantastic books to be historically accurate (after all, there are giants in the

146. "Manners, Morals, and the Novel," reprinted in Roger Sale's collection, *Discussions of the Novel* (Boston, 1960), p. 57. Three dated but helpful ingressions into the morass of Cervantes material are Jeremiah D. M. Ford and Ruth Lansing, *Cervantes: A Tentative Bibliography of His Works and of the Biographical and Critical Material Concerning Him* (Cambridge, Mass., 1931); Raymond L. Grismer, *Cervantes: A Bibliography* (New York, 1946); and Antonio Palau y Dulcet, *Bibliografía de don Miguel de Cervantes Saavedra* (Barcelona, 1950).

147. Phyllis Ackerman, "Five Baroque Don Quixote Tapestries," *Art Quarterly,* X (1947), 188–201. The article includes photographs.

Bible), and sallying forth in his great-grandfather's armor as if he himself were a knight. Subsequently his words and actions are such that he can truthfully declare, "since I am become a Knight Errant, I am valiant, courteous, liberall, well-manner'd, generous, gentle, bold, mild, patient, an indurer of labours, imprisonments, and inchantments. . . ."[148] In short, the bare-elbowed, hook-nosed madman becomes the embodiment of those lofty ideals which had thus far been reserved in literature for extraordinary heroes. When such a character is furnished with a practical-minded village droll for a squire, the realms of poetry and history converge. This is only the beginning, however. The relationship between the two protagonists becomes increasingly complex when the pragmatic Sancho embraces the knight's ideas, or the knight conducts himself as a veritable Solomon in matters aside from chivalry, or both of them together confront new situations which disclose new aspects of their thought and character. The reader may find himself pondering: What is the difference between acting heroically and being a hero?[149] Given the limitations of one's senses, beliefs, and reasoning, how is one to arrive at truth?

One of the minor fascinations of *Don Quixote* (as of Dickens' *Pickwick*) is that it seems to grow and assume its unique shape before the reader's eyes. Apparently the book started out to be a mere comic attack on chivalric romances, but then, after a few slapstick sallies, stirred up some important questions in Cervantes' mind. Moreover, it appears that Cervantes found his characters assuming wills of their own, somewhat in the manner of Pickwick, or perhaps of Falstaff. What began as a *novela* grew into a rambling, two-volume work.

As everyone knows, *Don Quixote* consists of a string of episodes which occur as its two heroes wander about Spain. In other words, like most of the fiction we have considered, *Don Quixote* is peripatetic. At one point Cervantes tells us that his knight and squire "mounted again and without taking any definite direction, as was the custom of knights-errant, they let Rocinante follow his own will, his master's inclinations . . . falling in behind.

148. *Don Quixote*, I, 552.

149. According to Hardin Craig, "The Elizabethans believed that the assumption of a surface affected the whole substance. To wear women's clothes endangered the masculine character, and the player's assumed passion over the death of Hecuba was as valid as any passion. Thus when Hamlet feigns insanity and when Edgar in *King Lear* pretends to be a Bedlam beggar, they do to a certain extent and in a certain puzzling way become the things they pretend to be" (*An Introduction to Shakespeare* [New York, 1952], p. 439).

. . . Proceeding in this manner, they came back to the highway and continued riding along, leaving everything to chance and with no plan whatsoever."[150] Confessing that Don Quixote could have no preconceived itinerary because he himself did not, Cervantes has his hero observe in Part II that "the Author of my Story is not wise, but some ignorant Prater, that at vnawares and without iudgement vndertooke it, hab-nab, as *Orbaneja,* the Painter of *Vbeda,* who being asked what he painted, answered, As it happens [i. e., Whatever it turns out to be]. . . ."[151]

True enough, not everything is woven in with equal skill. Indirectly speaking of himself once more, although ostensibly referring to the Moorish chronicler on whose writing the *Quixote* is supposed to be based, Cervantes says in Part II that to relieve monotony

in the first part he vsed the Art of Nouels, as one, of *The Curious Impertinent,* another of *The captiu'd Captaine,* which are (as it were) separated from the History, though the rest that are there recounted, are matters that happened to *Don Quixote,* which could not but be set downe: he [the imaginary Moorish author] was of opinion likewise, as he sayd, that many being carried away with attention to *Don Quixotes* exployts, would not heede his Nouels, and skip them, either for haste or irkesomenesse, without noting the cunning worke-manship, and framing of them, which would be plainely shewne, if they might come to light by themselues alone, without *Don Quixotes* madnesse, or *Sancho's* simplicities; therefore in this second part, hee would not engraffe loose Nouels, or adioyning to the Story, but certaine accidents that might bee like vnto them, sprung from the passages that the truth it selfe offers, and these[,] too[,] sparingly, and with words only proper to declare them. . . .[152]

On the other hand, some of the inserted stories, even in the first part, though taking place chiefly in the past, are concluded in the present, in the presence of Don Quixote and Sancho. For instance, the most beautified Dorotea, heroine of a sentimental love story in the book, meets Don Quixote and his friends in the Sierra Morena, and there swoons into the arms of the village barber. At such points in *Don Quixote* the antithetic lines of Neo-Aristotelian poetics—history and poetry—converge. Although he was to manipulate the technique more smoothly later on, as when he depicted Don Quixote and

150. Shelton's translation conveys these general thoughts, but for the sake of greater clarity I quote here from Samuel Putnam's version (New York, 1949), I, 161.

151. Shelton's *Don Quixote,* II, 20. One might, of course, argue that the knight's lack of planning is not the author's. Here as elsewhere, my comments reflect but one of the possible interpretations.

152. *Don Quixote,* II, 284.

Sancho at the wedding of Camacho (Part II), Cervantes suggests here the possibilities involved in blending romance with realism. This is not to hold him up as a man with a rage for order. Even in the second part he sometimes seems to have written just as thoughts came to him, almost as if, in Socratic fashion, he were testing ideas to find out what he himself really thought. Consequently his book sprawls with some of the ordered disorder of everyday life. It is full of inconsistencies and anachronisms. To say that *Don Quixote* has such flaws, however, is not to say that it lacks coherence. At its best *Don Quixote* succeeds in integrating a variety of elements, not merely collecting them; and from this derives its chief importance in the history of the novel. It achieves at least a rudimentary coherence simply by virtue of Cervantes' focus on his protagonists. Like *Lazarillo,* it has also a second and more sophisticated means to unity, namely that which is furnished by its anti-chivalric theme. Third, it is persistent in treating the themes of being and seeming. Fourth, and best of all, its complexity and coherence are solidly based on the fact that few of its incidents are fully disposed of at the time they occur. Like the chivalric romances it mocks, in other words, *Don Quixote* may seem at first to be little more than a number of separate episodes, but on closer acquaintance these episodes are seen to be absorbed into the minds of Don Quixote and Sancho, and to recur later on as subjects for argument.[153]

In the beginning, far from embodying important ideas which somehow "incandesced," thereby identifying philosophy and art, Don Quixote himself was a merely comic figure.[154] We are told at the outset that from too little sleeping and too much reading his brain has dried up.[155] And no matter what we are led to think later, we are still meant to laugh. Cervantes asks us, "Which of the beholders could abstaine from laughter, perceiuing the Mas-

---

153. This is noted in Gerald Brenan's *The Literature of the Spanish People* (Cambridge, Eng., 1953), p. 183.

154. I have in mind the concept-image relationship as discussed by René Wellek and Austin Warren, *Theory of Literature* (New York, 1956), pp. 98–113.

155. Robert Burton is able to cite learned authorities to show that too much study and contemplation are likely to bring on madness; that hard students are "most part lean, dry, ill-coloured, spend their fortunes, lose their wits, and many times their lives, and all through immoderate pains and extraordinary studies"; that such "are most part harmless, honest, upright, innocent, plain-dealing men"; and that *"Senes etiam decrepiti cerebrum habent concavum et aridum, ut imaginentur se videre . . ."* (*Anatomy of Melancholy,* I, 302, 304, and 425). What better description could one seek of the knight who sees flocks of sheep as armies and windmills as giants?

ters madnesse, and the seruants simplicity?"[156] Even in Part II he says that "if it make thee not laugh outright, yet it will cause thee shew thy teeth, and grin like an Ape: for *Don Quixotes* affaires must either bee solemnized with admiration or laughter."[157] Yet as we progress through the book we find more and more matter for thought. For one thing, we find that Don Quixote grows increasingly rational. As Mack Singleton has put it,

in the first chapters he never sees knights but insists on misinterpreting his senses by calling sheep, armed men; but in the later chapters he is almost always in the *actual presence* of the apparently Medieval and wonderful. The world puts forth all its efforts to present to him sensory stimuli which it is hoped he will interpret after his fashion. . . .[158]

The resultant elevation in Don Quixote's character is enhanced by Cervantes' use of dialogue. With the stunning exception of the *Celestina,* dialogue in practically all of the fiction from *Arnalte* to the *Diana* consisted of alternating rhetorical speeches, but in *Don Quixote* there seems to be real give and take between characters, especially between the knight and squire in Part II. In a word, we find more subtlety and less slapstick as we advance. Don Quixote is quite correct in saying that "Euery day, Sancho . . . thou growest wiser and wiser."[159] When Sancho displays considerable discretion as the governor of a land turned over to him in jest by the duke and duchess, Cervantes has one of his characters observe that "Euery day we see nouelties in the world, iests turn'd to earnest, and those that mocke, are mocked at."[160]

Understandably enough, Erich Auerbach is part of no great chorus when he maintains that one must overinterpret the book to find much of real seriousness in it. He thinks that good and evil are alike turned into fun in *Don Quixote,* and the world is presented "as play in that spirit of multiple, perspective, nonjudging, and even nonquestioning neutrality which is a brave form of wisdom."[161] I, too, believe that *Don Quixote* is more art than philosophy, but to say that Cervantes gives no answers is not to say that he raises no questions. Whereas much Spanish fiction is compounded chiefly of color and motion, the durability of *Don Quixote* derives in part from the glimpses

156. *Don Quixote,* I, 315.
157. II, 286.
158. Mack Hendricks Singleton, "Technique and Idea in Early Spanish Fiction," unpublished Ph.D. dissertation (Wisconsin, 1936), p. 236.
159. *Don Quixote,* II, 70.
160. II, 323.
161. *Mimesis,* tr. Willard Trask (New York, 1957), p. 314.

it affords through the superficial crust of life, reminding one of Emerson's observation that the world's highest minds have never stopped searching for the manifold meanings of every sensuous fact.[162]

The matter is crystallized in Don Quixote's statement concerning the object which he takes to be the helmet of Mambrino. That "which seemes to thee a Barbers Bason," he tells Sancho, "is in my conceit *Mambrino* his Helmet; and to another will appear in some other shape."[163] It also takes form in the answer given by the mysterious brass head. When Don Quixote asks if his adventures in the cave of Montesinos were truth or dream, the head replies, "there is much to be said, it partakes of all. . . ."[164] By such devices as these, a basic problem of life—which one may express as the jesting question "What is truth?" or "What is real?"—is made to seem implicit everywhere. The writer of *Lazarillo* had touched on the disparity between the false and the true, on the nature of a world based on deceit, wealth, titles, and trickery, but Cervantes gives us more data and treats the matter more directly. He depicts both the obvious make-believe of the world—the strolling players, the puppet show, the wise monkey, the magic head, the practical joke of Altisidora's "death"—and he depicts Don Quixote's rescue of a boy being whipped by his master, a kindly act which has such bad results that the boy cries out, "May God curse you and all the knights-errant that were ever born into this world!"[165] Wherein lies the right, the true, the real? In the *Coloquio de los perros,* one of his *Novelas ejemplares,* Cervantes has a character observe that what takes place in our imaginations may occur so intensely that we cannot distinguish between the real and the imaginary.[166] Little wonder, then, that Cervantes also has a wise father, speaking of Don Quixote in the more subtle Part II, advise his son to "feele the pulse of his vnderstanding, and since thou art discreet, iudge of his discretion or folly as thou seest best. . . ."[167]

Precisely here lies one of the finest qualities of the work. Despite its occasional verbosity, for which some would condemn it, *Don Quixote* stands in the front rank of western literature, as the *Arnalte* and *Amadís* and

162. "The Poet," *Essays: Second Series* (Boston, 1845), p. 4.

163. *Don Quixote,* I, 233.

164. II, 424.

165. Since Shelton obscures the issue at this point, I again cite from Putnam's translation, I, 273.

166. As noted earlier, this story was not translated in the Renaissance, but a modern English version is found in Putnam's *Three Exemplary Novels.*

167. Shelton's *Don Quixote,* II, 112.

Diana do not, because it is not merely an artifact shaped by an artist, completed, and set under glass. It is really finished, in fact it might be said to *exist,* only after it has been read, only after it has become a common ground where the minds of the author and reader have met. Too often Spanish fiction seems shallow. It is concerned with things merely for the sake of those things, not for the sake of any informing ideas. In *Don Quixote,* however, one is conscious of questions far beyond slapstick silliness and anti-chivalric spleen. And the view of these questions is never unilateral. Just as threads from many literary sources are interwoven to make up the action of *Don Quixote,* so various attitudes are interwoven to make up its thematic texture. That is, we are not presented with a single point of view, or even with two which constitute a warp and woof at perpendicular odds with each other; rather we are shown numerous possibilities which all contribute to the effect of the whole. We are shown a variety of attitudes which point to still others. This is one of the joys of the book. *Don Quixote* presents actions themselves, presents adventures, but does not tell the reader what to think of them. In *Don Quixote,* as Américo Castro has said, no "didactic or logical transcendency [is] superimposed on the process of living." The book succeeds in "showing that reality is always an aspect of the experience of the person who is living it."[168] The reader is forced to respond according to his own capabilities—or his own limitations.

In 1612, thanks to Thomas Shelton, it became the privilege of the English to be the first foreigners to read Part I of *Don Quixote* in their own language.[169] Then, eight years later, in 1620, Shelton's second part was added to his first.[170]

168. "Incarnation in 'Don Quixote,'" in *Cervantes Across the Centuries,* ed. Angel Flores and M. J. Benardete (New York, 1947), pp. 144, 166. For a consideration of some of the linguistic means by which Cervantes achieves his complex effects, see Richard L. Predmore, *El mundo del Quijote* (Madrid, 1958), esp. Ch. IV, "La realidad."

Quixote interpretations are legion, but two additional and particularly helpful maps of the morass (see above, note 146) are Helmut Hatzfeld's "Thirty Years of Cervantes Criticism," *Hispania,* XXX (1947), 321–328, and the same author's "Results from Quijote Criticism Since 1947," *Anales Cervantinos,* II (1952), 129–157.

169. César Oudin translated Pt. I into French, 1614; and François de Rosset, Pt. II, in 1618.

170. The latter was slightly altered. See Edwin B. Knowles, Jr., "The First and Second Editions of Shelton's *Don Quixote* Part I: A Collation and Dating," *HR,* IX (1941), 252–265. The work was reprinted only once again in the pre-Restoration period, in 1652. Among more recent editions of Shelton are those by Justin McCarthy (London and Philadelphia, 1895); James Fitzmaurice-Kelly (London,

Shelton was apparently an Irish Catholic who had received his education at the Irish College in Salamanca. For a while he lived in Paris, where he tried to teach Spanish, but he was staying in Brussels in 1607, the place and time of the Spanish reprint he used for his translation.[171] According to his own testimony, he wrote the latter "in the space of fortie dayes."[172] This amazing feat (Part I comes to nearly six hundred octavo pages) was "more then halfe inforced," he claims, being made "through the importunitie of a very deare friend. . . ." However this may be, the book was finished cursorily and left unprinted. "I cast it aside," says Shelton, "where it lay long time neglected in a corner, and so little regarded by me, as I neuer once set hand to reuiew or correct the same." Shelton was aware, then, that his translation might have borne some revision, though he himself was too busy for such a project. "My many affairs," he says, "prevent me from undergoing that labour." Whatever such affairs may have been, he was willing for some of his friends to undertake the publication of his work, provided "that some one or other would peruse and amend the errours escaped. . . ." Put together thus, Shelton's version of Part I was naturally full of inaccuracies. Unfortunately, Part II is no model of accuracy, either. Shelton may have rendered the sequel under pressure, too, but whether or not this is the case, one finds evidence in it that his knowledge of Spanish was still less than perfect. Most noticeably, he too often fell into the practice of equating Spanish words to the English ones nearest in sound, thus coupling a homonymic "closeness" of method with a consequential looseness of sense. To Shelton,

---

1896); A. W. Pollard (London, 1900); Royal Cortissoz (London and New York, 1906); and F. J. Harvey Darton (London, 1923).

It seems probable that an English *Don Quixote* was known to some readers even before 1612. Shelton himself tells us that his first part had been finished several years when it came to press, and, as Schevill says, "it must be remembered that the circulation of Mss. [one thinks of the *Diana*] was merely a continuation of mediaeval custom which only changed gradually after the invention of printing" ("On the Influence of Spanish Literature upon English in the Early 17th Century," *Romanische Forschungen*, XX [1907], 613). I would add that non-Spanish-reading Englishmen also could have read excerpts from *Don Quixote* in Paris editions of two of its stories, *Le curieux impertinent* (1608) and *L'histoire de Marcelle* (1609). At any rate, Shelton deserves credit for rendering the whole of *The History of Don-Quichote* as it first appeared in print.

171. J. George, "Thomas Shelton, Translator, in 1612–14," *BHS*, XXXV (1958), 157–164; and Edwin B. Knowles, "Thomas Shelton, Translator of *Don Quixote*," *Studies in the Renaissance*, V (New York, 1958), 160–175.

172. *Don Quixote*, I, ¶ 2ʳ. All quotations in this paragraph are from the same leaf.

discreto was "discreet," *admirar* was "admire," *trance* was "trance," *desmayarse* was "dismay," and *suceso* was "successe." At least sometimes, however, Shelton was acting on good authority. Perceval's *Bibliotheca* defines *Successo* as "successe" and gives "to dismay" as the first definition of *Desmayar;* and Minsheu's *Dictionarie* gives "successe" as the first meaning for *Sucésso,* and "to dismay" as the first for *desMaýr.*[173]

In spite of its weaknesses, Shelton's *Don Quixote* has a flavor and verve that no later version has matched. Shelton himself was not only a contemporary of Cervantes, which gave him an initial advantage over later translators, but he was also a contemporary of Shakespeare and the translators of the King James Bible. There were thus available to him a richness and strength of everyday vocabulary and idiom which could never afterwards be synthesized. Partly for this reason the first of the English translators of *Don Quixote,* obscure though he remains, fits comfortably enough into the procession of great translators of his day. Fitzmaurice-Kelly's remarks concerning him could be applied to the best of his tribe: "He had no sympathy for the arid accuracy that juggles with a gerund or toys with the crabbed subjunctive. . . . Shelton's view of his function was ampler and nobler than the hidebound grammarian's. He appeals to the pure lover of literature; and as a man of letters he survives."[174]

In time, Cervantes' book was to have considerable impact on English letters, but in the seventeenth century it was welcomed less warmly and read more superficially than one might guess. At first its strongest influence seems to have been on the drama,[175] but there also appeared very early an attractive narrative which is good enough to deserve special mention. Written by Robert Anton, a poet of satirical bent, *Moriomachia* (1613) may fairly be called the first English successor of *Don Quixote.* Borrowing from Cervantes both general concept and mode of treatment, Anton depicts a knight named Tom Pheander, whose adventures are meant to ridicule the literary

173. A modern dictionary provides the following comparisons: *suceso* (n. m.) "event, occurrence; happening, incident; issue, outcome, result; course of time"; and *desmayar* (v. t.) "to dismay, depress, discourage," and (v. i.) "to be faint-hearted, dispirited, dejected, discouraged"; and *desmayarse* (v. r.) "to faint, swoon." (*Cassell's Spanish-English Dictionary* [London, 1959].)

174. Introd., *The History of Don Quixote,* I, xlii.

175. E.g., *The Knight of the Burning Pestle* (*ca.* 1608); *The Second Maiden's Tragedy* (1611); *Amends for Ladies* (*ca.* 1611); *The Double Marriage* (*ca.* 1620); *The Cruel Brother* (1630); *The Triumph of Peace* (1634); *The History of Don-quixot* (announced 1651, 1658, and 1661); *The Disappointment* (1684); *The Married Beau* (1694); and *The Comical History of Don Quixote* (1694–1696).

traditions of knight-errantry, including damsels in distress, multitudinous combats, pastoral interludes, and even inflated rhetoric.[176]

Quite a different sort of English work to grow out of the Spanish one was the rather peculiar *Pleasant Notes upon Don Quixot* (1654). This was written by Edmund Gayton, a royalist Oxford don who had become a scribbling hack after losing his job as a teacher of physic. Briefly his *Pleasant Notes,* "which is accounted our Author's Master-piece,"[177] consists of jesting comments on excerpts drawn from the 1652 edition of Shelton's translation. Gayton's procedure was to copy out a passage and then play with it. Consider, for instance, such a "note" as the following:

There stood at the Inne door, two young women adventurers likewise.] These I beleeve had been dubb'd and dubb'd againe, and had devises in their Targets, for hotter adventures then ever the *Don* assaied; it was strange that the *Don,* (but that strong imagination is irresistible) being *gaunt,* (not *John a Gaunt* I meane) but fasting, and therefore of more exquisite sense, had not smelt out their profession from the evaporations of their saltpits: or that *Rosinante* had not by a merry neighing, discovered the approaches of two over-ridden jades. Their standing at the Inne door, was a sign of themselves and the house, and (though they were bound for *Sevil*) that their behaviour was not so.[178]

Clearly Gayton regarded *Don Quixote* in quite a different light from most modern readers. As E. B. Knowles has noted, he converts Don Quixote himself to "a sly coward," "an unabashed liar," "a vagabond," a "hypocritical thief," and a "mealy-mouthed courtier."[179]

Though Gayton is a tempting target, we should be cautious about condemning him for not being ahead of his time. Professor Knowles, who has found at least seventy-nine *Don Quixote* allusions in English books before 1660,[180] reports that most are "in comedies, light verse, and cheap prose. The person who most frequently refers to The Knight is the fourth-rate poet-scribbler John Taylor."[181] As a matter of fact, seventeenth-century readers in

---

176. The work was reprinted by Gustav Becker as "Die erste englische Don Quijotiade," *Archiv für das Studium der Neueren Sprachen und Literaturen,* CXXII (1909), 310–332.

177. Wood, II, 388.

178. *Pleasant Notes,* p. 6.

179. "Cervantes and English Literature," in *Cervantes Across the Centuries,* p. 270. See also Edward M. Wilson, "Edmund Gayton on Don Quixote, Andrés, and Juan Haldudo," *CL,* II (1950), 64–72.

180. "Allusions to *Don Quixote* before 1660," *PQ,* XX (1941), 583. These averaged less than one per year for the first thirty years after the initial publication of the book in Spain, hardly increasing in frequency until the 1630's and 1640's.

181. Knowles, *"Don Quixote* Through English Eyes," *Hispania,* XXIII (1940), 108.

Spain itself had relished Cervantes' book largely for its farcical qualities, and a few readers of our own day continue to regard the valiant knight of La Mancha as closer to Shakespeare's Adriano de Armado than to the high-minded philosopher-idealist he is more often taken to be.

At any rate, Gayton threw no new light on the book, nor, after the close of our period, did Milton's naughty nephew John Phillips. (In 1687 Phillips produced a farcical *Don Quixote* which has piqued some Cervantists.[182]) Therefore it is no shock to find that Thomas D'Urfey's stage version, *The Comical History of Don Quixote* (1694–1696), is prominent in Jeremy Collier's *Short View of the Immorality and Profaneness of the English Stage* (1698). Offsetting such treatment, Sir William Temple, also writing toward the end of the seventeenth century, declared that as a satire Cervantes' work "seems to be the best and highest Strain that ever was, or will be reached. . . ."[183] Moving into the eighteenth century, one cannot surely point to any particular time of general enlightenment, though one can at least be certain that the dimensions of *Don Quixote* were fairly widely advertised in 1742. In that year Henry Fielding declared in *Joseph Andrews* that the whole history of civilization was to be found in Cervantes' book.[184]

About a century and a quarter elapsed between Clerc's rather medieval *Arnalte* and Shelton's rather modern *Don Quixote,* during which period

182. E.g., Juan Suñé Benages and Juan Suñé Fonbuena, *Bibliografía crítica de ediciones del Quijote* (Barcelona, 1917), p. 232. One of the few students to suggest that the work is less deserving of censure as a translation than mild praise as an imitation is Ralph E. Hone in "Edward and John Phillips: Nephews and Pupils of John Milton," unpublished Ph.D. dissertation (New York University, 1954), p. 507.

183. Temple, *Works* (London, 1731), I, 246.

184. *The History of the Adventures of Joseph Andrews,* II, 4–5. Dr. Johnson also implied a great deal in asserting that "After Homer's Iliad, . . . the work of Cervantes was the greatest in the world, speaking of it . . . as a book of entertainment." (The words are those of Hester Piozzi in *Johnsoniana* [London, 1836], p. 91.)

Space and purpose forbid mentioning all the English works indebted to *Don Quixote*. Besides *Joseph Andrews,* however, one thinks of Butler's *Hudibras* (1663–1664), Lennox's *Female Quixote* (1752), Sterne's *Tristram Shandy* (1760–1767), Smollett's *Sir Launcelot Greaves* (1760–1762), and Graves's *Spiritual Quixote* (1772).

In addition to studies cited earlier, see James Fitzmaurice-Kelly, "Cervantes in England," *Proceedings of the British Academy,* II (1905–1906), 11–29; Gustav Becker, *Die Aufnahme des Don Quijote in die englische Literatur* (1605–ca. 1770) (Berlin, 1906); Edward M. Wilson, "Cervantes and English Literature of the Seventeenth Century," *BH,* L (1948), 27–52; and Carmine Rocco Linsalata, *"Don Quixote* in English Translation, 1612–1755," in *Smollett's Hoax: Don Quixote in English* (Stanford, Calif., 1956), pp. 3–12.

Englishmen received from Spain the *novela sentimental,* the chivalric romance, the picaresque story, the pastoral romance, the Moorish *novela,* the
unique *Quixote,* and a newly revived genre that we shall turn to in the next
chapter—the Byzantine romance.[185]

Later on there will be time for further conclusions, but already at this
point, surveying the handful of narratives we have glanced at, one is perhaps
struck more by variety than quantity, more by surface artistry than thought.
Perhaps one is also a bit more firmly persuaded of the wisdom in Samuel
Daniel's observation that literary standards "are continually in a wandring
motion, carried with the violence of vncertaine likings, being but onely
the time that giues them their power."[186] By 1620, nonetheless, the year of
Shelton's completed *Don Quixote,* the Spanish had helped England to open
some veins of fiction that were to prove quite as rich in their way as the
famous mines of Potosí.

185. One last disclaimer may not be superfluous: other lands besides Spain
contributed much to these genres.
186. Quoted from "A Defence of Rhyme," in *Elizabethan Critical Essays,* II, 383.

Chapter V

Labyrinths of Love

The Byzantine Romances

Persiles and Sigismunda

On April 19, 1616, four days before his death, Cervantes brought his life's writing to a close with the dedication of *Los trabajos de Persiles y Sigismunda* (1617). Though his *Persiles* was not really as incredible as the romances that he had taken to task in *Don Quixote,* it did, according to Cervantes' own avowal, dare to compete with the work of Heliodorus.[1]

A manuscript of Heliodorus' *Aethiopica,* most famous of the Greek romances, was discovered at the sack of Buda (1526), first printed in the original Greek (1534), and then translated into French (1547), Latin (1551), Spanish (1554), Italian (1556), and English (*ca.* 1569). Here at last, vigorously renascent, was an ancient model for long prose fiction, a work so appealing that it assumed a place in contemporary, not ancient, literature.[2] It had the attraction of adventure, which was offered also by the chivalric romances, but its marvels were more varied. It included some of the amorous anguish of the pastoral romances, yet avoided their slowness. And, for all of its talk of love, it had less sighing and stiffness than the *novelas sentimentales.* No wonder it was popular, both inside Spain and out.[3] Al-

1. An old but helpful introduction to the romance may be found in Rudolph Schevill, "Studies in Cervantes: I. 'Persiles y Sigismunda,' " *MP, IV* (1906), 1–24; (1907), 677–704.

2. According to Elizabeth Haight, Heliodorus probably wrote no later than the third century (*Essays on the Greek Romances* [New York, 1943], p. 62).

3. It was praised by Cervantes and Tasso, ranked by Pinciano with the *Iliad* and *Aeneid,* used as a source by Sidney and Calderón, and quoted by Shakespeare and Burton (Henry B. Lathrop, *Translations from the Classics into English from Caxton to Chapman* [Madison, Wis., 1933], pp. 161–165; see also Francisco López Estrada's introd., *Historia etiópica . . . ,* tr. Fernando de Mena [Madrid, 1954]; Moses Hadas' chapter on the novel, *A History of Greek Literature* [New York, 1950] pp. 287–298, and bibliography, pp. 317–318; and Samuel Lee Wolff's helpful though not entirely dependable *The Greek Romances in Elizabethan Prose Fiction* [New York, 1912]).

In London, about two years before the lively English version by William Underdowne (noted above), there appeared a little-known work called *Amorous and*

though other influences (for example, the Italian *novelle* and *Orlando Furioso*) may be traced in the romances included in the present chapter, each of these long adventure stories is to some extent indebted to Heliodorus' work.

Heliodorus' *Aethiopica*, like Achilles Tatius' *Clitophon and Leucippe,* is an involved and colorful story about the difficulties of two lovers who are kept apart by pirates and shipwrecks. The former work is more chaste and religious, and the latter more concerned with adventure, but in both, adventure is added to adventure, and peril to peril, until all but the most attentive and retentive of readers must get lost in the labyrinth. Structural complexity, it would appear, is one of the chief attractions the romances have to offer. Samuel L. Wolff explains that the ancient writers of such works were "interested rather in diversity than in unity, . . . liked the parts better than the whole, and lingered to elaborate whatever pleased."[4] Like Wolff, however, Moses Hadas thinks that the resulting

implausibilities are not due wholly to the artistic exigencies of form: they reflect an actual view of life. . . . In the Hellenistic world the links of causality seemed to have been broken and man abandoned to the caprices of fortune. When events are no longer calculable interest in them comes to lie in their very uncertainty. And if events in the outer world follow no discernible pattern, in the moral world choices are undeliberated, even unmotivated. . . . Emotion is reduced to sentimentality, which is fingered, probed, savored, for its own sake.[5]

Can it be that the author of *Don Quixote* believed his contribution to such a kind was his masterpiece? He leaves the matter in the air. *Persiles* will be either the greatest work of entertainment in Spanish, he says, or it will be the worst.[6] The decision rests with us.

In reaching some kind of evaluation of Cervantes' romance we might begin by noting that *Persiles* falls into two main parts. Its accurately translated subtitle in the anonymous 1619 English version is *A Northern History,* which refers to the fact that in the first two of its four books Prince Persiles of Thule and Princess Sigismunda of Frisland (disguised as Periander

---

Tragicall Tales of Plutarch, which contained *The Historie of Chariclia and Theagenes.* Charles C. Mish, who has compared this excerpt with Underdowne's translation, informs me that it includes practically all of Bk. 4 of the *Aethiopica,* that the text is slightly condensed so as to make it seem an independent episode, and that some extraneous material has been added.

4. *The Greek Romances,* p. 3.

5. *An Ethiopian Romance* (Ann Arbor, Mich., 1957), pp. vii–viii.

6. Dedication of *Don Quixote,* Pt. II, to the Count of Lemos. Omitted by Shelton.

and Auristela) are forced by circumstances to expend their energy wandering among remote islands in the exotic North. In the course of their travels they meet characters from Denmark, Norway, Scotland, Ireland, and England, and soon it becomes clear that to Cervantes, as to many other Spaniards, the North was as mysterious as Spain was to Englishmen. In the first half of his work Cervantes lets his imagination play with barbaric rites, lycanthropy, icebound ships, and cities where it is dark half the year and men carry flaming pine branches through the streets. In the final two books, however, he more conventionally sends his lovers through Portugal, Spain, France, and Italy. Here adventure remains prominent, yet one feels that the characters are traveling on firmer ground. Not only are the later adventures more plausible, but when the heroes leave Spain, it is even specified that they go on foot from "Parapignan . . . through Languedocke in Prouince."[7]

Another prominent characteristic of the *Persiles* is its nearly constant motion. In both the fanciful first part and the more realistic second part, the device of travel is as vital as it was in the *Diana, Don Quixote,* or any of the picaresque stories. But its effect here is more frenetic. As a way to introduce new characters or to arouse amazement by turning up old ones, or simply as a way to switch the scene from a barbarian cave to a royal palace, travel in *Persiles* seems especially important, both in technique and effect. It has been suggested that as real explorations became fewer, and as real fighting dimmed the glory of ideal combats, adventure in fact came to be replaced by adventure in fiction.[8] It has also been thought that the endless action and peregrination in much fiction of the time may be reflections of the inquietude of contemporary Spain.[9] But one can scarcely be sure in such a matter.

At least seeming to corroborate this second suggestion are the autobiographical strands to be found not only in *Persiles,* but also in the other romances soon to be discussed. The mender of plays in *Persiles,* for instance, is thought to be reminiscent of his creator, and the route followed by Periander

7. *Persiles and Sigismunda,* p. 297.
8. John Arthur Bourne, "The Life and Works of Gonzalo de Céspedes y Meneses with Bibliographical Notes on the Spanish Novel of the Seventeenth Century," unpublished Ph.D. dissertation (Emmanuel College, Cambridge, 1937), p. 3.
9. Agustín González de Amezúa y Mayo, *Formación y elementos de la novela cortesana* (Madrid, 1929), p. 17. Amezúa y Mayo had in mind the sixteenth century particularly, but also refers to the seventeenth. Note the similarity between his view and that of Hadas, cited earlier.

and Auristela in the closing chapters is similar to that which Cervantes took when he went to Rome. Furthermore, despite their exaggeration, the Spanish romances of sentimental adventure (to use Charles Mish's term) do contain incidents similar to those found in memoirs of the time.[10] After all, the guiding principles of the romances, *amor* and *honor,* were in some instances the guiding principles of the Spanish people. If, then, one finds in *Persiles* the movement, the color, the scope, and the mixture of sensuality and religion which are associated with that dangerous word "baroque," it is in part because these elements were found in seventeenth-century Spanish life.

This is not to say that Cervantes' final dream is lifelike. Quite the contrary. He himself insists that he is aiming for poetic truth. It is therefore unfair to regret that *Persiles* does not present individualized characters in particular circumstances at particular times. (One thinks of the exceptional little genre picture of the two university students who cause a commotion by pretending to have been slaves in Algiers.) Since Cervantes is writing a romance, one should resist the temptation to criticize his mingling of times, even though the chronology of *Persiles* is loose enough to encompass Rosamond, mistress of England's Henry II (d. 1189), and Philip III, reigning monarch of the day.[11] Furthermore, when it comes to characterization, one again should recall the special freedoms and restraints of a romance. Although there can be no character development because there is no real depth of character to begin with, there is a compensatory and many-splendored spectrum of one-toned persons ranging all the way from the vile witch Zenocia to the never-enough-praised Auristela, a creature so ineffably perfect that Aristotelian imitation may well have been Cervantes' aim. In creating Auristela, at least, Cervantes seems intentionally to be omitting the prose of nature so as to dazzle us with spirit. And the net result of such devices is neither inartistic nor inconsistent with his aims. It is simply artful in a way that few moderns will appreciate.

At least one other characteristic of *Persiles* which is too important to

10. See Joaquín del Val, "La novela española en el siglo XVII," in *Historia general de las literaturas hispánicas,* ed. Guillermo Díaz-Plaja (Barcelona, 1953), Vol. III, p. LXXI. Mish gives not only a good label but a good discussion of the genre in England in his unpublished Ph.D. dissertation, "English Prose Fiction, 1600–1642: A Survey" (University of Pennsylvania, 1951).

11. Though he remains unnamed, Philip is adjured to "driue away the Moores, like him that pluckes the serpent out of his bosome before hee gnaw his intrailes . . ." (p. 286).

neglect is its olla-podrida quality.[12] Together with autobiographical bits, Cervantes has tossed in scraps of fact and fancy from Vergil, Garcilaso de la Vega (the Inca), Lodovico Ariosto, and the *Amadís*. He has added ideas and episodes from Núñez de Reinoso, and a *novella* from Giovanni Giraldi. He has seasoned generously with popular and traditional matter. And he has included exemplary narratives, probably from his own storehouse, as well as matters which must have sprung fresh from his imagination. Surely these varied ingredients, whether from life or literature, might have been blended to convey some general meaning or some complex of meanings. But I cannot see that they are. In order to indicate what the book is all about, one might even choose to borrow the tapestry metaphor of Rodríguez de Montalvo. Américo Castro, seeming to have done this, writes that the *Persiles* "is a representation of love in agony, . . . the title of which might well be 'The sergas of Persiles.' Its real protagonist is Suffering. . . ."[13] Among other things, this is a good way to say that Cervantes has allowed various elements of his story to crowd into the foreground one after the other in such a fashion that little interest is ever aroused in his characters, even the chief ones. Imitating the *Aethiopica,* in other words, Cervantes gives no preview (or, it may be, no sign of remembrance) of his own achievement in *Don Quixote*.[14] At least in Part II of the *Quixote* he had managed to integrate numerous kinds of strands into a meaningful whole; in the *Persiles* he offers quite a different sort of tour de force. Depending on one's sympathies, the result is a medley or a muddle. To me it seems that even though the incidents of the romance are more or less related to a single pilgrimage to Rome, Cervantes has let himself be lured in too many directions, and too frequently lingered to elaborate whatever happened to please him.[15]

12. For the sources referred to here I have gone back to Rudolph Schevill and Adolfo Bonilla, introd. to Vol. I, *Persiles y Sigismunda* (Madrid, 1914), and J. Palomo Roberto, "Una fuente española del *Persiles*," *HR,* VI (1938), 57–68.

13. "The Prefaces to *Don Quixote*," *PQ,* XXI (1942), 87.

14. Mack Singleton tries to resolve embarrassing problems by demonstrating that although published over a decade later than *Don Quixote,* Pt. I, the *Persiles* was actually composed much earlier ("The 'Persiles' Mystery," in *Cervantes Across the Centuries,* ed. Angel Flores and M. J. Benardete [New York, 1947], pp. 227–238).

15. In fact he himself has a character complain that the lingering is sometimes too protracted (*Persiles,* p. 182). Of course here, as always, it is impossible to affirm what an ironic author "means." In a later passage we read that "the Authour, who derideth others, is very impertinent in this historie, and sheweth himselfe ridiculous. And so he endeth this troublesome discourse, in saying that *Periander* was giuen to vnderstand, that some were weary of his long narration: who therefore purposed to abridge the same; and not, through default of iudgement that could not be excused,

The pilgrimage to Rome is naturally the chief evidence for those who find unity of purpose in the book. The nameless English translator, coming early, and happily oblivious of any such purpose, presented his version as a product of mere importunity and idleness, apologizing that it is better to busy oneself with trifling than with nothing.[16] Nonetheless, perhaps partly because it is Cervantes' work, the degree of "seriousness" in *Persiles* has long proved a snag. William C. Atkinson finds in the book not only a "deep moral preoccupation," but believes that it is an "allegory of the redemption of man from his burden of original sin through the teachings and the sacraments of Mother Church."[17] Joaquín Casalduero believes that from the tense opposition of North and South there arises, in true baroque fashion, unmistakable unity. For him, *Persiles* shows how man, plagued by tribulation, may arrive safely at his destination if guided by virtue and faith.[18] Certainly the lover-pilgrims do progress to Rome because it is the seat of the Holy Roman Catholic church, and certainly Cervantes was influenced by Núñez de Reinoso's *Los amores de Clareo y Florisea* (1555), for which the author himself had offered a didactic, allegorical explanation. But it is not certain that *Persiles* is best viewed as an allegory. Of course it is good to inquire in what ways the inset stories or even the main plot may be considered exemplary. It is good to be conscious of the apothegms and sententiae scattered through the book. However, to regard the protagonists as allegorical instead of merely idealistic, to regard the whole narrative as a technicolor sermon is going rather far.[19] As we watch the two lovers shoved across the map, and as we see how seldom character necessitates event, we are conscious not so much of any invisible, adorable, or ultimate reality behind and guiding the pilgrims or their story, as of the dangers of pirates and witches and shipwrecks *per se*. To be sure, the pilgrims travel to Rome. To

---

abuse the patience of such as hearkned vnto him . . ." (p. 186). We also see here, by the way, that *Persiles,* like *Don Quixote,* masquerades as a translation even in the original.

16. *Persiles,* A4ʳ. "To the Reader," however, he suggests that the variety of the book *"may rob some houres from thy untimely sleep; and the seriousnes of it, diuert Idlenesse from bringing-foorth worse effects."*

17. "The Enigma of the *Persiles,*" *BSS,* XXIV (1947), 246, 248.

18. *Sentido y forma de "Los trabajos de Persiles y Sigismunda"* (Buenos Aires, 1947). See also Juan J. Remos, "*Persiles,*" *Anales Cervantinos,* V (1955–1956), 159–182. Both a view and a summary of commentaries are presented by Alberto Sánchez in "El 'Persiles' como repertorio de moralidades," *Anales Cervantinos,* IV (1954), 199–223.

19. I certainly do not mean to denigrate the views of other readers, especially when my own familiarity is greatest with the English version. Perhaps it is fairest simply to admit that the romance has produced widely varying opinions.

be sure, we see virtue rewarded. But above all, the *Persiles* is a work which dares compete with Heliodorus, and, as in the *Aethiopica*, the *dulce* is more important than the *utile*.[20]

In the English translation the qualities of fantasy and adventure seem a bit heightened by the handling accorded to religion. In the original, the Spaniard Antonio baptizes his barbarian wife in the Catholic faith and teaches her that the Holy Roman Catholic church is ruled by the Holy Spirit and governed by the pope, vicar and viceroy of God on earth, and legitimate successor of St. Peter, first *pastor* after Jesus Christ.[21] In predominantly Protestant England, readers were simply told (by the wife) that Antonio "learned mee his Catholike religion, & baptized me in this riuer, though not with such ceremonies as he saith are obserued in the Church. . . ." Elsewhere Protestant sensibility was not spared a description of *"our Lady Church at Gadaloupe,"* nor even the scene in which the pilgrims kiss the threshold of the gate to the Holy City. The translator goes so far as to say that the pilgrims went to Rome "to be instructed in the truth of religion, which in these Northerne parts was a little erroneous."[22] Times being as they were, the bookseller, Matthew Lownes, was not afraid to present a papistically flavored work of fiction. (Just the year before, King James had been so eager to please Catholic Spain that he had had Raleigh beheaded.) At the same time, however, the translation is modified a bit.

Lacking the translator's name, a discussion of the English *Travels of Persiles and Sigismunda* must necessarily seem bland. We know only that certain comments by the translator were presumably passed on to the bookseller, Lownes, who professes not to know who brought the work to light. Significantly, neither translator nor bookseller mentions Cervantes' name. Although *Don Quixote*, Part I, had been printed in English seven years before, we here read only that *"The Authour is a Spaniard; whose stile becomes him well, in his own mouth: and his Works of this kinde, haue*

---

20. Some, of course, including Pinciano, have found symbolic depths in Heliodorus, too. See Albinio Martín Gabriel, "Heliodoro y la novela española," *Cuadernos de literatura: Revista general de las letras*, VIII (1950), 215–234.

21. *Persiles y Sigismunda* (Madrid, 1914), I, 45–46. Cervantes' religion has been variously regarded. Helmut Hatzfeld expresses the opinion that "Velázquez' coldness and distance from the Divine reminds us of Cervantes' shocking objectivity, lack of distinction, indifference and almost cynical matter-of-factness *in sacris*. The picture he gives of Auristela's instruction in religion [in the *Persiles*] reflects the spirit of Velázquez' picture [*La Coronación de la Virgen* (1641)]" ("Artistic Parallels in Cervantes and Velázquez," *Estudios dedicados a Menéndez Pidal* [Madrid, 1952], III, 270).

22. The references are to pp. 32, 243, 351, and 391.

*raysed his name, and approued his spirit; not alone in his owne Country,
but in others."*[23] Some of this information is wrong, of course. First and fortunately, Cervantes wrote no other Byzantine romance; and second, although the translator's words might imply that he himself worked from
the Spanish original, he in fact used the 1618 *Travaux de Persiles et de
Sigismonde* by Vital d'Audiguier. He might have done better to use the
other French translation, also of 1618, by François de Rosset, for D'Audiguier's is not very faithful. In the introductory matter to *Les travaux,*
D'Audiguier not only complains of Cervantes' diffuseness, but mentions his
own alterations and brags of producing a book that is better than its source.[24]

Conceivably Chandler is right in saying that the rather undistinguished
English *Persiles* was called for again in 1639; of this I have found no other
evidence.[25] We can be sure, though, that Fletcher and Massinger found in it
the basis for their sensational *Custom of the Country* (*ca.* 1620); and we
can be fairly sure that Defoe did *not* find in it—as Coleridge claimed—the
idea for *Robinson Crusoe*.[26] Readers of today, I think, are most likely to find
a rich inventiveness and variety, a poetic precinct where actualities need
not be insisted on. In laying the *Persiles* down, however, we well may have
the feeling that here is a persuasive illustration of Keats's belief that "a
mighty providence subdues the mightiest Minds to the service of the time
being. . . ."[27]

The Pilgrime of Casteele

Two years after the English *Persiles,* Edward All-de printed *The Pilgrime
of Casteele* (1621), another romance of sentimental adventure. English interest in Spain was mounting now toward a peak. The year before,

23. *Persiles*, A4ʳ.

24. See Juan Givanel Mas, *Catálogo de la colección cervantina* (Barcelona,
1941), I, 93–97; and Esther Josephine Crooks, *The Influence of Cervantes in France
in the Seventeenth Century* (Baltimore, 1931), *passim*. Except for the closing chapters, apparently finished somewhat hurriedly, the original *Persiles* is said to contain
some of Cervantes' finest prose. One would not guess this from the English translation.

25. *The Literature of Roguery* (Boston, 1907), I, 208. The only recent printings
that I have seen from the translation are the two stories excerpted in J. B. Trend's
Spanish Short Stories of the Sixteenth Century (London, 1928).

26. *Notes and Lectures upon Shakespeare,* ed. Mrs. H. N. Coleridge (London,
1849), II, 73.

27. Letter to J. H. Reynolds, May 3, 1818, in *The Letters of John Keats,* ed.
Hyder E. Rollins (Cambridge, Mass., 1958), I, 282.

the completed *Don Quixote* had appeared, and controversy over the Spanish marriage was growing hot.[28] Like the title page of *Persiles,* however, that of *The Pilgrime* gives no clue to the identity of either its author or translator.[29] The introductory matter reveals only that the titular pilgrim—he is to prove another traveling lover—has been entreated by special friends to appear in England. His story is not even dedicated to anyone in particular, on the theory that his good spirit and *"the sweetnesse of his Conuersation"* will make him welcome anywhere.[30]

No one could guess from this that the author was honored at home as the Cicero of Castile, the Phoenix of Spain, the Prince of Dramatic Poets. No one could guess that the work was based on *El peregrino en su patria* (1604), by one of Spain's greatest and most prolific geniuses, Lope de Vega Carpio.[31] It is significant yet not surprising that Lope's name meant nothing in England.

Since some scholars hold that Lope could not conceal himself even in his most nonsensical fiction, and since romances seem to have been conducive to a certain amount of self-revelation, one might anticipate touches of autobiography in the *Peregrino.* Certainly there is an alteration of everything "real" which gets into the romance, but it seems that Lope did make some attempt to create an idealized image of himself in both the main character, Pánfilo de Luján, and Pánfilo's good friend Jacinto. The name "Pánfilo," though certainly no neologism, seems appropriately suggestive of Lope's amatory nature, particularly when coupled with "Luján," a name associated both with Lope's birthplace and his mistress, a beautiful blonde actress named Micaela de Luján. Lope customarily referred to Micaela as "Camila Lucinda," and though the lady could not write, he placed verses signed

28. Lucy Aikin declares that the most important political event in the reign of James was the petition sent by the House of Commons to the king in 1621, voicing grievances, e.g., "The expectation of the popish recusants of the match with Spain, and feeding themselves with great hopes of the consequences thereof" (*Memoirs of the Court of King James the First* [London, 1823], II, 277).

29. According to William A. Jackson's notes for the revised *STC,* the copy at Worcester College, Oxford, contains MS notation that William Dutton is the translator.

30. A2ᵛ. I cite from a 1623 copy.

31. Lope's career was by no means complete at the time, but one of the values of the *Peregrino* is that it lists more than 200 plays he presumably had written already. According to literary legend he turned out about 1,600 sonnets, 1,800 plays, and 400 *autos sacramentales* (allegorical or religious plays).

Though the English knew nothing of him, Lope had sailed with Philip's Armada, and later claimed to have used as cannon wadding some verses in praise of a lady.

"Camila" at the beginning of the *Peregrino*. It was also to her that he addressed his beautiful eclogue "Serrana hermosa," included in the text of the *Peregrino* and regarded by some as the single document that sheds most light on his life. Surely it is no coincidence, then, that Jacinto, who is credited with the poem in the romance, wins the lady in it named "Lucinda."[32]

One would err to make many equations, however. Lope apparently derived his title from an Italian source, Jacopo Caviceo's *Il peregrino* (1508), and he was probably indebted not only to Jerónimo de Contreras' *Selva de aventuras* (1565), itself derivative, but also to Heliodorus and Achilles Tatius. However tinged with his own amours, in other words, and however modified by the sunlight and tears of his native land, Lope's *Peregrino* is still a romance, its ultimate forebears over a thousand years old.[33]

Like Heliodorus' *Aethiopica* and Cervantes' *Persiles,* and like its original, the English *Pilgrime* plunges the reader into a turmoil of adventure from the start. The hero, mysteriously washed ashore at Barcelona, is said to have suffered in a shipwreck that is not described until Book III, and his identity and name—Pamphilus—are withheld until later in the story. The central plot which gradually unfolds is rather cleverly worked out. Primarily it concerns two runaway lovers, Pamphilus and Nisa, who are repeatedly separated in their search for each other. But it also concerns another pair, Celio and Finia, siblings of the first two, who are engaged in a parallel pursuit. In following the activities of these various sweethearts, the reader is taken on a tour of Toledo, Valencia, Seville, Saragossa, Barcelona, and—via flashback—even North Africa.

Because the contents of *The Pilgrime* are not widely known, and because they differ from those in the original Spanish version, perhaps a more detailed summary may be forgiven. Pamphilus is washed up on the Barcelona shore, as he tells his fishermen rescuers, after a shipwreck on his return from Rome, whither he has gone for "the indulgences of the *Iubile"* when

---

32. Américo Castro, "Alusiones a Micaela Luján en las obras de Lope de Vega," *RFE,* V (1918), 256–292, includes a brief bibliography of the subject. More recent is the study by S. Griswold Morley, "The Pseudonyms and Literary Disguises of Lope de Vega," *UCPMP,* XXXIII (1951), 421–484. What seem to be more or less direct comments on Lope's amours are found in the translation on pp. 14 and 72.

33. Rudolph Schevill underlines contemporary admiration of Heliodorus and notes that one of Lope's characters refers to him as that "griego poeta diuino" (*The Dramatic Art of Lope de Vega* [Berkeley, Calif., 1918], pp. 152–153, 262).

Clement VIII was pope (1600).[34] Recuperating in the fishermen's cabin, he hears a singing voice, and, going to discover its source, finds two men waving "Harquebushes" in his face. He is invited to sup with the troop of which the men are members, however, and one of the band, who never appears again, tells *The History of Doricles.* Although Doricles is the leader of this very group, his story does not really become relevant until Pamphilus learns that Nisa, the heroine, is his prisoner. Alarmed, Pamphilus breaks in to see the girl, only to be shot by Doricles and sentenced to death. Fortunately he manages to mollify his executioners by an affecting prayer to an image of the Virgin. Then he flees to the city, becomes involved in a broil, is imprisoned once again, and thus meets Everard, an incarcerated knight who tells *The History of Mireno.*

Book II takes Pamphilus, now pardoned and released, to the famous Montserrat. Together with two fair boys whom he has encountered on the way, he soon is hearing *The History of Aurelia,* which is related by one of the hermits of the place. Then he separates from the boys, rescues his friend Everard from some marauding Moors, and proceeds to Valencia. Here, like any good tourist of the day, he visits a madhouse. Unlike others, he encounters a beautiful young man who resembles his sweetheart. Of course it really *is* Nisa. Apparently she was confined for her wild actions when she thought that Doricles' men had hanged Pamphilus. Now the lovers have scarcely begun to get reacquainted when the authorities separate them again, and, because of his protests, beat Pamphilus and forcibly eject him. Improbably enough, he awakens in the arms of another young man (this one really *is* a young man) who turns out to be none other than Nisa's brother Celio. And here, by the way, as at other places in the story, the author varies his design with a bit of appliquéd philosophy. "A Christian said the stranger, ought never to bewaile the destinies, nor thinke that good or euill fortune depend of them," for destiny is governed only by God.[35] And to seal up the matter there are references to Democritus, Chrysippus, Epicurus, and Boethius, as, indeed, there are learned allusions stitched in throughout the work. Celio, who does not recognize Pamphilus, tells the patient hero and the reader part of Pamphilus' own life story, then confesses that he is searching for Finia, Pamphilus' sister. The second book ends with Pamphilus' rescue of a knight, Jacinth, and details of the latter's sister's attraction to the hero.

34. *Pilgrime,* p. 2.
35. *Pilgrime,* p. 53.

Book III relates how Nisa is purchased from the madhouse by an Italian earl seeking a fool. (One thinks of Velázquez' pictures of the fools at the Spanish court.) Since the various madmen may reasonably be expected to display their wit before Nisa is selected, Lope has the chance to display all sorts of peculiar erudition. At last, however, Nisa's new master places her on a ship, and after the inevitable shipwreck, from which Nisa of course escapes, she coincidentally meets Pamphilus' sister in Marseilles, at which point the reader is allowed another instalment of the central story. The remainder of Book III is then taken up with Moorish episodes, coming to a climax with another shipwreck—in fact the same one which occurred just before the beginning of Book I.

Book IV introduces a detachable but effective narrative which George Borrow deemed "the best ghost story in the world."[36] Then it sees to the uniting of miscellaneous lovers. The artificial but inevitable ending of the whole may be suggested by a single sentence: "In this manner in one Day, and in one time, entred into the noble *Leonicios* House; *Aureliana, Pamphilus* Mother, *Nisa,* and *Eliza, Iacinth, Tiberia,* and hee who was most dispaired of, *Celio. . . .*"[37] The little Eliza mentioned here has just been created by the author for the sole, specific, and obvious purpose of having someone to mate with Thesander, a youth who has grown attached to Nisa. Thus everyone is satisfied.

The chief justification for this long summary is its use in showing what happened to Lope's work in the process of transmission. The Spanish opening is a bit more effusive than the English version's "VPon the shore of *Barselon,*" although both it and the passages immediately following are recognizably derived from the Spanish. There are significant changes very shortly, however. The fifteen-stanza song, heard by the pilgrim while recovering in the fishermen's cabin, is omitted altogether. So is the six-page poem spoken by Pánfilo to that image of the Virgin when he is about to be hanged. And so is the poetic lament inspired by his imprisonment in Barcelona. Even if some critics did not feel that the chief value of the Spanish story is its wealth of verse, such changes would be important. Still more important is the omission which occurs when Pamphilus is released from prison and sent on his way with a "thousand louing imbracings" from his friend Everard. At

---

36. *Wild Wales,* II, in *The Works of George Borrow,* ed. Clement Shorter (London, 1924), XIII, 5. The story has been printed separately by Alfonso Reyes as *Las aventuras de Pánfilo* (Mexico City, 1957).

37. *Pilgrime,* p. 148.

this point in the original, Lope announces that great festivities are then taking place in Valencia. In fact, the pilgrim arrives at a particular square in Valencia just as a drama is about to begin. Three famous performers are commencing the presentation of *El viaje del alma,* one of Lope's most celebrated religious plays. Composed earlier than the narrative part of the *Peregrino,* the *Viaje,* which seems actually to have been performed about the turn of the century, tells in verse how the Soul is persuaded by a pilot (*el Demonio*) to embark with Desire on the ship of Delight, ignoring the warnings which Memory and Reason shout from the shore. In the course of the trip, the voyagers encounter the ship of Penitence, piloted by Christ, toward whom the Soul is finally drawn. Longer than all of the narrative which has preceded it, this *auto* or *representación moral* brings the first book to a close and succeeds in dominating it completely. In Jacobean England, morality and mystery plays scarcely were packing in crowds, but in theocratic Spain, where strength and unanimity of belief made religion a suitable subject for popular spectacles, Lope's religious dramas, colorful and lyrical, had considerable appeal.[38] It is therefore important for our understanding of Lope, the *Peregrino,* and the *Pilgrime* to realize that the English translation omits this play entirely and goes on to tell of Pamphilus' trip to the Montserrat.

It may be recalled that at the beginning of Book II Pamphilus encounters two young men while traveling to this sacred, serrated mountain of the Catalans. Their pale faces and blonde hair reveal them to be Flemish or Ger-

---

38. Though literary history has long assumed that English miracle plays died a natural death, it has recently been suggested that the English authorities, wishing to wash their hands of Rome, put a deliberate end to them (Harold C. Gardiner, *Mysteries' End* [New Haven, Conn., 1946]).

Many references to Spanish religious drama might be cited. A broad view is provided by Marcelino Menéndez Pelayo, "Autos y coloquios," *Estudios sobre el teatro de Lope de Vega,* I, ed. Enrique Sánchez Reyes, in *Edición nacional de las obras completas* (Santander, 1949), XXIX, 23–137; and Bruce W. Wardropper, *Introducción al teatro religioso del Siglo de Oro* (Madrid, 1953). Arturo M. Cayuela, "Los autos sacramentales de Lope. Reflejo de la cultura religiosa del poeta y de su tiempo," *Razón y Fe,* CVIII (1935), 168–190, 330–349, has impassioned praise for Lope and laments lack of modern interest; and Henry R. V. Fox, Lord Holland, throws some cold water on the whole subject: "It was difficult for him [Lope] to divest any of his writings of all poetical merit; and in his Autos, the patience which could wade through such nonsense would no doubt be occasionally rewarded with some striking passages" (*Some Account of the Lives and Writings of Lope Felix de Vega Carpio and Guillen de Castro* [London, 1817], I, 207–208). See also Homero Serís, *Manual de bibliografía de la literatura española* (Syracuse, N. Y., 1948–1954), I, 283–286, 831–832.

The *Peregrino* is of particular interest for introducing Lope's *autos* in print.

man, just such pilgrims as seem to have traveled into Spain in considerable numbers,[39] and Lope, if not his translator, has the three youths strike up a conversation quite in keeping with the fact that they are approaching the site where Loyola avowed the religious life, and where, in fact, it was sometimes supposed the castle of the Holy Grail had stood. One of the travelers tells Pánfilo that he has come to Spain seeking religious asylum. He praises the Inquisition, mentions the errors of Luther, and lauds the religion of Rome. Fast on the heels of this there follow stories relating miracles wrought by the Virgin. Nor is this the end. The boys compose Latin verses to the Holy Lady of the shrine—one of the most celebrated in Spain—and then go on to speak with the holy men nearby. Only at long last does Pánfilo meet Everardo in Valencia, and then, quite fortuitously, it turns out to be the very day on which there is to be a presentation of *Las bodas de la alma y el amor divino*, a symbolic play commemorating the marriage of Philip III and Margaret of Austria.[40] Hence we find another drama in the final pages of the second book. Virtually all of Book II, in other words, was cut from the English version.

The reason lies close at hand: like all translators who work with an intermediate version, the writer was at the mercy of a middleman. Whoever he was, the translator of the *Peregrino*, like the translator of *Persiles* two years earlier, made use of a French version by Vital d'Audiguier, in this case *Les diverses fortunes de Panfile et de Nise* (1614).[41] Surely he knew that D'Audiguier had confessed his version was inaccurate. Surely he knew that after labeling Spanish writing as vain, verbose, extravagant, boring, and difficult, D'Audiguier had gone on to justify his own reshaping of the *Peregrino*. And just as surely he knew that D'Audiguier had complained on the grounds that Lope had so many ideas that he could express them only confusedly, talking of everything at once. According to D'Audiguier, Lope had dragged in long digressions in order to vary his story or swell his book or waste paper. In the midst of his tale of love and adventure, he even gave speeches in praise of the Holy Inquisition. Now, asks D'Audiguier, is this the

---

39. Rudolph Schevill, "Some Forms of the Riddle Question and the Exercise of the Wits in Popular Fiction and Formal Literature," *UCPMP*, II (1911), 198–199.

40. Early in 1599 Philip III and his sister, Doña Isabel Clara Eugenia, welcomed Margaret and Albert of Austria, their future consorts, who had come to Spain from Italy to celebrate their double wedding. Lope performed in the nuptial festivities, and on April 18 the renowned Villalba put on the play referred to here.

41. The projected subtitle of the English version appears in the Stationers' Register, ed. Edward Arber (London, 1877), IV, 59: *"The Fortunes of LLAMPHILUS [sic] and NISA."* The Spanish book was called simply *El peregrino en su patria*.

way to charm a mistress, especially if she is a Huguenot? Perforce or by choice, the English translator was bound by D'Audiguier's views.[42]

Regarding the story simply as a story, one might justify the remodeling. With so much cut out, the basic lines of the narrative are easier to discern.[43] In fact removal of some of the religious and poetic appendages makes the *Pilgrime* less distinctive but more Heliodoran than the original *Peregrino*. And this is true to an even greater extent than I have so far indicated. Later in the *Peregrino* there come two more plays—the semi-dramatic and song-filled *La maya* and the allegorical *El hijo pródigo,* based on the story in St. Luke. Added to the first two plays, these occupy about forty per cent of the entire work. In all, including the plays, the matter relevant to the two blonde pilgrims, and a variety of amorous, religious, narrative, humorous, and descriptive poems which Lope may have inserted to clear his desk, the 1604 Barcelona edition contains approximately two hundred and eighty pages which are omitted from the English version. Putting this another way, the English version omits about sixty per cent of Lope's romance! Small wonder, then, that it has only four books, the Spanish five. When speaking of methods of translation, one may hardly cite a more remarkable example of remodeling.

It is not true, however, that a didactic romance has been converted to a merely amorous-adventurous one. Although the plot of the Spanish *Peregrino* is many-sided, it scarcely will be accused of being multi-leveled. Of course the original story contains allegorical patches, but it is itself no allegory. Lope is willing enough to proffer edifying allusions and comments, but few readers will be tempted to seek in such a "galimatias"—the word is D'Audiguier's—for any underlying, unifying theme. The nearest approach to such a theme, both in the Spanish and English versions, is made toward the end of Pamphilus' peregrinations, during which he has played

42. Perhaps even knowing Spanish, the Englishman would not have transmitted Lope's romance unchanged. In a time of increasing freedom it might be all right to refer here and there to Roman Catholicism, but it also might be asking for trouble to laud the Inquisition. Captain John Stevens (d. 1726), many years later, was still acutely aware of the problem. One work he calls "Too religious to bear in English"; another is "Extraordinary devout & consequently unfit for English"; and a third is "Too godly to be translated" (quoted by Robert H. Williams, "A Manuscript Document on the Translations from Spanish by Captain John Stevens," *RLC,* XVI [1936], 152).

43. In the comparatively recent edition by Francisco J. Garriga (Barcelona, 1935), the *autos* and other "additions," said to be interesting only to the erudite are removed to let the narrative flow freely.

the role of courtier, soldier, captive, pilgrim, madman, herdsman, and lackey. Here the author lays aside his plot to discuss the merits of the active life. At first (in the words of the translator) he says only that his story has been told "To the end that you . . . may learne to know, how trauailing abroad brings honour, & profite, and many times the contrary." Then he adds that even though "All consisteth in the disposition of Heauen, whose influence[s] guide the passages of our life, as it pleaseth them," man has the divine gift of free will, and it is "a weaknes vnworthy of a gentle heart, not to dare hazardously to enterprise any thing. . . ." How can one obtain anything of value without running after it? Man's success lies in his courage to keep striving, to defend himself from the "perilous assaults of Fortune."[44] At least such ideas occurred to Lope, seemed appropriate to what he had written, and elicited enough of his attention to receive rather full expression.

Most modern readers have proved immune to the *Peregrino*'s delights.[45] Its inventiveness, variety, and ingenuity have seemed overbalanced by confusion and shallowness. If one wished, however, one might attempt an explanation of these weaknesses. Setting aside the fact that some of our own contemporary writers have courted confusion, a reader who regrets that Lope finds delight in disorder might be reminded that this, after all, is a freedom claimed by more than one baroque artist. Even when baroque art has logic at its core, it often has an air of riot. Thus the exuberant complexity of the *Peregrino* is in some ways similar to that in the canvases of Rubens. The theatricality of the romance might even be compared with that of El Greco, who placed an impossible but effective spotlight beneath the bridge in his view of Toledo. Then, too, the fundamental plot of the *Peregrino*— as we see more clearly by looking at *The Pilgrime*—is reasonably simple. It is observation rather than condemnation to say that in presenting it, Lope left little in the inkwell.

As for the second charge, shallowness, one might wonder whether Lope's

44. *Pilgrime*, pp. 140–141. No matter how many excuses their authors give, the romances of sentimental adventure seem partly governed by fate—not the grand fate of ancient tragedy, but a decadent sort of fate that delights in games of symmetry and is more superstitious than the ancient variety (Alfonso Reyes, " 'El Peregrino en su Patria', de Lope de Vega," in *Boletín de la Academia Argentina de Letras* [Buenos Aires, 1937], p. 646). The matter is also noted, among other places, in Arturo Farinelli's *"Peregrinos de amores en su patria* de Lope de Vega," *Homenatge a Antoni Rubió i Lluch* (Barcelona, 1936), I, 581–602.

45. It is even suggested by Ludwig Pfandl that the *Peregrino* is a superficial parody of better works of the same genre (*Historia de la literatura nacional española en la edad de oro,* tr. Jorge Rubió Balaguer [Barcelona, 1952], pp. 286–289).

temperament was unsuited to reflection, or his adventurous life simply left him too little time to develop a mature philosophy.[46] In any case, despite its autobiographical tinges, the characters and commentary in the *Peregrino* reveal little depth, little of Lope's "self-interiority." For all of their motion, the people of the narrative, like most of those in his plays, are mere mannikins. The fictional-dramatic parallel is a tempting one to pursue, as a matter of fact, for Lope's Heliodoran romance, like his writing for the stage, has a certain colorful, kaleidoscopic attraction in spite of its shallowness. Since Lope has given us such a swirling and intriguing vision of love and travel and adventure—and even religion in the original—perhaps it is a bit ungrateful to expect a Quixote or a Hamlet from him as well. It is asking pears of the elm tree.

Modern readers of the English *Pilgrime* are rare. Charles Mish, the only commentator I know of, makes the interesting observation that Lope "used the epic form to commendable advantage; the antecedent action related by the characters is comparatively brief, the foreground story clearly dominates the interest, and the plot, though it is not without complexity, never suffers from obscurity or confusion."[47] Mish regrets, though, that the ingenious romance "should have been translated in such a turgid style." He believes it necessary "to unravel the mysteries of the punctuation and to re-cast the phrasing so as to make sense. . . ."[48] Readers must judge for themselves. Truly the translator has no outstanding virtues such as the colloquial energy of Mabbe, and yet, in spite of its awkward passages—its thrums and knots—*The Pilgrime* seems to me a workmanlike piece of writing, the product of industry more than art, but sufficient to convey some sense of the original's verve.

Contemporary English readers seem to have reacted more favorably than they had to Cervantes' *Persiles*. In 1623, when Spanish interest was high, two issues of a second edition were called for. (It was in February of the same year that Prince Charles and Buckingham, disguised in false beards, set out on their own pilgrimage through "Casteele." James addressed the two in a letter in June as his "sweet boys and dear venturous knights, worthy to be put in a new romanso.")[49] Furthermore, Fletcher's tragicomedy called *The*

---

46. The latter suggestion is made by Salvador de Madariaga, "Paralelos anglo-españoles," in *Ensayos anglo-españoles* (Madrid, [1923]), p. 184.

47. "English Prose Fiction," p. 100. For a reader of the English version, as we have seen, the effect of focus is enhanced by the omission of non-narrative passages.

48. "English Prose Fiction," pp. 103, 104.

49. Quoted by Aikin, II, 325.

Pilgrim, based on the translation, was already on the boards by the Christmas season of 1621–1622.[50] In other words, Lope's *Pilgrime of Casteele* both deserved and won its brief hour on the stage, though few would mistake it for one of the great books of its time.[51]

Gerardo

In 1622, three years after *Persiles* and one year after the first edition of *The Pilgrime,* Leonard Digges published his translation of what Pfandl deemed the last of the major Heliodoran romances.[52] *Gerardo the Unfortunate Spaniard* depicts a youth who calls himself a pilgrim and has a variety of fervid adventures, mainly amorous, and it does, expectedly, reveal something of its author's life. Considerably more sensational in tone than either *Persiles* or *The Pilgrime,* it is structurally more reminiscent of Ariosto. That is—to borrow Montaigne's complaint against Ariosto—its author seems "faintly to hover and flutter from tale to tale, . . . skipping from bough to bough, alwaies distrusting his owne wings, except it be for some short flight. . . ."[53]

Gonzalo de Céspedes y Meneses must have been a roaring boy when, in 1615, he composed the first part of the *Poema trágico del español Gerardo.* (Two years later he capitalized on his success by writing a sequel.) At any rate, it seems to have been his conduct in love that landed him in prison long enough to write the book. As Digges puts it, *"in the time of fiue yeres of his Imprisonment, vnder the borrowed Name of* Gerardo, [he] *personates himselfe in his owne misfortunes. And so partly with truth, partly with fiction, makes vp a first and second Part."*[54] Naturally Digges pretends that all the colorful misfortunes of young Gerardo are so many seamarks directing a reader in the channel of morality. In the preface which he borrowed for his translation of Claudian's *De raptu Proserpinae* (1617), he had previously

50. Baldwin Maxwell, "The Date of *The Pilgrim*," *PQ,* XIII (1934), 350–356.

51. A supposed 1628 edition is noted by Hugo A. Rennert and Américo Castro, *Vida de Lope de Vega* (Madrid, 1919), p. 156; Luis Guarner, ed., *El peregrino en su patria,* in *Novelas* (Madrid, 1935), II, 11; and Remigio Ugo Pane, *English Translations from the Spanish: 1484–1943* (New Brunswick, N. J., 1944), p. 195. Pane also lists an edition of 1632—probably a metathetic error for 1623.

52. *Historia de la literatura,* p. 289. Some writers (e.g., Luis Guarner, ed., *El peregrino . . . ,* II, 8) would exclude *Gerardo* from the genre.

53. *The Essayes* (1603), tr. John Florio, p. 238.

54. *Gerardo,* A3ʳ. It is suggestive that Céspedes y Meneses elsewhere used the pseudonym "Gerardo Hispano."

relayed the belief that one might find three different levels of meaning in that story—historic, symbolic, and allegorical.[55] But the reader well may be dubious concerning any profound purposes in *Gerardo*. It is, after all, a long way from saying to doing.

Since he is the only identifiable English translator of a Spanish romance of sentimental adventure, Digges deserves a special word or two. Apparently he was a quiet, bookish man. Son and grandson of two of the most distinguished mathematicians of the time, he had plenty of family precedent for publication, his grandfather, also named Leonard, having chosen specifically to write in English "to store his natiue language and benefite his Countrey men. . . ."[56] When Thomas Digges, the father of the future translator, died in 1595, young Leonard was about seven. As it turned out, his mother was left with a fortune sufficient to draw forth a number of suitors, among them (whatever his reasons) Thomas Russell, a man half her age. Thus the overseer of Shakespeare's will became the stepfather of one of the Spanish translators. The relationship may be significant. Leslie Hotson, at any rate, declares that "In all Shakespeare's Stratford circle, . . . the only person of definite literary talent was . . . Leonard Digges; and we know that the younger spirit took heat from Shakespeare's fire and feeling."[57] Certainly we do have warm praise for Shakespeare from the quill of Leonard Digges.

After leaving University College, Oxford, in 1606, Digges retired to London for a while. Later, says Wood, he "travelled into several Countries, and became an accomplish'd Person," in fact "spent many years in good letters in transmarine Universities. . . ."[58] Hotson adds, "in particular, at Madrid."[59] Hence Digges's knowledge of Spanish. As to how his Spanish interest may have begun, Hotson has several suggestions: (1) that his stepfather's friend John Davies introduced him to James Mabbe; (2) that the Spanish ambassador, Digby, had occasion to know him through Dudley Digges, his brother; and (3) that he was swayed by his near neighbors and friends the Porters, who had some Spanish blood and figured in Anglo-Spanish affairs. In any case, Hotson concludes that young Digges went along with Mabbe when Digby and his train set out for Spain in 1611. Later on, we know, Digges, like Mabbe, retired to his college to live. There he brought forth *Gerardo*,

55. *The Rape of Proserpine,* ed. H. H. Huxley (Liverpool, 1959), p. xii.
56. *A Geometrical Practise, Named Pantometria* (1571), A4ᵛ.
57. *I, William Shakespeare* (New York, 1938), p. 214.
58. *Athenae Oxonienses* (London, 1721), I, 600.
59. *I, William Shakespeare,* p. 237; see also pp. 238–239.

and there, in 1635, he died. We have already seen Wood's summation: "He was esteemed by those that knew him in *Univ. Coll.* a great Master of the *English* language, a perfect understander of the *French* and *Spanish,* a good Poet and no mean Orator."[60]

At a time when more than a few Englishmen were curious about Spain, Digges's particular turning of the tapestry revealed a highly involved series of tragic love stories grouped in two parts and a number of "discourses." Everything in *Gerardo* is given a certain amount of coherence by the survival of the protagonist (though he sometimes fades from sight) and a single ostensible moral (namely, loose loving is bad). The pattern is so complex, however, that as soon as one steps back from a part of it, the whole becomes blurred. Although the author has apparently tried for unity in diversity by using some of his characters in successive tales, Mish justly complains that this merely

snarls the time relationship of the episodes hopelessly, and considerably impairs the verisimilitude of the main story. It is hardly reasonable, for instance, to suppose that a lady piqued by a fancied slight on the part of the hero could, after abandoning him in a huff, pick up a band of robbers and become their chief so quickly as to enable her to capture her erstwhile lover in the next sequence.[61]

Nor is the reader reassured when, later on, Gerardo discovers that the mysterious slave-girl who effects his escape from some Moors is the same ubiquitous lady, long since presumed dead. (One thinks, perhaps, of those seventeenth-century buildings with façades having a clever but illogical double functioning of members, such as a molding that serves as a sill.) Even with the dubious advantage of such doubling, incidents in *Gerardo* seem discrete. Céspedes y Meneses made use of elements that are pastoral, chivalric, Italianate, Moorish, picaresque, and pseudo-religious; but instead of blending them, he manipulated them in such a way that the reader is almost always

---

60. I, 600. It is of incidental interest that Edward Blount, who brought out Digges's *Gerardo,* published also Mabbe's *Rogue* and the First Folio. Digges had a finger in each of these. He wrote verses praising both Shakespeare's *"wit-fraught Booke"* and Mabbe's talent at deciphering difficult Spanish (First Folio [1623], leaf following A3, and *The Rogue* [1622], I, A4ᵛ). Hotson explains that in his youth Digges had known Heminges and Condell (p. 244). Ben Jonson, who knew some Spanish, also wrote verses for the First Folio and was a friend of Mabbe. And Mabbe, in turn, was not only a major translator of Spanish, but among those who praised Shakespeare in the Heminges-Condell volume. Although the relationships of these men are not clear, an interesting fact does emerge: the first collection of Shakespeare's plays was launched with the aid of Hispanophiles.

61. "English Prose Fiction," p. 105.

more conscious of the parts than the whole. Most moderns, notwithstanding the appeal of certain episodes, would regard the total result as ruinously confusing. But, then, neither Céspedes y Meneses nor his translator could predict how hard it would be for posterity to read the romance in the same spirit that its author wrote. Digges says particularly that the reader will find delight in the *"weauing and contexture of the Worke."*[62]

When it comes to *Gerardo*'s ostensible moral, as we have seen, the book cries wine and sells vinegar. In the first place it presents sensual, not merely rhetorical love; and in the second place, it furnishes its hero with no less than four ladies. The ending, at least, is edifying. First, mistakenly thinking Gerardo dead, his sweetheart Nisa retires to a nunnery. Then, discovering that he is really alive, she gives up her habit to marry him. Finally, though, when the day of the wedding comes, Gerardo himself is missing. Fortunately for our comprehension he has left a note giving thanks to God for (in Digges's words) *"vnspeakeable bounty, in raising me from the bondage of a vicious life. . . ."* Avowing the religious life himself, he asks, *"should not I, by falling into the reckoning of my sinnes, striue to expiate some one, by leauing to the quiet possession of my gracious Maker, a Spouse, admitted to his* Hymenean *rites?"* When Gerardo's brother takes this news to Nisa, she is already in her habit again. Without knowing Gerardo's decision, she has reached the same one for herself. And thus the book ends.[63] Surely this is exemplary. Surely, too, the author has amply shown that wanton lust leads to misery. But ever since the first couple of discourses, Gerardo has seemed rather like the teetotaler who must drink the whole jug before he believes that the cider is hard. After Discourse One, in which his sweetheart Clara accuses him of rape, tries to kill him, and finally slays her husband and herself, Gerardo still has much to learn, and the reader much to see: a naked woman sprawled in a pool of blood, a eunuch whose windpipe is slit, a mulatto stablehand in a strawy rendezvous with a beautiful lady, and even a naked lover trapped in a chimney where a husband has a fire built. Was it possible to believe the conventional claim that such a work was a fiction-coated moral pill and not a moral-coated fictional comfit? Unless the reader

62. *Gerardo*, A3^r. Years later, in crying up the translation of Scudéry's *Artamenes* (1655), Humphrey Moseley assured his readers that *"Our Author hath not shew'd more strength of Brain in the admirable Turnes and Mazes of this Work (which makes it reputed second to none) than He hath at last in tying all up . . ."* (V, A2^r).

63. *Gerardo*, p. 471. Much earlier, Heliodorus had had his lovers not only married, but also consecrated as priest and priestess of the Sun and Moon.

had a knack for finding sermons in everything, it would certainly seem doubt-ful.[64]

Stylistically the Spanish *Gerardo* leans toward Gongoristic fustian, espe-cially in its earlier parts. E. G. Mathews cites a number of passages to show how the English translator has pruned, perhaps with the thought that the original was too euphuistic, inclined to sound old-fashioned if translated verbatim.[65] At the same time, Digges also made small additions, sometimes strengthened expressions, and, often with happy results, made the language more colloquial.

Earlier we had occasion to consider Digges's censorship, his rejection of a *"by-discourse"* for *"smelling of Papisticall Miracles. . . ."* Mathews identifies the passage in question as one that concerns a woman who took her stepson as a lover, causing her husband to murder the boy. The woman has since spent ten years of penance in the wilderness, thus winning God's grace.[66]

More interesting is Digges's rationalization of the Fernando-Camila story:

all alone towards midnight he [the lover Fernando] got him to the Nunnery wall. He had no sooner climbed to the top of it, but hee might heare a voice iust vnderneath him, calling out, Is it *Fernando?* Who replide, 'Tis I, sweet, I come. But with this, I come, and his sudden haste to fasten the thred-Ladder, for his better getting downe on the other side, with the darknesse of the night together, and his owne want of heed, hee stumbled vpon a great loose stone which fell from the wall and him, & (it seemed) guided by *Camila's* destiny, or higher Prouidence, lighted vpon the vnfortunate Creatures head; the waight of it was such as gaue her no leaue to cry out, onely *Fernando* might heare by one soft mortall groane, the execution done, and his bitter losse.[67]

This was not what Céspedes y Meneses had described. In the Spanish, Fer-nando also scales the wall, but then sees in the garden a crackling fire. It turns out to be an eerily menacing sort of vision, in the midst of which is Camila. And the next day, her body disfigured and covered with bruises,

64. External evidence on the subject is given in Céspedes y Meneses' own *Soldado Píndaro,* a weaker attempt in the same genre, in which he affirms the pur-pose of a fiction writer to be diversion and delight (reprinted in Vol. XVIII of *Biblioteca de autores españoles . . . : Novelistas posteriores a Cervantes,* ed. Cayetano Rosell [Madrid, 1851], p. 361).

65. Indispensable on this subject is Mathews' "Studies in Spanish-English Cul-tural and Literary Relations, 1598–1700," unpublished Ph.D. dissertation (Harvard, 1938).

66. Mathews, pp. 367–368.

67. *Gerardo,* p. 451.

Camila is discovered to be dead. Apparently her supernatural retribution seemed too "papisticall" to Digges.[68]

Since Digges was not a very talented poet, it is well that he chose to omit or alter much of the verse in his source. The lyrics of Céspedes y Meneses were undistinguished at best, and it is not surprising that the Englishman seldom managed to strike from them a spark of lyricism. As for his prose, Mathews concludes that Digges, like Bartholomew Yong, "transmitted his original intelligently and forcibly, and has demonstrated in some passages that a greater original might have stimulated him to be more consistently at his best." Fitzmaurice-Kelly was even willing to say that Digges's prose matches the finest of its day in brilliance and picturesque force. And Bourne is scarcely less lavish with praise.[69] Perhaps all would agree, however, that from the distance of more than three hundred years, it seems a mistake for Digges to have lavished time and talent on so perishable a commodity. *Gerardo* still retains a certain interest as a labyrinth of rather Italianate *novelas* on a single theme, but somehow the whole thing would be much more fun if it were a fraction of its nearly five hundred pages.

In its time, the romance was marketed in several forms. During the same year that it was put on sale in octavo by Blount, it was snatched up by dramatists, just as *Persiles* and *The Pilgrime* had been. Fletcher and Massinger took from it two stories and the names for nearly all the characters of *The Spanish Curate* (1622). In the next year, this time teamed with Rowley, Fletcher made use of the Jayme-Ismenia tale for *The Maid in the Mill*. Nor is this all. The sensational Roberto-Isdaura story furnished materials for two more plays—Rowley and Middleton's *The Changeling* (1622) and Manuche's (?) *The Bastard* (1652). Later on, the same story appeared in debased form in *The English Rogue*,[70] and in 1683, over sixty years after Digges's translation, it was printed under the guise of *The Famous History of Auristella*. The romance itself, however, was not printed again for three decades. After Henrietta Maria moved into the English royal household, Spanish romances in general seem to have sunk from view for a while. Then at last, in 1653,

68. It should be noted, nevertheless, that Digges included elsewhere "a blacke and dismall apparition" which understandably leaves Gerardo with "his haire standing on end" (p. 296).

69. Mathews, p. 367; Fitzmaurice-Kelly, "Un hispanófilo inglés del siglo XVII," *Homenaje á Menéndez y Pelayo* (Madrid, 1899), I, 55; and Bourne, p. 176.

70. *The English Rogue* (I, 1665; II, 1668; III–IV, 1671), the picaresque work by Richard Head and Francis Kirkman, is not to be confused with the Alemán-Mabbe narrative.

Gerardo bobbed up again, and as late as 1657 William London thought it belonged in his *Catalogue of the Most Vendible Books in England.*[71]

Don Fenise

The last translation of a Greco-Spanish story was *The History of Don Fenise. A New Romance, Written in Spanish by Francisco de las-Coveras. And Now Englished by a Person of Honour* (1651). It has proved to be the source of some confusion. Although the anonymous translator suggests that the reader compare *Fenise* with its original, he makes the comparison nearly impossible by providing only the name of a non-existent author—Coveras. The reader has no way to know that the original Spanish book was signed with the name "Francisco de las Cuevas." Even if he did, it might take him some time to discover that this, in turn, was really the pen name of a minor writer named Francisco de Quintana. Seemingly to cast still more murk, the translator gives a title which is so far removed from the original one that, to the best of my knowledge, the world lay in Cimmerian darkness until 1912, when Hugo Rennert pointed out that the English *Fenise* is based ultimately on *Las experiencias de amor y fortuna* (1626).[72] In 1934 Franklin P. Rolfe scattered the remaining darkness by showing that the version used had appeared anonymously in Paris in 1636, and that it was called *La Fenise, histoire espagnol.*[73]

The English preface has puffing praise for the book. Quoting with approval an unnamed French "wit," it declares that *"The Plots are so well mannaged; the Passions cleane and naturall; the Language chosen and proper; and the whole Discourse so perfectly well wrought, that I am sorry it was written by an Enemy to our Country."*[74] In structure, style, and perhaps faithfulness to life, in other words, the book is highly commended. Spaniards, too, were flattering. Francisco Palau, who read the book twice, praised not only its pithy, pure, and elegant language, but also its warnings to wanton youth.[75] Others compared it with the *Aethiopica*, although, like *Gerardo*,

---

71. London, Ee4[r]. He must have included it grudgingly, for he regarded romances as "the trash of writings" (C2[v]).

72. *The Spanish Pastoral Romances* (Philadelphia, 1912), p. 188.

73. "On the Bibliography of Seventeenth-Century Prose Fiction," *PMLA*, XLIX, 1078.

74. *Fenise*, A3[v]–A4[r].

75. *Experiencias de amor y fortuna* (Barcelona, 1633), ¶ 2[r].

it lacked a central plot and focused attention on a single hero instead of a pair of pilgrim-lovers.[76]

Coming along some two and a half centuries later, Rennert postulated a bit cynically that Quintana's contemporary Spanish success was due to the influence of Lope de Vega, his dedicatee. Rennert thought such success merely demonstrated "how easily the public taste was satisfied."[77] Quintana himself had apologized for his digressions, but such adjectives as Rennert applies—"wearisome," "commonplace," and "dull"—would have wounded and puzzled him, for he had aimed at success via the strange and marvelous, as well, of course, as the exemplary.[78]

Like *Persiles, The Pilgrime,* and *Gerardo,* Quintana's romance has some situations of interest. There is, for instance, the hero's digging of a tunnel to rescue a lady in "Argier." But there are too many situations, too many reappearances of long-forgotten characters, too many strains on credibility. And the seams between sections are crude. At one point a character finishes a story with these words: "Behold deere *Fenise* the successe of my loves, if the recitall thereof hath beene too long pardon me; I did it but to divert you from thinking of what you have left at *Cartagene* [his sweetheart]. It is now my brothers part, to tell us the occasion, which made him absent himselfe from *Madrid,* and not participate of all these marvellous felicities." Whereupon, without respite, the romance continues: *"Fenise* found this history extreamly pretty and well entermixed, saying that for its raritie it merited to be consecrated to posteritie; which gave subject to *Charles* to endeavour to merit like praise, in recounting his fortunes: which he thus begun."[79] And patched in here is *The History of Don Charles and Violante,* which in turn is followed by *The Prodigious History of a Sonne and His*

76. Both Lope de Vega and Juan Pérez de Montalván, a *novela* writer soon to be discussed, compared the romance with Heliodorus' work (*Experiencias,* ¶ 5ᵛ and ¶ 8ʳ). Considering the warm relationship between Lope and Quintana, I am inclined to wonder if the name of the book's hero, "Feniso," is not a thinly veiled compliment to the great dramatist, the "fénix" or "phoenix" of Spain. In the *Experiencias* itself, Quintana refers to Lope as the *"dignissimo* Fenix de Europa" (¶ 2ᵛ).

77. *The Spanish Pastoral Romances* (Baltimore, 1892), pp. 97, 99. "It is written," says Rennert, "in the bad taste of much of the prose of the time, with a piling-up of epithets and constant resort to antithetical clauses" ([Philadelphia, 1912], p. 191). Rennert's reason for mentioning it in his study is to confute those critics who have carelessly labeled it a pastoral romance.

78. *Experiencias,* ¶ 7ᵛ.

79. *Fenise,* p. 264.

Mother. The effect is that of a crazy quilt. Subordination lacking, there can be no order. Furthermore, as might be expected, the reader almost always has the feeling that he is being given only the argument of the book, embroidered, to be sure, with moral and rhetorical flourishes, but consisting, after all, of mere events.

As for edification, the translation offers such sentences as these: "contentment is the most excellent paint wherewith a woman can beautifie her selfe." And: "I gave her presents; for it is long agoe since liberalitie hath beene the mother of love. . . ." And even: "necessity . . . is the mother of invention."[80] Another mode of edifying is by example. A lady who has slain her lover asks, "Is there in the whole world a woman of so little courage, that could support so many injuries, without giving an exemplary chastisement to all ingrates?" And a youth who tempts his own mother to an assignation finally has "his heart touched with a very sensible repentance; judging that all these miseries were come unto him by divine punition. . . ."[81] In *Don Fenise,* however, the *Gerardo*-type plots (the singular would be inaccurate) are not notably exemplary.

One might gather from the scraps already offered that the language of the translation is moderately clear. Usually it is. The Englishman, following the French translation of the Spanish, manages pretty well until he tries a purple patch. Then it is hard to believe that a scant sixteen years after *Fenise,* Thomas Sprat was advocating a lean style, his famous "close, naked, natural way of speaking."[82]

Despite all one is tempted to say against it, Quintana's *Fenise* was of interest to readers of its time. Its action is repetitious and disjointed, its characters less intriguing than the factors in some algebraic equations, its structure as maze-like as its author could make it, and its English style unobtrusive at best. Nevertheless Gerard Langbaine, as late as 1688, remembered it clearly enough to recognize that Aphra Behn took from it the plot for her *Dutch Lover* (1673), and Thomas D'Urfey his *Banditti, or A Ladies Distresse* (1686).[83]

80. *Fenise,* pp. 53, 116, 195.
81. *Fenise,* pp. 303, 315.
82. *The History of the Royal-Society of London* (1667), p. 113.
83. *Momus Triumphans* (1688), pp. 3, 7.

In 1652, a year after *Fenise,* the printer Bernard Alsop resurrected an English romance from the preceding century. It was R. C.'s tangentially interesting *Troublesome and Hard Adventures in Love,* which we have noted earlier as an imitation of Montemayor and Gil Polo (see Ch. IV). Just as *Fenise, Gerardo,* and *The Pilgrime*

Conclusion

At least three generalizations may be drawn from the romances considered in this chapter. First, they are rather cosmopolitan. To be sure, they tell of Spanish cane-tourneys and serenades under balconies. They show pilgrimages to the Montserrat and Guadalupe. They even depict a celebration in honor of Philip III's wedding. And they have autobiographical echoes. In fact, compared with the chivalric romances, these newer stories reveal positive steps toward realism, including steps in the process by which the incredible hero of older literature gradually evolved into the recognizable man of the new. But these romances are not wholly Spanish. Dependent on travel for movement, and designed to entertain with variety, they shift their settings from Spain to Africa to Italy to France, and then back to various parts of Spain. Don Fenise finds his Laure in the Alps, and Persiles and Sigismunda are captured by savages in the exotic North. Furthermore, passing through translators' hands, the romances have become cosmopolitan in a more subtle sense. It could be argued that denationalization was a significant factor in enabling some Spanish works to gain a moderately wide audience in Renaissance England. On the one hand, their Spanish quality was of interest in satisfying curiosity, but to the extent that such books could hurdle the usual cultural barriers, they were, on the other hand, capable of nestling at greater ease by English firesides. After all, the Spanish and English shared, at least to some extent, a common medieval heritage, and as Mabbe reminded his countrymen, there was "not so great a distance betwixt Hierusalem and Samaria, as some imagine."[84] Then, too, the Spanish romances sometimes seem to have a certain cosmopolitan tone simply because other nations were producing fairly similar books of their own.

---

contain elements of the pastoral romance, so *Adventures in Love* contains the shipwrecks, pirates, and separated lovers of the Byzantine romance. (Its Ismenia-Lexander story, though lifted directly from Gil Polo, goes back to the tale of Cnemon in the *Aethiopica*.) Before the turn of the century Sidney had managed to combine the same elements to form a best-seller. In about 1634 his *Arcadia* was commended by Sir William Alexander as "the most excellent Work that . . . hath been written in any Language that I understand" ("Anacrisis," in *Critical Essays of the Seventeenth Century,* ed. Joel Elias Spingarn [Oxford, 1908], I, 187). But readers of *Adventures in Love,* either in 1594 or 1652, must surely have been less than rapt. R. C.'s romance is an unfinished, badly proportioned labyrinth of labors, not only for the lovers it depicts, but also for a reader in whose path it lies.

84. *Devout Contemplations* (1629), unsigned leaf preceding A1.

A second generalization which might be made—and another one related to travel—is that the Spanish romancers show a greater interest in diversity than unity. As Wolff says of their Greek predecessors, authors of the kind "liked the parts better than the whole, and lingered to elaborate whatever pleased." Episodes therefore tend to be separable units rather than integral parts of a whole, as may be seen in the handling of Lope's ghost story, or Quintana's use of *The Prodigious History of a Sonne and His Mother.* The advantage of the technique is its ability to amaze. It might be explained, perhaps, as an early step in solving the problem of presenting the multiple events of long fiction. In an aesthetic work of any period, however, the attention is strained, unfairly strained, when elements are not presented so as to lure one onward from point to point, furnishing change and forestalling ennui, at the same time that a basic, informing unity gives each element intensified significance. Despite his rambling, Cervantes had demonstrated in *Don Quixote* the effectiveness of combining unity with variety. In more primitive forms of fiction—in Cervantes' own *Persiles*—writers seem content at times to consider only the object immediately at hand. Since the Spanish were consciously imitating a Greek form, it is no wonder they did not transcend what B. E. Perry refers to as the Greek "capacity for contemplating only one thing or one aspect of a thing or person at a time, purely for its own interest and without regard to the ulterior implications or associations. . . ."[85] Cervantes, of course, manages to send his pilgrims to Rome in a good cause; Lope de Vega concludes with a plea for the active life; and Céspedes y Meneses selects tonally similar stories which show that a man who sows thorns must meet with prickles. All these are gestures in the "right" direction. But they do not prevail over the piecemeal manner in which the romances are presented. In these stories of sentimental adventure, plot elements are generally juxtaposed in such a way that one must look very hard indeed to find that sort of unity which is achieved in some literature by a tension of opposing forces. Moreover, the romances are atomized not only by diversity, seemingly offered for the sake of diversity, but also by complexity. In such stories as these, complexity is partially a result of diversity. Unfortunately, it is also an end in itself. It was supposed to be fun to be lost in the maze.

Third and most important, the complexity of the romances is almost entirely a matter of external action. Since we come three hundred years later, know what the novel was to achieve, and have learned to bring more than

85. "The Early Greek Capacity for Viewing Things Separately," *Transactions of the American Philological Association,* LXVIII (1937), 404.

mere attention to the fiction we read, the romances' prolonged focus on externals is almost certain to convey to us an impression of vacancy. Unless we remind ourselves that the world of romance has laws of its own, we may wait a long time in hope of coming to a situation in which characters are as important as what happens to them. The fact is that one had best not wonder if Jacinta's harsh treatment of Gerardo is based on human probability; one is not meant to notice that her actions occur merely to keep the story on the go. In the romances, to put it another way, the emotion or will of a character is not often presented as an interior, felt impulse. Emotion and will are more apt to be means of fulfilling the demands of some idealized value, especially *honor* and *amor*. Hence, even when a character pauses to express his feelings, it may be that emphasis shifts away from physical action only to turn to rhetoric. If looking for some kind of human emotion, one will not turn first to the love-laments in the romances of sentimental adventure. Though today we still have romances (and it is silly, of course, to rail against them for not being something they were never intended to be), thoughtful modern readers have generally come to regard action and rhetoric in the best fiction as modes of illustrating a subject rather than as the subject itself; and to such readers, the Byzantine romances are bound to seem artificial, melodramatic, and sentimental.

This third point suggests a corollary: long before the time of Cervantes and Lope de Vega, the apparent shallowness of fiction had troubled the conscience of some readers and given rise to allegorical interpretation. From Fulgentius, who allegorized ancient myths, down through Petrarch and Tasso, writers tried to justify imaginative literature on allegorical grounds. Among Elizabethans, Fulke Greville declared that Sidney aimed in the *Arcadia* "to turn the barren Philos[o]phy precepts into pregnant Images of life. . . ." Sidney's end, said Greville, was "not vanishing pleasure alone, but morall Images, and Examples, (as directing threds) to guide every man through the confused *Labyrinth* of his own desires, and life. . . ."[86] And to convey these images and examples, Sidney himself had said, a poet substitutes a golden world for nature's brazen one.[87] With reason enough, Sir Francis Bacon grumbled that fiction was often written first, and its exposition devised later.[88]

86. *The Life of the Renowned Sr. Philip Sidney* (1652), pp. 18 and 245.
87. *The Defence of Poesie* (1595), C1ᵛ. In the same sentence in which he says this, Sidney refers to Theagenes, hero of the *Aethiopica,* as epitomizing the true lover.
88. *The Second Booke* . . . , in *The Twoo Bookes of Francis Bacon of the Proficience and Advancement of Learning* (1605), p. 19.

Perhaps in the golden world of *Persiles,* Cervantes comes closer than any of the other Spanish romancers to projecting morality in action. Though his characters are such stuff as dreams are made on, the fabric of his vision is not wholly baseless; despite all their detours, the goal of Cervantes' pilgrims is Rome. Lope, in contrast, writes unmistakable allegory in the dramas inserted in the *Peregrino,* yet is content in his main plot merely to create a world of adventure. In the abbreviated English *Pilgrime,* therefore, we have little beyond action, little but—as Jonson said of Shakespeare—"excellent fancy, brave notions, and gentle expressions, wherein he flowed with that facility that sometime it was necessary he should be stopped."[89] As for the other Spanish romancers, we may safely invoke Bacon's skepticism. Their dreamchildren are a world away from *Don Quixote,* where Cervantes had succeeded in reaching both above and below the surface of the materials he worked with.

Weak as they now seem, the Greco-Spanish romances appeared at least seven times in England between 1619 and 1653, that is, the period between the debut of *Persiles* and the second edition of *Gerardo.* Of these seven editions and issues, five appeared in the years 1619–1623, when general interest in Spain ran high. Perhaps equally significant, both of the remaining ones appeared in the 1650's, when commerce, colonization, and a far-flung war revived interest in both Spain and the New World. In the years between, the 1630's and the troubled 1640's, interest in Spain was relatively low. Under the influence of Charles's French queen, whose favorite book was D'Urfé's *Astrée,* the chief foreign interest was France. As a matter of fact, three of the four Spanish romances considered in this chapter came into English through French. The Spanish seem to have contributed more Heliodoran narratives to English literature than did anyone else, including the English themselves, but Leonard Digges was the only translator who worked directly from the Spanish. Perhaps as a consequence, his is the only work enlivened by an occasional flash of Englishry.[90]

---

89. *Timber,* ed. Felix E. Schelling (Boston, 1892), p. 23.

90. Considering the period 1600–1642 and including *Don Quixote,* Mish counts ten romances of sentimental adventure ("English Prose Fiction," p. 76). Of these, only Thomas Gainsford's *Trebizond* (1616) was, presumably, not a translation. Although *Argenis* (1621) was written by John Barclay, a Scot, it was first composed in Latin. *Eromena* and *Donzella Desterrada,* both by a resident of London, Francesco Biondi, were translated from Italian in 1632 and 1635, respectively. Toward the close of the preceding century, of course, not only Sidney, but such writers as Greene and Rich had used similar narrative elements.

Combining love and adventure with varied though lesser amounts of morality, the Spanish romances of sentimental adventure offered much for readers of their time to admire, but, gradually and naturally, men of taste moved on to approve something else. By the mid-eighteenth century, when England discovered—or perhaps rediscovered—the novel, the old romances, when read at all, must surely have struck sophisticated readers as tangled, stilted, and sentimental. Nevertheless, Persiles and Sigismunda, Pamphilus and Nisa, Gerardo and Fenise had furnished many hours of delight to readers of their time, and it has yet to be demonstrated that people of a later time have always sought gratification at a level much higher.

Chapter VI

Delight in Severall Shapes

The Novelas

In the preface to his *Incognita* (1692) William Congreve tries to distinguish between romances and what he calls "novels." Compared with romances, he says, *"Novels are of a more familiar Nature; Come near us, and represent to us Intrigues in practice, delight us with Accidents and odd Events, but not such as are wholly unusual or unpresidented, such which not being so distant from our Belief bring also the pleasure nearer us."*[1] By "novels" Congreve intends what we might call long short-stories, novelettes, or *novelas*.[2] More important than labels, however, is his significant and basic distinction between familiarity and fantasy in fiction. Although the distinction is inadequate as a means of differentiating *novelas* from romances (some

---

1. I quote from the 1713 ed., A4^v.

2. Or perhaps even "novels." Cervantes' word *novela* was translated as "novel" by both Shelton (*Don Quixote* [1620], II, 20) and Mabbe, who rendered part of Cervantes' collection under the title *Exemplarie Novells* (1640). John Minsheu (*A Dictionarie in Spanish and English* [1599], p. 176) had earlier defined *novela* merely as "newes," but the year before, John Florio (*A Worlde of Wordes*, p. 241) had already defined the Italian *novella* not only as *"a noueltie, a discourse, a newes, a message,"* but as *"a tale, a nouell. . . ."*

Since Cervantes' shorter fiction sometimes approaches the "totality" and "essential unity of impression" required by Poe in the tale and by Brander Matthews in the short-story, and since it also resembles in some ways the modern novel or novelette, it has seemed best here to retain Cervantes' own label (Poe, "Review of New Books: *Twice-Told Tales*," *Graham's Lady's and Gentleman's Magazine*, XX [1842], 298–300, and Matthews, *The Philosophy of the Short-Story* [New York, 1931]; Henry Seidel Canby wrestles a bit with terminology in his helpful *Short Story in English* [New York, 1909], pp. 161–162; and T. Atkinson Jenkins discusses sources of the word "novel" in a suggestive essay called "On Newness in the Novel," *PMLA*, XLII [1927], xliii–lix). One of the best studies of the Spanish *novela*, that by Caroline B. Bourland, reveals its author's stand in its title—*The Short Story in Spain in the Seventeenth Century* (Northampton, Mass., 1927). A work with a contrasting title is Peter N. Dunn's *Castillo Solórzano and the Decline of the Spanish Novel* (Oxford, 1952).

novelas are further from life than are some episodes in the romances), and although its application depends on subjective decisions, it is both helpful and increasingly relevant as we approach the rise of indisputable novels such as Richardson's and Fielding's. Even more important here, it might have been applied to some Spanish *novelas* at least seventy-nine years before Congreve wrote.

No one is quite sure when the Italian word *novella* was naturalized in Spain, but as late as 1590, in a prologue to his translation of Cinthio's *Hecatommithi,* Gaitán Vozmediano expressed hope that some of his countrymen might for the first time try to compose *novelas* in Spanish.[3] It seems that most Spanish critics disdained the form. Since the infinitive *novelar* was used synonymously with the word meaning "to lie," it comes as no surprise that in the 1613 preface of his *Novelas ejemplares,* seventy-nine years before Congreve, Cervantes not only claimed to be the first to *novelar* in Castilian, but did so with some reason.

Cervantes went on to explain that the short narratives previously printed in Spanish had all been translations, whereas his own were neither imitated nor stolen.[4] In considering this statement, Cervantes' disciples have sometimes minimized the possibility that the master may have been claiming difference in origin as much as in kind, but they have compensated by

3. Noted by Ludwig Pfandl, *Historia de la literatura nacional española en la edad de oro,* tr. Jorge Rubió Balaguer (Barcelona, 1952), p. 333. For brief discussions see Agustín González de Amezúa y Mayo, *Cervantes: Creador de la novela corta española* (Madrid, 1956), I, 349–355; and *Formación y elementos de la novela cortesana* (Madrid, 1929), pp. 71–83.

4. In Madrid at one time there was even an Academia Imitatoria, "founded for the purpose of imitating the writers of Italy" (noted by Samuel Putnam, *Three Exemplary Novels* [New York, 1950], p. 229), but Spaniards were nevertheless slow in taking up the *novela.* D. P. Rotunda suggests that "because it lacked moral scope direct imitation of Boccaccio's work was carefully shunned" ("The *Guzmán de Alfarache* and Italian *Novellistica,*" *RR,* XXIV [1933], 129). To balance the usual statement of Spain's debt to Italy (and even Cervantes was indebted), one might also recall Robert H. Williams' statement concerning her independence: "from 1600 to 1700 some forty novelistic works in Spanish attained a total of over four hundred editions published in other languages, while the number translated into Spanish in all that time scarcely exceeds a dozen. For most of the latter a single printing sufficed; several, indeed, never even got to press, but survive to this day in manuscript" (*Boccalini in Spain* [Menasha, Wis., 1946], pp. vii–viii). Foreign books were simply hard to come by in Spain. Readers who were interested in current literature "were obliged to depend for their supplies upon the chance of securing copies of the prohibited books smuggled in with bales of merchandise" (George Haven Putnam, *The Censorship of the Church of Rome* [New York, 1906], I, 35).

laboring to show just how his *novelas* are different from the short fiction written earlier. The present survey has touched already on some of this earlier fiction, most notably the *novelas sentimentales* of San Pedro and Flores. Long before the time of the latter two writers, however, Spain had produced an outstanding author of short narratives in Prince Juan Manuel (1282–*ca.* 1349), nephew of Alfonso the Wise, whose *Conde Lucanor* (or *Libro de Patronio*), a collection of fifty apologues, was completed even before Boccaccio's *Decameron*. Coming after San Pedro and Flores there had been (to name only those translated into English) writers like Antonio de Guevara, Melchor de Santa Cruz, Pedro Mexía, and Antonio de Torquemada, all of whom, with their anecdotal proto-fiction, helped further to prepare the way for Cervantes—though their own little-of-everything was nothing-in-the-main.[5] Moreover, despite the fact that the fully developed Spanish *novela* might be said to begin with Cervantes' *Novelas ejemplares,* other earlier stories which the English translated were to be found intercalated not only in the *Diana* and the *Quixote* itself, but in Gracián Dantisco's *Galateo español* (1582?) and Alemán's *Guzmán* (I, 1599; II, 1604). It is possible to conclude that all these works merely vindicate Cervantes' claim to innovation. Nevertheless, it seems only right, before turning to the *Novelas ejemplares* and the fiction of Pérez de Montalván —the other *novela* writer in our range—to refer more specifically to at least a part of the evidence.

Abyndaraez and Xarifa

The oldest story to be noted, and the first to be translated, was the *novela morisca* already mentioned as appearing in the Montemayor-Yong *Diana*. Called *Abyndaraez and Xarifa* and dating from the mid-

5. To sidestep the harrowing task of extirpating bits of narrative, as I have said, I have omitted all books which are not themselves predominantly fictional (see *Appendix D*). The only exception is the Italian *Galateo,* into which a Spaniard inserted a *novela* (see below).

The historian of short narratives in Spanish must of course consider still other works, e.g., Juan de Timoneda's *Patrañuelo* (1566?) and Antonio de Eslava's *Noches de invierno* (1609)—the latter containing a story analogous to that in Shakespeare's *Tempest*. Both of these are books of genuine fiction, though both, in accord with Cervantes' claim, are also indebted to Italian art. (See Marcelino Menéndez Pelayo, *Orígenes de la novela,* III, ed. Enrique Sánchez Reyes, in *Edición nacional de las obras completas* [Santander, 1943], XV, 3–217; and Edwin B. Place, *Manual elemental de novelística española* [Madrid, 1926].)

sixteenth century, this narrative is both historically and technically notable for displaying some of the qualities that have been praised in later Spanish fiction.[6] Its unknown author was able to create noble yet moderately credible characters, and to handle a simple plot with skill, both restricting and developing his materials. Though his finished work is naturally much more an imitation than a reproduction of nature, he nevertheless may be said to have stayed in touch with "real life."

Axa and the Prince

*A*xa *and the Prince,* another early story, deserves more detailed comment because we have not discussed it earlier and because it has been overlooked so long by students of English fiction.[7] It apparently did not appear in England until 1640, when William Style brought forth a courtesy book called *Galateo Espagnol.* Style's source was the Spanish *Galateo* by Lucas Gracián Dantisco, but this, in turn, was derived from the well-known Italian *Galateo* (1558) by the diplomat, poet, and cleric, Giovanni della Casa. Attitudes on translation being what they were, Gracián Dantisco had inserted in Della Casa's book a full-length (and, some would add, Italianate) *novela,* intending it to illustrate some remarks by Della Casa on how a story should be told.[8] Afterwards, when Style came along, he naturally translated both the remarks and their *exemplum.*

Relevant as they are, one might turn with special curiosity to the *Galateo*'s comments on storytelling, but unfortunately they plumb no depths. A reader is told, among other things, that a good story will have in it no "uncivill words, or obscene passages. . . , especially if Women bee in the company," and its plot will be "layd so neatly, and artificially, that

6. That it nevertheless may be indebted to an Italian source is suggested by J. P. Wickersham Crawford, "Un episodio de 'El Abencerraje' y una 'novella' de Ser Giovanni," *RFE,* X (1923), 281–287. The *Diana* itself, as noted earlier, is indebted to the Italian *novelle,* e.g., the Felix-Felismena story, imitated from Bandello.

7. For a fuller commentary see my *"Axa and the Prince:* A Rediscovered *Novela* and Its English Translator," *JEGP,* LX (1961), 48–55.

8. Although the story was being acted on the Spanish boards in Gracián Dantisco's time, he gives no hint of its source. That this source might be Italian is the view of Menéndez Pelayo, *Orígenes,* III, 215. D. P. Rotunda reports that Giambattista Basile's *Pentamerone* contains the same plot, but Basile was only about seven when Gracián Dantisco wrote ("Gracián Dantisco's Rules for Story-Telling," *RR,* XXI [1930], 235–236).

the Auditors, may bee fed with pleasure of it. . . ."[9] Furthermore, "Tales and stories should bee such, that besides the entertaynement, and pleasure of them, there may bee also drawn from them, good examples, and moralls. . . ."[10] Rambling and obscurity are to be eschewed, and simplicity commended. The author asks, "what shall wee say of the coyned phrases, of some Ideots, that labour to speake in metaphors, and high and excellent straynes, as they conceive"?[11] Nothing, quite clearly, very favorable. A good story, according to the literary dicta of the *Galateo,* will be refined, artistic, moral, lucid, and simple.

To bait Della Casa's edifying hook, Gracián Dantisco inserted "The tale of the great Soldan, and of the loves of the beautifull Axa and the Prince of Naples." The story relates how a Persian soldan of great valor has lost his sight and can be cured by none of the physicians in his kingdom. When a Christian doctor assays the case and fails, he is naturally thrown into a dungeon. Furthermore, he is given tidings that in eight days he will become food for some lions. Thus encouraged to stall for time, the doctor manages to think of a prescription which will turn the difficult trick, but among its hard-to-come-by ingredients are the blood and heart of an exemplary young man, one who is noble, valiant, fair, wise, esteemed, and clear of complexion. Soon such a paragon—none other than the Prince of Naples—is captured and brought back to the reluctant doctor. Again the latter stalls, this time maintaining that the young man is too troubled, "his humours . . . not setled."[12] Obviously a potion made from his blood and heart while he is in such a state would be a waste of time and skill. The soldan's daughter Axa is thereupon brought forth as a sort of seductive sedative, and, as the reader may anticipate, the beautiful princess soon finds herself hopelessly in love with the handsome prince. When the prince reciprocates, Axa robs her father of great riches (including a magic sword and ring), and together with the physician the lovers steal away through a secret passage which brings them to a bark on a river that flows to the sea.

Meanwhile the soldana, an enchantress on the side, sets out in pursuit of the three, and, when she is finally foiled by their escape, seeks revenge by

9. *Galateo,* p. 125. Note that the advice pertains to oral narration. Like an elegant parlor game, the skilful telling of *novelas* seems to have been an adornment not only for the man of birth, but, later on, for *le bourgeois gentilhomme* who aspired both to become a gentleman and (perhaps more important) to act like one.

10. *Galateo,* p. 126.

11. *Galateo,* p. 153.

12. *Galateo,* p. 131.

magically arranging that the first woman the prince embraces will make him forget Axa. The prince returns home and greets his mother with an embrace, and the charm goes into effect.

The details of the plot gradually multiply, but at last the magic ring becomes the means of restoring the prince's memory. At the inevitable recognition scene the prince falls to his knees before Axa, the king and queen receive her as their daughter (she has been christened, so readers need not be offended), and at last she and the prince inherit the Neapolitan throne, beginning a "long reigne, with happy peace, and prosperity."[13]

A world away from Congreve's definition, *Axa and the Prince* is a romantic, featherweight concoction that mingles the perennially attractive elements of suspense, exoticism, violence, travel, and love. To these is added the ingredient of magic, which is quite as important here as in a tale by the Grimm brothers and may perhaps be said to constitute the major difference between this story and the more realistic Spanish *novelas* which developed in the early years of the seventeenth century. This is not to say that magic is a weakness in *Axa,* for it is not a device which the author resorts to when cornered. On the contrary, it is frankly an important part of the proceedings. The wide-eyed, childlike nature of the entire work, in fact, inclines one to indicate rather than criticize what looks suspiciously like inadequate motivation (Axa's decision to rob her father comes as something of a shock) and even unpremeditated structure (the doctor, having played his role, seems forgotten rather than disposed of). After all, one does not go hunting butterflies with a shotgun.

In presenting his English version of the *Galateo* to the ten-year-old Prince of Wales, William Style apologized that the little duodecimo *"was first penned by a Courtyer. Therefore if it bee not well translated, no marvaile, for how should a plodding Lawyer, make a neate construction, of a quaint and polite Gallants meaning?"*[14] Plodding or not, Style was a legal writer of some note, a cultivated gentleman who elsewhere spoke indignantly of those blockheads who hold "it vain, if not impious to speak or understand more than their own mother-tongue."[15] He himself, knowing Spanish reasonably well, proved a competent translator. In *Galateo Espagnol* he demonstrates a commendable willingness to subordinate himself to his source, retaining as many of its ideas as possible and adding few; and his

---

13. *Galateo,* p. 152.
14. *Galateo,* A4ʳ.
15. *Narrationes Modernae* (1658), A1ᵛ.

final product, if not a work of art, is certainly a fair approximation of its Spanish original.

Novelas in *The Rogue*

Also among the older *novelas* to be Englished were those in Mateo Alemán's *Guzmán de Alfarache,* robustiously translated by James Mabbe as *The Rogue* (1622).[16] The most ambitious recent study of Cervantes' *Novelas* is naturally much concerned with Cervantes' contributions to the genre, and yet its author, Amezúa y Mayo, admits that these earlier stories by Alemán are also true *novelas.* At one point, though insisting on the aesthetic gap between them and Cervantes' short fiction, he even affirms that Alemán and Cervantes *together* opened the road of the *novela* in Spain.[17]

Since *The Rogue* is primarily picaresque, it is interesting to find that among the handful of narratives inserted in the course of its hero's adventures, at least two are distinguishable not only structurally, but by strains of gentility and even idealism.[18] In order to show that such stories may be lifted out for inspection, it might be indicated that at least three were later published separately, and another, though more firmly attached, was borrowed from Masuccio's *Il novellino.* At this point one again recalls Cervantes' claim to be the earliest Spaniard to write *novelas* which are neither imitated nor stolen.

Alemán's *Ozmin and Daraxa,* inserted in Part I, Book 1, is our second oldest *novela morisca.* It concerns a beautiful Moorish girl, Daraxa, who is taken to Seville by Queen Isabella and placed in the custody of a Spanish gentleman, Don Luys de Padilla. In order to be near Daraxa, her Moorish lover, Ozmin, gains employment as a gardener to Don Luys, and finally, after some jousting and killing, manages to win her. The queen asks both to

---

16. The work as a whole is discussed in the next chapter.

17. *Cervantes,* I, 427, 436.

18. It may be helpful to note that three *novelas,* ten fables, and sixty-five *cuentos* are listed in Malcolm Jerome Gray's *Index to Guzmán de Alfarache* (New Brunswick, N. J., 1948). Rotunda observes that "Alemán does more than interpolate Italian *novelle* of entertainment in his work. At times he adapts them to Spanish tradition and makes them serve an exemplary or illustrative end; at others he molds his own episodes from the background and motifs of his models. In this, indeed, he becomes a precursor of the master, Cervantes" ("The *Guzmán de Alfarache* . . . ," p. 133).

become Christians, and they assume the names of Isabell and Ferdinand.[19]

Concluding Part I of *The Rogue* is another *novela,* a violent little story reminiscent of Bandello and set in Rome. Two attractive lovers, Dorido and Clorinia, are in the habit of conversing through a hole in a wall near Clorinia's home. When this latter-day Thisbe first put her hand through the hole, her lover "tooke it, and kist it againe and againe, blessing and stroking his face therwith, neuer suffering it to depart from his mouth."[20] But a spurned admirer of the heroine goes to the hole, pretends to be Dorido, and, when Clorinia gives him her hand, chops it off.

The next story, from Book 1 of Part II, is the one borrowed from Masuccio. It relates how the constable of Castile offers a diamond ring to Don Luys de Castro or Don Rodrigo de Montalvo, depending on which can tell the better love story. Finally, however, he gives the ring to neither but to a young gentlewoman who has riskily spent a night in bed with Don Rodrigo (who did not know it) in order that Don Rodrigo might be gulled, and Don Luys and his mistress disport.

A fourth *novela* brings Book 2 of Part II to a close. This one is set in Seville and concerns a rich and virtuous young lady, Dorotea, who is wooed and wed by a personable goldsmith, Bonifacio. Unfortunately a dastard named Claudio manages to lure the lady to his own bed, in fact to have his way with her for a while. But one night his house catches fire and the two are discovered naked. Dorotea returns to her husband, and the villain—like the hero in *Gerardo*—retires "to the top of a mountaine in a desert place, where in a holy course of life hee ended his dayes, betaking him-selfe to the Religious Order of Saint *Francis.*"[21]

In sum, the first of these stories in *The Rogue* is a Moorish *novela,* the

---

19. This tender tale (whose heroine may be found "distilling ropes of Pearles in round orientall drops downe her louely cheekes" [*Rogue* (1622), I, 72]) contrasts most strikingly to its setting. When it begins, Guzman has just said "my Companion was so bang'd about the chappes, that he durst not dare to speake, for feare he should spit out his grinders" (I, 64). Then, after nearly forty pages of pleasantly mingled sentiment, chivalry, realism, and rhetoric, the author yanks the reader back to a picaresque plane—and Mabbe does this very well—by telling of a sudden argument. "What a Diuell . . . meane you by this?" cries a carrier to Guzman. "Marry gupp with a murraine, you are a fine Gentleman indeed; doe you thinke to ride a cock-horse on free cost?" (I, 101). Mabbe's version of the story has been edited and reprinted in J. B. Trend's *Spanish Short Stories of the Sixteenth Century* (London, 1928).

20. *Rogue,* I, 258.

21. *Rogue* (1623), II, 208.

second and fourth are Italianate, and the third is borrowed directly from
Masuccio. More of *The Rogue* later, however.

Novelas in Don Quixote

Known in his time as the Spanish Boccaccio, Cervantes, too, was indebted to Italy. According to Amezúa y Mayo, Cervantes' *novelas*
share with some of the Italian *novelle* a quickened awareness of the value of
unity of plot; a consequent suppression of semi-relevant commentaries and
erudition such as had disfigured much early fiction and semi-fiction; a com-
pensating fondness for rather full development (a fondness discernible
in sixteenth-century Italian stories, but carried further by Cervantes); an increasing alertness to the possibilities of dialogue; and a relative disinterest
in nature and setting, which were to become important in later times. All of
these bonds with Italian writers, says the Spanish scholar, are insufficient to
negate Cervantes' claim to be the first to *novelar* in Castilian, because what
matters most in Cervantes' *novelas* is his own: their spirit, their genial vision
of life, their lack of concern for supernatural marvels, their elevated aims, and
their revelation of the hearts and minds of characters.[22] What Cervantes did to
the Italian *novella* was to make it both human and Spanish, borrowing but
also transforming.

The first of his *novelas* to appear in English were those in Part I of *Don
Quixote*. Betrayed either by the printer or Thomas Shelton's own carelessness,
the English public was warned that Cervantes (or at least one of his per-
sonae) had affirmed these "tales, and digressions" to be "in some respects lesse
pleasing, artificiall and true, then the very Historie it selfe."[23] But Cervantes
had protested that they were no *less* pleasing. Possibly he included them on
the grounds that inserted narratives were a customary mode of expanding
long fiction, but he may also have wished to equip his unorthodox book with
a few things that would be relatively familiar and hence acceptable.[24] After

22. *Cervantes*, I, 460–465. Most of these views seem basically sound, though one
may find widely varied opinions concerning any and all of Cervantes' *novelas*. (E.g.,
Bourland writes: "Cervantes excelled . . . in describing the scenes in which his
stories take place" [p. 8].) Another major study is Joaquín Casalduero's *Sentido y
forma de las Novelas ejemplares* (Buenos Aires, 1943).

23. *Don Quixote*, I, 278.

24. The latter idea is attacked by J. D. M. Ford, "Plot, Tale, and Episode in *Don
Quixote*," *Mélanges de linguistique et de littérature offerts a M. Alfred Jeanroy*
(Paris, 1928), pp. 311–323. See also Edward C. Riley, "Episodio, novela y aven-
tura en 'Don Quijote,'" *Anales Cervantinos*, V (1955–1956), 209–230.

the success of Part I, at any rate, he showed a greater willingness to let his main actors take the center of the stage.

The chief intercalations in *Don Quixote* are *The Curious Impertinent* (Shelton's time-honored mistranslation of *El curioso impertinente*); *The Captive's Story;* the story of Marcela and Chrysostome ("Grisóstomo," of course); the story of Cardenio, Dorotea, Luscinda, and Fernando; and the story of Quiteria and Camacho. Of these, only the first two are readily detachable, for the knight and his squire come into the others as observers.

Taken chronologically as they appear in the text, the first, that of Marcela and Chrysostome, is a melancholy, Montemayoran affair, replete with sheep and languishing verse, yet startlingly intensified by the death of the pining swain. (One might hesitate to regard this tale as detachable had it not been published separately in 1609.) The second, that of Cardenio *et alia,* sprawls through half a dozen scattered chapters.[25] Although it is not particularly exemplary, its adventures resemble those in *Las dos doncellas,* one of the more Italianate *novelas* in Cervantes' later and professedly monitory *Novelas ejemplares.* Fortunately, since the characters in both stories are little more than cardboard cutouts, one can at least be grateful that the beautiful Dorotea, one of the inamoratas in the *Don Quixote* version, expands for a while into the rather credible girl who aids the barber and curate by playing the role of the Princess Micomicona, to the end that Don Quixote may have a bona fide damsel to succor. The third story, the elegant but somewhat tedious tale of *The Curious Impertinent,* requires three chapters. First brought into England in dramatic form, this is an Ariostan narrative of a Florentine gentleman who perversely insists on tempting his nearly flawless wife with the charms of his best friend, an upright man, until wife and friend capitulate and all are brought to sorrow.[26] The fourth narrative, usually called *The*

25. Shakespeare scholars have been tantalized by the name because a now-lost play called *Cardenio* was performed by the King's Men in 1613. In 1653, when Humphrey Moseley had it recorded in the Stationers' Register, he attributed it—perhaps erroneously—to "Mr Fletcher and Shakespeare." (See Kenneth Muir, *Shakespeare as Collaborator* [New York, 1960], pp. 148–160.)

26. Abraham S. W. Rosenbach, "The Curious-Impertinent in English Dramatic Literature before Shelton's Translation of Don Quixote," *MLN,* XVII (1902), 358, notes that the story's introduction to the English stage was in *The Second Maiden's Tragedy,* licensed October 31, 1611. Aphra Behn's much later play called *The Amorous Prince* (1671) has been cited for showing "how much that was objectionable could be infused into the story" (James Fitzmaurice-Kelly, "Cervantes in England," *Proceedings of the British Academy,* II [1905–1906], 25).

It has been thought that the story is symbolic, a microcosm following the same

Captive's Story, derives from Cervantes' own experiences as a slave in Africa, and resembles his later *Amante liberal,* another of the *Novelas ejemplares.* And a fifth is the story of Quiteria and Camacho, in which a lover's trick to catch a wife is interwoven with Sancho's delight at the stewpots and wine bags of a wedding feast.

These and other stories in *Quixote* have the effect of incidental *divertissements,* however; the stories in the *Novelas ejemplares* are works in their own right.

Exemplarie Novells

In the year of Style's *Galateo,* 1640, which was twenty years after Shelton's completed *Quixote* and only one after Lawrence's metrical *Arnalte,* the venerable Mabbe brought forth Cervantes' *Exemplarie Novells.*[27] Because Mabbe chose to emphasize the lighter, more romantic aspects of Cervantes' collection and hence translated only half of the original twelve stories, some critics have lamented, saying that Englishmen were thus deprived of the more thoroughly Spanish *Rinconete y Cortadillo* and *El coloquio de los perros.* Pity 'tis, 'tis true. One can only reply that, without Mabbe's partial translation, some seventeenth-century readers might have remained altogether ignorant of Cervantes' narrative skill.

At the beginning of the present century Martin Hume offered the opinion that Cervantes' stories were "for the first time . . . worthily translated into English by Mr. Maccoll. . . ."[28] Yet Mabbe has usually been praised for his general accuracy, his flowing style, and his conveyance of Cervantes' spirit. Starkie thought him the greatest prose stylist of his time. Fitzmaurice-Kelly called him the best translator, excepting Edward Fitzgerald, that we have in

---

laws as the cosmos of *Don Quixote* (Marcel Bataillon, "Matrimonios cervantinos," *Realidad,* II [1947], 172; and Bruce W. Wardropper, "The Pertinence of *El curioso impertinente,*" *PMLA,* LXXII [1957], 587–600). Karl Solger (1780–1819) even suggested that not only this *novela,* but also the others in *Don Quixote* are related allegorically to the work as a whole. Be this as it may, in Pt. II Don Quixote is told that one of the criticisms of Pt. I has been that the "Author put in it a certaine Nouell [N. B.] or Tale, intitled the *Curious Impertinent,*" and "that it was vnseasonable for that place, neither had it any thing to doe with the History of *Don Quixote*" (II, 20).

27. Reprinted in full by S. W. Orson, 2 vols. (Philadelphia, 1900). See also *The Spanish Ladie and Two Other Stories from Cervantes* [*The Jealous Husband* and *The Liberall Lover*] (London, 1928).

28. *Spanish Influence on English Literature* (London, 1905), p. 146. Hume refers to N. MacColl's two-volume version published in Glasgow, 1902.

the language. And William Godwin waxed most lyric of all: "Perhaps the most perfect specimen of prose translation in our language," he wrote, "is to be found in the Six Exemplary Novells of Cervantes, turned into English by James Mabbe. . . ."[29] The truth is that Mabbe's translations are very good. If they lack some of the verve of his writing elsewhere, they are nonetheless readable and, for the most part, reasonably accurate. But true also is P. E. Russell's observation that, "admirable as they are, [they] have little more than an antiquarian interest."[30]

Before moving on to the stories themselves, we owe Mabbe himself a word. Born in 1572, son of John Mabbe, a London goldsmith, the future translator entered Magdalen, Oxford, in February, 1588, when interest in Spain was high. In 1594 he received his B. A. and was elected to a fellowship, and four years later he was awarded his M. A.[31] Perhaps a more important date than these, however, was August, 1605. Still at Oxford, already thirty-three, and having done none of the work for which he is remembered, Mabbe was at this time requested to give the official welcome to King James and Prince Henry upon the latter's matriculation. Perhaps it was then that Mabbe met Sir John Digby, a fellow Magdalen alumnus who had come up to Oxford with Henry and, as we have seen, was to prove important in Anglo-Spanish affairs. In 1610, at any rate, when appointed ambassador to Spain, Digby sent not only for Magdalen's chaplain, John Sanford, whom he asked to go along as embassy chaplain (Sanford was inspired to turn out the Spanish grammar noted earlier), but for Mabbe, whom he also took along, possibly as secretary but more probably as tutor for his stepson, Lewis Dyves, a boy of twelve with whom Mabbe formed a lifelong friendship.[32] Whatever his position, Mabbe sailed for Spain with the ambassadorial party in the

29. Walter Starkie, prologue, *The Jealous Husband* (Valencia, 1945), p. 14; James Fitzmaurice-Kelly, "Un hispanófilo inglés [Digges] del siglo XVII," *Homenaje á Menéndez y Pelayo* (Madrid, 1899), I, 49; and Godwin, *Lives of Edward and John Phil[l]ips* (London, 1815), p. 246.

30. "A Stuart Hispanist: James Mabbe," *BHS, XXX* (1953), 84. Russell's comment, however, refers to *all* Mabbe's translations. For a glimpse of Mabbe's own views on translation see above, Ch. III, pp. 32–33.

31. About 1603 he began a six-year investigation of the civil law, which resulted in his request "to be admitted to the Degree of Bach. of that faculty; but whether he was really admitted," Anthony à Wood tells us, "it appears not" (*Athenae Oxonienses* [London, 1721], II, 28). For additional biographical data see not only Russell, but Fitzmaurice-Kelly, introd., *Celestina* (London, 1894), and introd., Vol. I of *The Rogue* (London, 1924); and also Arthur W. Secord, "I. M. of the First Folio Shakespeare and Other Mabbe Problems," *JEGP, XLVII* (1948), 374–381.

32. See Russell, p. 77.

spring of 1611. Wood reports that the translator took advantage of his situation by improving himself "in various sorts of Learning, and in the Customs and Manners of that and other Countries." Doubtless he did. Together with Digby he remained in Spain for several years, and in 1613 was appointed to— perhaps rewarded with—a lay prebend at "the Cath. Ch. of *Wells. . . .*"[33] Though it was in this very year that Cervantes' *Novelas* appeared, history gives no hint as to whether Mabbe, before coming home, tried to meet the man he later called one of the prime wits of Spain. After another trip abroad in 1620, he brought out his version of Alemán's *Guzmán.* And in 1623 he again requested Oxford's leave and favor to return abroad, perhaps because Digby was negotiating in Madrid for Prince Charles's marriage to the elusive "golden Ladye."

After this date our knowledge of Mabbe is limited largely to a knowledge of his works. Now over fifty, a learned man who had been "conversant with the Muses" for many years, he had already proved himself well equipped to be an interpreter of Spanish books. In 1629 he gave still further evidence of his Spanish interest by making a translation of Fonseca's *Discursos,* which he dedicated to his patrons and friends, Dyves and Sir John Strangwayes, and their wives. A massive, 648-page folio, this was clearly the product of no passing fancy for Spanish. Next he published a translation of Rojas' vastly different *Celestina* (1631), which he followed in 1632 with another religious book, his *Christian Policie,* based on the *República y policía cristiana* by Fr. Juan de Santa María. Then at last, in 1638, the year in which he retired to the home of the kindly John Strangwayes in Dorset, his *Exemplarie Novells* was registered with the Stationers' Company. Appropriately, he dedicated the little anthology to Susanna, daughter-in-law of Sir John. What happened to Mabbe after this is unknown. He stepped off the stage so quietly, perhaps about 1642, that one cannot say whether or not he lived to see the Strangwayes mansion garrisoned for the king.

Our main concern, however, is his translation from Cervantes. After dedicating six *novelas* to Susanna and assuring her that a lady who has wrought with her needle deserves recreation, and after playfully signing himself "Don Diego Puede-Ser,"[34] Mabbe begins his book with *A Storie of Two Damsells*

33. Wood, II, 28. Mabbe was prebendary of Wanstrow, near Frome.
34. Mabbe had beguiled readers with this pun (Mabbe > Puede-Ser) for many years. Students have assumed, therefore, that he pronounced his name "May-be," yet the possibility that his name was pronounced as a monosyllable is suggested by his signature, "Mab" or "Mabb."

(from *Las dos doncellas*). It seems that Theodosia and Leocadia, the titular damsels, have both been wronged by the same scambling, outfacing, fashion-monging rogue, Marco Antonio, and the *novela* consists of telling how the girls track him down. Having pursued him to Barcelona, they finally find him just as he is being hit by a rock in a waterfront brawl. Somewhat chastened, he gives himself to Theodosia, and the left-over Leocadia, for whom things momentarily look bleak, is allowed to match with Theodosia's conveniently willing brother. In due time Marco Antonio recovers, both couples decide to go on a pilgrimage to Santiago, and both arrive home in time to settle a feud which has arisen among their fathers.

Within the fifty-four pages of this "book" (the word is Mabbe's), which Fitzmaurice-Kelly regards "the poorest of the series,"[35] we follow the lovers on a triangular tour that crosses Spain from south to northeast to northwest and back to south, all without gaining a notion of anything particularly Spanish. We do encounter occasional bits of "real life," as when dawn comes to an inn and we read that daylight "entred in by many chinkes and crevices, which commonly all your lodgings in Innes are seldome without."[36] But we are really in a fantasy land. Not that there is any of the supernatural or totally impossible. It is simply that a gilded style and approach, coupled with improbable action, create an artificial impression. Although the main story-line is simple and there are few superfluous characters or events, the general effect is so frivolous that we may wonder about the relevance of criticizing the work for not being more life-like. After all, if the muleteer it depicts is no Sancho Panza, Cervantes and Mabbe doubtless saw this as clearly as we. The really unfortunate fact is that despite the potential attraction of disguises, flights, fights, love, jealousy, and mystery, this particular mixture of the old ingredients makes little impression on one's pulse, quite possibly because Cervantes never really felt it, either.

The second of the "books" in Mabbe's collection is *The Ladie Cornelia* (from *La señora Cornelia*). In this story Cervantes plays up the part of Don Juan de Gamboa and Don Antonio de Ysunca, two Spanish youths, embodiments of gentlemanly virtue who are ostensibly studying at the university of "Bolonia." His chief subject, however, is the clandestine love of Cornelia and the Duke of Ferrara. It seems that family pressure has kept the duke from courting Cornelia openly, and yet his intentions are so honorable that readers are not supposed to be distressed when his ardor results in making

---

35. *The Life of Miguel de Cervantes Saavedra* (London, 1892), p. 236.
36. *Exemplarie Novells* (1640), p. 14.

him a bachelor father. Opportunely for the combustion of cloak-and-dagger
episodes, Cornelia's *honor*-minded brother, Lorenzo, does not learn of his
sister's liaison until the story is under way. Then one night the whole situation flashes into action: Cornelia's baby is mysteriously passed out a door
into the hands of Don Juan; shortly afterward, his sympathies are aroused
and his sword unsheathed by a street fight between Lorenzo's men and the
duke; and the swooning Cornelia, wandering distractedly through the streets,
requests shelter from Don Antonio. To complicate matters still further,
Cornelia next flees into the country. It is only after fairly prolonged difficulties that the Spanish students, Cornelia, the duke, and Lorenzo are all
united under the same happy roof. And fortuitously—many happenings in
the *novelas* do seem fortuitous—it is a curate's roof.

The Ladie Cornelia, for all its woe, is a pleasant story. Some of its situations
are intriguing, and its general atmosphere has a Cervantean warmth and
wholesomeness. Offsetting this good, however, is its pervasive melodramatic
quality. For instance, there is little need to marry the duke's servant, Fabio,
to Cornelia's maid, Sulpicia. Nor does it seem necessary for the duke to
arouse the ire of his helpful friends by feigning the desire to marry a peasant
wench when in fact he has already discovered the lost Cornelia. Then
again, a Caroline reader would have been quicker than we to agree with
the Spanish lads, who think the duke has "put upon them the most discreet,
and most savourie conceit in the World."[37]

Rather similar to the Heliodoran romances, but fortunately shorter (it is
only seventy pages), is the third of the *novelas* Mabbe rendered. *The Liberall
Lover* (from *El amante liberal*) derives in part from Cervantes' reading,
but also from his own military, maritime, and Algerian experiences.[38] Hence
it is the more surprising that the story is so lacking in personal touches. As it
begins, the lover Ricardo is a slave on the island of Cyprus, lamenting to a
fellow slave named Mahamut. Properly importuned, Ricardo speaks of his
love for Leonisa, the fairest damsel in Sicily, and of his princox, sugar-paste
rival, Cornelio. He tells how a band of Turks suddenly descended one day,
kidnapping Leonisa and himself, and how the two of them have since been
separated. Now, as the story progresses, both he and his sweetheart fall into
the hands of a master known as the "Cadi" ("a minister of *Mahomet*"[39]),

37. *Exemplarie Novells,* p. 106.
38. That Cervantes particularly liked the story is indicated by his further use of
it in *Los tratos de Argel* and *Los baños de Argel.*
39. *Exemplarie Novells,* p. 167.

who harbors a lust for Leonisa. To make things symmetrical, his wife Halima soon burns to be bedded by Ricardo. Since the heroine is supposed to be delivered as a present to the "Grand-Signior," these two unlikely couples, together with Ricardo's friend Mahamut, set sail for Constantinople. The Cadi is all the while plotting to throw his wife overboard. But she is no fool; she plans to do likewise with him. Both plots are squelched when Ricardo, aided by some Greek Christians, takes command of the ship and sails for Sicily. Once arrived at the harbor of their home city, he and Leonisa, *au grand sérieux,* declaim for the benefit of each other and their public, including Ricardo's old rival, to whom Ricardo, for no good reason, offers not only some thirty thousand crowns of loot, but also (at least momentarily) the fair Leonisa. Everything works out all right, however, for Leonisa decides that she prefers the "liberall" Ricardo. Luckily, too, a clergyman is handy once again, for he "instantly married them."[40] To make another pair happy in the usual fashion, both Ricardo's friend *"Mahamut, and Halima* were reconciled to the Church, who impossibilited of fulfilling her desire in being *Ricardo's* wife, contented her selfe in matching with *Mahamut."*[41] Only the fastidious will complain that Halima still has the Cadi for a husband or that Mahamut and Halima have not previously shown the slightest interest in each other. As Puck says, Cupid is a knavish lad.

Even so short a summary may indicate some of the widescreen allure that such a plot must have had. In addition to sailing adventures, *amor,* and intrigue, moreover, there is also the appeal of words. Mabbe, according to his custom, indulges in some alterations and additions, but by and large his rhetorical colors derive from Cervantes. When Mahamut asks Ricardo to tell his story, he says in part,

I earnestly entreate and beseech you, and conjure thee, by that which thou owest to those good offices I have done thee; the good will I beare thee, the love I have showne thee, and by that which ought to obliege thee thereunto; in that wee are both of one and the same Country, and bred up in our Child-hood together; that thou wilt deale freely with me, and lay open unto me what is the cause which makes thee so exceeding sad and melancholy?[42]

All this requires nearly twice as many words as Cervantes had found necessary. In the language of either writer, however, it seems a strange and stiff way for one friend to ask another what ails him.

40. *Exemplarie Novells,* pp. 176–177.
41. *Exemplarie Novells,* p. 177.
42. *Exemplarie Novells,* p. 111.

The first of Mabbe's selections which seems very Spanish is the next, *The Force of Blood* (from *La fuerza de la sangre*). Though some have called it Italianate, Cervantes' own words have led others to think it is based on an actual incident. In either case, it conveys a more individualistic impression of life and approaches closer to that delicate balance between reality and romance which is characteristic of much good fiction, old and new.

The story tells what happens to a respectable family when its quiet course is suddenly diverted by the rape of its blameless daughter. Leocadia is returning home one night from a pleasure trip with her family when she is kidnapped by some licentious young blades and hustled off to the home of one of them. Because she is blindfolded and swooning she does not know where she has been carried and cannot defend herself; but before Rodolfo, the young man, has led her, blindfolded again, to a place in the city whence she can find her way home, she has memorized the details of his chamber and stolen a silver crucifix. Time passes, Rodolfo goes to Italy, and Leocadia, in secret, brings forth his son. Seven quiet years slip by, and then one day, while taking a message for his grandmother, the little boy is trampled by a horse. Because he is injured badly, the child is hurried to the home of a kindly old bystander who has been drawn forward by the mysterious "force of blood."[43] This bystander, it turns out, is none other than the boy's own paternal grandfather. Hence the two families of the story become acquainted, Rodolfo's parents learn of their son's transgression, and the silver crucifix becomes ocular proof. The young man is summoned home, falls in love with Leocadia (whom he does not recognize), and after some impertinent delays is wedded to her. Since Rodolfo is rather worse than a spoiled brat, possibly it is more realistic than exemplary that he is given the privilege of marrying a beautiful and virtuous woman with whom he has fallen in love. At any rate, bad is offset, not defeated, by good.[44]

43. The meaning behind the title of the story is partially clarified in *Don Fenise* (1651): A certain Fernand did not know who his mother was, but when confronting her, "he felt something in his soule which provoked him to take pittie of this poor Lady, the force of the blood whereof their hearts were formed, gave him the feeling" (p. 267). Clifton Cherpack traces the literary use of this strange power back to the *Aethiopica* (*The Call of Blood in French Classical Tragedy* [Baltimore, 1958], p. 7).

44. Perhaps it should be added that "There was little or no public opinion against the sowing of wild oats in any form and if the testimony of the [seventeenth-century] novela is to be trusted, the young gentleman of the period, however distinguished his family or his personal attainments, did not feel himself dishonored by casual episodes of the basest character" (Bourland, p. 31).

This story moves faster and seems far more compact—save for its rather protracted ending—than most fiction of the time. The descent of Rodolfo and his roaring boys into the well-ordered world of Leocadia's family, a down-at-heels family with a noble name, is sudden and, because of its intensity, shocking. In fact each of the two main parts of the story begins in unexpected violence (the second climax is the trampling of the child), then, wave-like, subsides into quiet, in each case in Rodolfo's bedroom. Because of its meaningful contrasts and successful evocation of setting, and because its violence is somehow made credible, *The Force of Blood* is a story worth returning to.

Perhaps of greater historical interest, though otherwise less appealing, is Mabbe's fifth story, *The Spanish Ladie* (from *La española inglesa*). As in his much longer *Persiles,* Cervantes here writes of England, and, in contrast to those of his countrymen who portray Elizabeth as a libidinous beast, he depicts the great queen, for the most part, as indulgent, tolerant of Catholics, and even acquainted with Spanish.[45] As we shall see, however, Mabbe obscures Cervantes' generosity.

The Spanish Ladie is mainly concerned with a Spanish girl, Isabella, who is kidnapped and taken to live in "the famous [but unnamed] Northern Island."[46] There she is not only raised by "Christian" foster-parents, but wooed by the "Christian" hero, her foster-brother. When told of the couple's desire to wed, the queen sends the young man, Ricaredo, on a mission to prove himself. He returns in triumph, incidentally rescuing Isabella's real parents from their Turkish captivity, and of course is welcomed warmly at the "Northern" court. All seems about to end happily when the "chiefe Bedchamber Ladie to the Queene" begins to stir up trouble for the lovers on behalf of her son, Arnesto, who desires Isabella for himself. Ricaredo remains true to his sweetheart, however, even after a dose of poison from the bedchamber lady has destroyed Isabella's beauty (temporarily, it turns out). His less charitable parents deport Isabella's whole family to Spain and arrange for his marriage with someone else, "a Northern Damosell, who was

45. The chronology of events in the story cannot be untangled. Fitzmaurice-Kelly writes: "All we can safely say is that the tale must have been written after May 26, 1605, when the English Envoy, the Earl of Nottingham, arrived in Valladolid to ratify the treaty of peace between Spain and England. As Sr. Icaza shrewdly remarks, Cervantes was not the man to praise Elizabeth and Essex while war was waging between the two countries" (MacColl's ed., I, xxiv). But *cf.* Mack Hendricks Singleton, "The Date of *La española inglesa*," *Hispania*, XXX (1947), 329–335.
46. *Exemplarie Novells*, p. 209.

likewise (like them) a close and concealed Christian."[47] But Ricaredo vows to follow Isabella. He is long delayed, even taken as a slave to Algiers, and it is only by the greatest good fortune that he finally arrives in Seville just where and when his heartbroken fiancée is about to take the veil. Then, at last, all ends happily.

Among this *novela*'s points of interest is its change in Mabbe's hands. No close comparison with the original is necessary to find that Mabbe has converted England to the "Northern Island," and Roman Catholicism to the "Christian" religion, which is carefully distinguished from "the religion of the Countrey." Frank Pierce, noting these and other alterations, writes as follows:

The subject of clandestine Catholics in Elizabethan England is, to say the least, striking in its originality . . . , but Mabbe has deliberately and thoroughly falsified the effect; for the peculiar virtue of this tale (otherwise just another *novella*) lies in the intertwining of topicalities with the ordinary stuff of adventure, thus heightening its probability and illustrating the extent of Cervantes' understanding of the possibilities of this *género chico*. Mabbe, on the other hand, shatters the subtle proportion of naturalistic fact and idealistic fiction and invests the story with an improbability unacceptable to the author.[48]

Even granting some of Pierce's contentions—and some are irrefutable— Mabbe's changes are not enough to hide the fact that Cervantes' story is really about England.[49] For instance, he merely changes the name of London to the anagram "Mundolin," a device which might be thought to whet the curiosity more than puzzle the intellect. Furthermore, the ratio of fact to fantasy, sufficiently slight in the original, is still capable of provoking a certain amount of interest. In reading of Ricaredo's encounter with the Turks,

47. *Exemplarie Novells,* p. 212.

48. "James Mabbe and 'La Española Inglesa,' " *RLC,* XXIII (1949), 84. Of all the *novelas,* this one is changed most by Mabbe, particularly when it comes to his treatment of Ricaredo's motive for going to Rome. Mabbe says only that it was fitting for Ricaredo to go elsewhere in Christendom to settle his conscience, but Cervantes had had his hero say, "I arrived in Rome, where my soul was cheered and my faith was fortified. I kissed the feet of the Chief Pontiff, I confessed my sins to the Grand Penitentiary [the Cardinal Penitentiary presiding over the Apostolic Penitentiary]; he absolved me of them, and handed me the necessary credentials which should give testimony of my confession and penitence, and of the submission I had made to our universal mother, the Church" (for clarity I cite from MacColl, I, 171).

49. E. Allison Peers, however, believes that "From the beginning of this romantic and idealistic story to the end, there is no indication that Cervantes had any knowledge whatever of England" (*Cervantes in England,* Publications of the Institute of Hispanic Studies, Lectures and Addresses, No. 6 [Liverpool, 1947], p. 2).

for example, one is reminded of traditional accounts of the English vessels which met the Armada. Ricaredo has "Shippes that were light laden, and were quicke and nimble; and such excellent saylers, that they would turne and winde, and come off and on, as if they had beene plied with Oares. . . ."[50] There is even a glimpse of customs, as when Ricaredo refuses to sail up the Thames joyously because of the death of his commander. He mixes his signs, "One while the Trumpets sounding loud, and shrill; and another while low, and hoarse; one while the Drummes did beat lively, and the Flutes goe merrily, and another while dead, and softly, answering each other with mournefull and lamentable notes."[51]

However, the collection's most convincing compound of fact and fancy is *The Jealous Husband* (from *El celoso extremeño*), the last and best story of the lot. In contrast to *The Spanish Ladie,* which whisks its characters through Spain, England, France, and Italy, to say nothing of Algiers, virtually all of this story takes place in Seville, and, more specifically and significantly, in the household of one man, Felipe de Carrizales. It is the lot of rich old Felipe to love Leonora, a tender child whom he marries and mews up in his house. The old man blocks his windows, instals a tornell (such as nuns have in convents), hires an old Negro eunuch as guard, and forbids entry even to a male cat or a male figure in a tapestry. His hopes, of course, are doomed, for there is always a June-blooded squire in the tale of January and May. In this case it is one Loaysa, a cunning rogue who disguises himself as a patch-eyed cripple, insinuates his way into the trust of the eunuch, Luys, and succeeds in winning the affection of the whole female part of the household. Finally, at the climax of the story, Felipe discovers Loaysa in bed with Leonora. At this point, where conventional codes would have him rage, hot for bloody revenge, the old man seizes a dagger, true enough, but then simply and humanly crumples. He calls for a scrivener, makes a will that leaves both Leonora and her parents rich, and entreats her to marry her lover. Then, within a week, he dies; and before another week has passed, Leonora, dejected and wretched, goes to a nunnery.

Here is the most touching tale in the collection. Of course it has flaws. For example, we are to think that Leonora's virtuous resistance to Loaysa is so strenuous that both of the young people are exhausted, and the girl falls asleep in the arms of the boy. Yet genuine pathos is generated by the old man's disillusionment and by Leonora's inability to explain her innocence.

50. *Exemplarie Novells*, p. 224.
51. *Exemplarie Novells*, p. 230.

As these latter facts imply, the story has a bit of characterization. One is apt to remember not only the foolish old man who stakes his happiness on the fallibility of a child, but also the frustrated and aging duenna, Marialonso, and the deftly drawn, weak-minded Negro, Luys, with his love of wine and music.

Doubtless another reason that *The Jealous Husband* seems convincing is that, compared with the other *novelas,* more details of its Spanish background have come into English. There is a sprinkling of Spanish words, even some proverbs that are inserted intact. There is a description of the popular tunes of the day, mention of how Felipe's slaves are branded, and a glimpse of the hard, near-desert life of Felipe's native region, the Estremaduran plains.

As for Mabbe's treatment, *The Jealous Husband* is the story in the collection that is most notable for its traces of good old Elizabethan gusto. After Loaysa climbs into the loft above and between the outer and inner doors of the house, we read that the eunuch

Luys presently tinded a waxe candle, and . . . *Loaysa* drew out his Ghitterne, and playing upon it with a soft and sweete touch, suspended the *Negro* in such sort, that hearing it, hee was almost out of his little wits. Having played a pretty while, hee tooke out a new collation, and gave it unto his Scholler, who in swallowing downe his sweet meats, dranke so deepe of the bottle, that it made him more besides himselfe then the musicke.[52]

By this time

the poore *Negro* had foure fingers thicke of wine swimming in his braine, hee could not hit right upon any one of the frets, or make any true stoppe; and yet notwithstanding *Loaysa* made him beleeve that he had learned alreadie two tunes, and the jeast was, that the good silly *Negro* did verily thinke so indeed.

When Loaysa finally gets a chance to perform for the ladies of the house, there is not one who can resist his charm.

There was not the oldest amongst them which did not fall a dancing; nor the yongest which did not tricke it with their armes a kembo; but very softly, and with a strange kind of silence, having set Sentinels, and spyes, to give them notice, if the old man should chance to wake.

The muted merriment of this scene—one of the most memorable in the fiction of its day—is a prelude to that in which Leonora's old governess breaks forth into lively song. She begins,

52. Quotations in this paragraph are from pp. 289–310, *passim.*

Mother,
Keepe me not under locke and kay,
For who can hold what will away?
If I doe not my selfe containe,
Your watch and ward is all in vaine.

Perhaps the most striking touch in the whole volume, however, does not occur until Luys, fearful of his awakened master, stumbles drunkenly up to the refuge of his loft. There,

covering himselfe over head and eares with his poore bed-blanket; he sweated, and did so sweat for feare, one drop overtaking another, that his shirt was dung-wet. And yet for all this, hee did not forbeare tampering on the Ghitterne, which hee hugged close in his bosome, wronging the strings with his untunable fingering; such and so great (now fie upon him) was the affection which hee bare to Musicke.

For the moment, at least, the elegance of Mabbe's collection is shattered. At such a time one sees clearly enough how readers have sometimes confused realism—for life *is* touched here—with a depiction of the seamy side of life.

Having completed a brief survey of all of Mabbe's *novelas,* it is natural to wonder not only how they are exemplary, but whether or not any valid generalizations may be made concerning their "realism." One cannot resolve such problems both briefly and adequately, but it is worthwhile to raise and ponder them because of Cervantes' importance in the history of the novel.

As for their relation to life (and I mean the phrase to be broader than mere "lifelikeness"), the weaker *novelas* show Cervantes disappointingly ready to marry off characters irresponsibly, to whip up sentimentality when genuine emotion would do, to overuse chance, and generally to manipulate his raw materials so that their relevance is largely restricted to their mutual relevance in the stories. The whole man is not writing here.

Yet Amezúa y Mayo contends that Cervantes humanized the Italian *novella.* Even when not at his best, true enough, Cervantes does have a knack for infusing his fiction with a certain warmth. When he is in top form, he is capable of making us glimpse what he describes, even feel it to some extent, and therefore suspend some of our disbelief. Beyond this, he sometimes does more than merely expose types of character; he takes short steps toward analyzing them. In *The Jealous Husband,* most notably, Felipe de Carrizales seems to have a mind as well as a role. But more typical of the collection is *The Spanish Ladie,* which, despite patches of realistic detail, is largely concerned with action that is carried on by puppets. An enthusiastic apologist, confronted with such a work, might respond that Cervantes has not so much failed to report life as created a golden world from some of the raw materials of nature's brazen one. Naturally readers differ widely. My own belief is that among Mabbe's six *novelas, The Force of Blood* and *The Jealous Husband* come nearest to conveying Cervantes' greatest skills: the successful interweaving of life and romance, and the suggestion of general truths.[53]

It is this suggestion of general truths that would seem to entitle the *novelas* to be called exemplary. Presumably the stories operate not in the old, medieval way of laying down rules, but, at least according to Cervantes, in two other ways: by example and diversion. First he says that "if you look closely there is not one of them that does not afford a useful example."[54] Believing that moral efficacy lies more in illustration than precept, he has tried to depict virtues and vices in action. "If it were not that I do not wish to expand upon this subject," he continues, "I could show you the savory and wholesome fruit that is to be had from each of them separately and from the collection as a whole." Then he puts forth his second claim: he also has written because "decent and pleasing pastimes are profitable rather than harmful." As Cervantes himself knew, this second claim to utility might be advanced for a walk in the park or a game of billiards, or for anything else which combats the sin of boredom. There is no gainsaying that such things have a certain kind of value, but Cervantes' first and more significant claim can be more specifically substantiated, and perhaps most clearly in *The Jealous Husband*. As the song of the old governess puts it, *"If I doe not my selfe*

---

53. Amezúa y Mayo protests that not one of the *novelas* is totally absurd or impossible (*Cervantes,* I, 486), and Francisco A. de Icaza shows that even in *The Two Damsells* some episodes are parallel to historical facts (*Las novelas ejemplares de Cervantes* [Madrid, 1928], I, 226–231).

54. Quoted from Samuel Putnam's translation of Cervantes' prologue in *Three Exemplary Novels,* p. 5. The point is made explicitly if not convincingly in *The Spanish Ladie,* which concludes as follows: "This Novell may teach us, what great power vertue and beautie have, since that both of them together, and each of them by themselves are of force, to make even their enemies in love with them. As likewise how that heaven knowes from the greatest adversities and afflictions, to draw the greatest benefits, and comforts" (p. 267). Cervantes' claims have been widely discussed. See, e.g., William J. Entwistle, "Cervantes, the Exemplary Novelist," *HR,* IX (1941), 103–109; Américo Castro, "La ejemplaridad de las novelas cervantinas," *NRFH,* II (1948), 319–332; and Enrique Sordo, "Notas al margen: Realidad y ficción de las Novelas ejemplares," *Cuadernos de Literatura,* III (Madrid, 1948), 271–283. Though not about Cervantes, a helpful discussion of "illustrative tales" is found in Donald M. Beach's "Studies in the Art of Elizabethan Prose Narrative," unpublished Ph.D. dissertation (Cornell, 1959).

containe,/ Your watch and ward is all in vaine." Whatever else this story does or does not do, it conveys a sense of the serious consequences of regarding a human being as a thing. (From his own Algerian captivity, Cervantes knew what it meant to be the property of another man.) Antithetically to the husband in *The Curious Impertinent,* who insists on exposing his virtuous wife to the most severe temptation, the jealous Felipe subjects Leonora to the most severe repression. From the results of the experiments of these widely differing husbands a reader may infer that somewhere between lies the virtuous mean.[55] Further support for Cervantes' claim may be found in *The Force of Blood.* One thinks, for instance, of the noteworthy passage which occurs when Leocadia's father refuses to denounce his daughter for her loss of virtue. "God is offended," he says, "with our sayings, our doings, and our desires; and since that thou neither in thought, word, nor deed, hast offended him, account thy selfe honest, for I shall hold thee so, and shall never looke upon thee but like a kinde and loving Father."[56]

Nevertheless, Singleton goes so far as to say that "Cervantes could be very wily at times. If anybody thinks he is not being wily when he defends the *Novelas ejemplares* as being exemplary in a Counter-Reformation society, I think he is wrong."[57] Perhaps Mabbe felt thus. Though both the scholar and businessman in him would have prompted him to retain Cervantes' proclamation of exemplariness in his title, Mabbe goes on to say that he presents not *exempla* but *"matters of harmlesse* Merriment, *and* Disports" which are *"pleasing andd elightfull [sic]. . . ."*[58] As I have suggested earlier, it is noteworthy that when the book appeared a second time, it was called *Delight in Severall Shapes* (1654).[59]

55. In an earlier manuscript version of *El celoso extremeño,* incidentally, the adultery between Leonora and her pursuer takes place. In the printed version of 1613, Cervantes violates both reason and art to prevent it.

56. *Exemplarie Novells,* p. 190.

57. "The 'Persiles' Mystery," in *Cervantes Across the Centuries,* ed. Angel Flores and M. J. Benardete (New York, 1947), p. 237.

58. *Exemplarie Novells,* A3ᵛ.

59. Charlotte E. Morgan, *The Rise of the Novel of Manners* (New York, 1911), p. 53, reports that Mabbe also brought out four of the Cervantes stories in 1638. Apparently Miss Morgan relied too heavily on an entry in the Stationers' Register, ed. Edward Arber (London, 1877), IV, 445, which under November 27, 1638, records four *True Tragicomicall Histories* (*The Liberall Lover* and *The Jealous Husband* are omitted). Although no such edition is known, the entry serves as a hint that a collection of Cervantes' stories was contemplated well in advance of the time one appeared.

Cervantes' *novelas* reappeared in Sir Roger L'Estrange's *The Spanish Decameron*

In his original 1640 dedication Mabbe compared his several stories with the dishes at a banquet, commending them to an English reader for their variety, and mentioning particularly their changing scenes, pretty passages, strange episodes, and happy endings. He could have said more. Appearing as late as they did, nearly thirty years after their Spanish models, his translations still would have had a certain amount of freshness simply because English book-sellers in the three intervening decades had had relatively few important new *novelas* to serve. Robert Greene's popular tales and Forde's *Ornatus and Artesia* (1634) were both warmed-over fare in the seventeenth century, and Boccaccio's *Decameron,* though translated for the first time in 1620, had long since seen its salad days. Perhaps the most serious new competition was offered by the psychological analysis in *Love and Valour* (1638), a translation from the lumpy French story by Vital d'Audiguier (whom we have noted as a translator), and the distinctly personal style and realistic touches in Richard Brathwait's *The Two Lancashire Lovers.* The latter did not appear, however, until the same year as the *Exemplarie Novells.*

The preface of the 1654 issue of Cervantes' collection (probably not by Mabbe, since he would have been eighty-two at the time) offers the additional information that "a *paire of our best Poets* [Beaumont and Fletcher are identified in the margin] did not scorn to dresse two of these *Stories* for our *English Stage,* and (were they yet alive) they might justly confesse that they gather'd some of the *fairest Flowers* of their *Reputation,* from our *Authors Garden-plot.*"[60] It is important to students of English literature that dramatists like Beaumont, Fletcher, Heywood, Middleton, Rowley, and probably others turned to Cervantes' garden, even though one must add that the immediate source for most of these writers was probably the Rosset-D'Audiguier translations of 1615.[61]

(1687), which was partly plagiarized from Mabbe, and in Dr. Walter Pope's *Select Novels* (1694). In the eighteenth century Mabbe's original translation was revived, but attributed to Shelton. Some form of *El celoso extremeño,* by the way, served as the source for the Bickerstaffe-Dibdin opera, *The Padlock* (1768).

60. *Delight,* A2ᵛ.

61. This is the opinion of Edwin B. Knowles, "Cervantes y la literatura inglesa," *Realidad,* II (1947), 275. I know of no real basis for the statement by Antonio Palau y Dulcet that Mabbe's book is a modified form of an unpublished manuscript translation by Shelton (*Manual del librero hispanoamericano* [Madrid, 1950], III, 455).

Some of the plays which either possibly or certainly borrow from Cervantes' collection are: *Las dos doncellas,* used by Fletcher and Beaumont (and Jonson?) for *Love's Pilgrimage* (1616); *La señora Cornelia,* used by Fletcher for *The Chances*

Significantly, any direct influence of the stories on early English fiction seems to have been rare. Notwithstanding Mabbe's rhetorical and translating skill, one gropes in vain for a seventeenth-century equivalent to Sir Walter Scott's statement that he was a constant reader of Cervantes' *novelas,* and that it was these which inspired him to excel in fiction.[62]

Pérez de Montalván's *Aurora* and *The Prince*

Like Mabbe, the Spanish *novela* writers who came after Cervantes were also attracted most by the amatory, patrician elements in the master weaver's richly varied web. It is sad to relate that the golden age of the Spanish *novela* both begins and comes to a climax with the *Novelas ejemplares.* Such a man as Juan Pérez de Montalván, who was not the weakest among Cervantes' successors, could no more weave another *Jealous Husband* than strike the sky with his fist.

When his *Sucesos y prodigios de amor* (1624) first appeared in Madrid, Montalván was only twenty-two. The son of a bookseller of Jewish extraction —a man who sold books to Philip III and became the friend of Lope de Vega —the young man had talent, opportunity, and ambition. He was a successful playwright at seventeen, a licentiate in theology at eighteen, and fairly soon afterward was ordained a priest, graduated as doctor of theology, and appointed to an office in the Inquisition. More important to us is that during his short and busy life he was much encouraged by Lope. Lope's influence is apparent not only in many of the young man's nearly sixty plays, but also in his fiction.

When two *novelas* from his *Sucesos* first appeared in London in 1647, Montalván's English translator was only twenty-two. England was then in civil turmoil, but Thomas Stanley went about having his genteel translations

---

(ca. 1617?); *El amante liberal,* used by Heywood for *The Fair Maid of the West* (I, ca. 1610; II, ca. 1630); *La fuerza de la sangre,* used by Middleton and Rowley for *The Spanish Gipsie* (1623), and by Field, Fletcher, and Massinger for *The Queen of Corinth* (1617). Other useful *Novelas ejemplares,* not translated by Mabbe, were: *La ilustre fregona,* used by the writers of *The Fair Maid of the Inn* (1626)—Massinger, Webster, Ford, and Fletcher (?); *La gitanilla,* used by Middleton and Rowley for *The Spanish Gipsie* (cf. above); and *El casamiento engañoso,* used by Fletcher for *Rule a Wife and Have a Wife* (1624). Edward M. Wilson, "Cervantes and English Literature of the Seventeenth Century," *BH,* L (1948), 27–52, notes the sort of use made of Cervantes' stories in *The Chances, Love's Pilgrimage,* and *The Queen of Corinth.*

62. Cited by George Ticknor, *History of Spanish Literature* (Boston, 1891), II, 141, from Lockhart's biography of Scott.

printed privately for presents. Born in 1625 in Cumberlow, Hertfordshire, son of Sir Thomas Stanley, the future poet and translator had first been tutored at home by William Fairfax, son of the translator of Tasso. Then, before he was fifteen, he had gone to Pembroke Hall, Cambridge, "where he became a very early proficient in all sorts of Polite Learning, not without the assistance of the said Mr. *Fairfax,* as well during his stay in that University, as afterwards in his more advanced Years."[63] Possibly "It was Here he composed those *Madrigal's Poems,* and other Pieces, which together with some Translations out of the *French, Italian,* and *Spanish,* were published in one Volume after his Return from his Travels."[64] After receiving his M. A. in 1641, at any rate, Stanley did make a Grand Tour, and upon his return became "the central figure in a circle of Cavalier poets."[65] "Most of his friends," writes Osborn, "devoted themselves to rescuing the remnants of the golden age; by translation and imitation they made available the glories of past literatures."[66] Stanley married in 1648, was elected to the Royal Society in 1661, and died in 1678, a respected and admired man of letters.[67]

In his translation of Pérez de Montalván's *La hermosa Aurora,* Stanley retells the story of a Sicilian princess, Aurora, who irks her stepmother and is packed off to an island in the "Tyrrhen Sea." In time a handsome young

63. Wood, I, f. 284.

64. From the anonymous memoir prefixed to the 1701 edition of Stanley's *History of Philosophy,* a1ʳ.

65. James M. Osborn, "Thomas Stanley's Lost 'Register of Friends,'" *Yale University Library Gazette,* XXXII (1958), 123. Mild though he seems to have been, Stanley did not shrink from politics altogether. In 1657 he published *Psalterium Carolinum,* a partial verse rendition of Charles' *Eikon basilike,* set to music by Dr. John Wilson.

66. "Thomas Stanley's Lost 'Register . . . ,'" p. 145.

67. No matter where one finds information about him, there is praise. Edward Phillips, a friend and fellow translator (see below), describes him in the *Theatrum poetarum* (1675), II, 184, as

> a Gentleman both well deserving of the Common-wealth of Learning in general, by his . . . Lives of the Philosophers, and his Learned Edition of *Aeschylus;* and also particularly honoured for his smooth Air and gentile Spirit in Poetry; which appears not only in his own Genuine Poems, but also from what he hath so well translated out of ancient Greec [*sic*], and modern Italian Spanish and French Poets, as to make his own.

To his contemporaries, Stanley's four-volume *History of Philosophy* (1655–1662), alluded to by Phillips, loomed as an imposing contribution to learning, though he is better remembered now for his verse.

prince, Pausanius, on his way to the court to see Aurora, is shipwrecked near her island. Since he has never met the princess, Pausanius is deceived by her pretending to be Clelia, a lady-in-waiting with whom she trades names. A romance between the royal pair springs up and fares well, but only until the king spoils everything by coming to take Aurora back to Sicily. Then the king's right-hand man, Clearchus, who loves the real Clelia, intercepts a message addressed to Prince Pausanius and signed "Clelia." Meeting in a wood, the presumed rivals have a chance to duel by the dramatically flickering light of burning brands. (Neither is sufficiently bothered by Clelia's apparent perfidy to give her up.) But all's well that ends well. First Pausanius is rescued from the island by friends he thought drowned at the time of his shipwreck, and then he goes to the Sicilian court, makes a friend of Clearchus, learns that his sweetheart is a princess, and, finally, weds her.

Now and again this highly romantic tale pauses for a bit of verse or an amorous letter, but for the most part it moves along in graceful narrative prose. Taken as a whole, it rather reminds one of certain Shakespearean comedies. It provides a romantic island setting, a spirited, exiled princess pretending to be her own handmaiden, a shipwrecked prince, and a rivalry between faithful lovers. Heightening a generic sort of resemblance to such plays or to Lodge's *Rosalynde* is the fact that nothing about the *novela* seems particularly Spanish. It might have been written almost anywhere.

In Stanley's English, *Aurora* is not without charm. Moreover, it is close to its original with regard to incident, generally close in detail, and cavalier only with names. "Sicily," for instance, began as "Syracuse." Even here Stanley is not irresponsible, however, for he has announced in his introduction that if the reader "finde the Names of Persons or Places differ from the Originall, let him suppose it done for the better accommodation of the Scaene."[68] For the most part he follows his source closely. In fact Montalván was lucky to have his verses rendered not merely by a competent and conscientious translator, but by a man who himself was a poet. No one is apt to exclaim over Stanley's renditions of the songs in *Aurora*, and yet they are carefully done, far better, surely, than more slavish translation would have permitted.

Stanley's second *novela*, based on Montalván's *La prodigiosa*, appeared as both *Ismenia and the Prince* and *The Prince*. It is more tangled and perhaps less interesting than *Aurora*, but of a basically similar type. It opens with a striking scene in which a man clad in skins is seen descending from "the top of

68. *Aurora, & The Prince* (1647), A2ʳ.

Caucasus, a Mountain in *Armenia. . . ."*[69] This character proves to be an exiled Albanian prince named Gesimenes, and at length it becomes clear that the main story is based on the fact that his half-brother Lucander was at one time his competitor in love. When the lady in question produced a child by Gesimenes, Lucander took steps to butcher the infant and have its pieces delivered to Gesimenes. Actually, however, a servant managed to whisk the royal baby to safety so that it might grow up in seclusion. Now the grown Ismenia, ignorant that such is her background, comes upon the mountain hideaway of the royal hermit and, most chastely, begins to live with him. Later on she also has the good fortune to encounter a handsome and younger man—also a prince—who finds it hard to resist her in her "Tygresse" skin sarong. Though their love becomes mutual, its course is not smooth until Gesimenes defeats the wicked Lucander, proves himself to be legitimate, finds his preternaturally patient lady, attains the Albanian crown, discovers Ismenia to be his daughter, and witnesses her marriage to the handsome young prince.

It is probably true that practically all literature has its moral aspect, but to search for a way in which such a work as this stands guard over morals is to look for a hare on a housetop.[70] In English as in Spanish, coincidences are pushed to the greatest extreme. The pastoral atmosphere, rather appealing in *Aurora,* is here so extended as to become a bit ludicrous; Aurora charms the birds with her singing, but Gesimenes takes up residence with lions. Literary questions of motivation and characterization seem almost irrelevant to such a work because, without being an actual fairy tale, it assumes some of the privileges of the kind. Of course Renaissance English readers would have known how to take all this. Ever since Barnabe Riche's *Farewell to Militarie Profession* (1581) they had had rather similar stories.

Both of Stanley's *novelas*—one of the prince of Albania and one of the princess of Sicily—are woven of the same stuff, but the colors in *The Prince* seem a little more flashy, the pattern more confused, and the finished result less unified. Perhaps the most charitable remark one might make is that Shakespeare could have transmuted them both into something not unlike *The Winter's Tale.* As it is, bringing only competence and grace to his work, Stanley neither transcends nor transforms. At least on the basis of these two stories, Douglas Bush is quite right in deeming Stanley a smooth and genteel writer who exemplifies the long-range shift in translators' motives, "the dwin-

69. *Aurora . . . ,* p. 45.
70. Like Cervantes' stories eleven years before, the eight *novelas* in the *Sucesos* professed to be exemplary.

dling of humanistic and patriotic seriousness into the cultivation of a polite accomplishment."[71]

The bibliographical career of Stanley's tales is tangled because of their appearance together at least twice (1647 and 1650) and in collections with some of his other works at least three times (1647–1648, 1651, and 1652). Since variant title pages indicate that the stories were also issued twice more (1648 and 1650), their total number of appearances is raised to seven. Even if none of these printings was large, and even if Stanley's accompanying compositions were really the chief attraction, *Aurora* and *The Prince* must have been at least moderately well known in England for a while.[72]

Montalván's *Illustrious Shepherdess* and *Imperious Brother*

About a decade after Stanley's 1647 debut, Edward Phillips brought out two more translations from the same collection, *The Illustrious Shepherdess* (from *La villana de Pinto*) and *The Imperious Brother* (from *El envidioso castigado*). Phillips was the son of Edward Phillips, a secondary of the crown office in the court of chancery, and of Ann, only sister of John Milton. That Milton was Edward Phillips' uncle is of more than incidental interest, for the poet, when his sister was widowed, seems to have felt a moral obligation to help both of her sons. In 1639 the future translator began going to lessons at his uncle's lodgings in the home of a tailor in St. Bride's Churchyard, and later, when Milton moved to Aldersgate, the boy went to board with him. Aubrey, in explaining that Milton's first wife, the royalist Mary Powell, was unhappy with her husband, declares "she found it very solitary: no company came to her, often-times [she] heard his Nephews beaten, and cry."[73] Edward later told how the boys read from the Greek Testament on Sundays, went through the Pentateuch in Hebrew, read some of Matthew in Syriac, made "a good entrance into . . . *Chaldee*," and, somewhat anticlimactically, studied French and Italian.[74] Disappointingly he omits Spanish from his list, though he says specifically that Milton himself knew the language.[75]

71. *English Literature in the Earlier Seventeenth Century* (Oxford, 1948), p. 64.

72. Of greatest bibliographical aid is Margaret Flower, "Thomas Stanley (1625–1678): A Bibliography of His Writings in Prose and Verse (1647–1743)," *Transactions of the Cambridge Bibliographical Society*, I, Pt. 2 (1950), 139–172.

73. Quoted by J. Milton French, *The Life Records of John Milton* (New Brunswick, N. J., 1950), II, 64.

74. Noted in his biography of Milton, reprinted in *The Early Lives of Milton*, ed. Helen Darbishire (London, 1932), p. 61.

75. Prof. French has called to my attention that Antonio Francini, in some versi-

It was in 1656, at the age of twenty-six, that Edward brought out his two stories from Spanish, either one of which his uncle would have been quick to designate a "meer amatorious novel."[76] Later on, one hopes, Edward may have redeemed himself in his mentor's eyes with his *New World of English Words* (1658).[77] At any rate, though he ended up teaching "School in the *Strand* near the *May-Pole,* lived in poor condition . . . [,] wrote and translated several things meerly to get a bare livelihood, [and] was out of Employment in 1684 and 85,"[78] he and his brother John managed to turn out some forty works between them; and, as William Godwin puts it, "In the age in which they lived they were to the full as well known, and as much objects of attention to literary men, as almost ever falls to the lot of authors of a subordinate talent."[79]

Phillips' *Illustrious Shepherdess* is scarcely the brief sort of narrative that is usually conjured up by the name "short-story." Indeed, it stretches to some ninety octavo pages, and its companion volume, *The Imperious Brother,* to eighty-four.[80] In some remarks to the reader, however, noting that England has been "profusely entertain'd," perhaps even satiated, by French gallantry, Phillips has the wit to turn the very length of his stories to advantage. He suggests that "it will not be amiss to give a taste of the Spanish Reserve and Gravity: and (since things of this nature are swell'd to such an excess of voluminousness) to correct one extream with another, by publishing an Adventure as concise as the rest are tedious."[81] That is, we are meant to compare his translation not with other *novelas,* but with the long French romances. The same comparison is invited in his dedication to the Marchioness of Dorchester. After ad-

---

fied praise prefixed to Milton's *Poems* in 1645, says that Milton spoke it at that time. This is one of several hints that Phillips may have translated directly from Spanish (as Ralph E. Hone assumes in his "Edward and John Phillips," unpublished Ph.D. dissertation [New York University, 1954], p. 163). In the biography of his uncle, by the way, Phillips refers unsympathetically to "the Wheedling, Lisping Jargon of the Cringing *French*" (p. 69).

76. Quoted by John J. O'Connor, "A Note on the Meaning of 'Novel' in the Seventeenth Century," *NQ,* CXCVIII (1953), 477–478.

77. Later still, it has been said, he earned the honor of founding English biographical literary history. In his *Tractatulus de carmine dramatico poetarum veterum* (1669) he assayed a sketch of literary history which provided the basis for his better known *Theatrum poetarum,* an index to poets of all times and places (René Wellek, *The Rise of English Literary History* [Chapel Hill, N. C., 1941], pp. 16–17).

78. Wood, II, 1117.

79. *Lives of Edward and John Phil[l]ips,* p. 1.

80. The two are bound together in some copies.

81. *The Illustrious Shepherdess,* A8.

dressing her ladyship in words that seem to have come bubbling through honey, Phillips dares to affirm that Montalván

hath made his Hero *to perform somwhat of so gallant, that in the narrow Limits to which he is confin'd, and his due regard to Likelihood and Possibility, a particular, of which there are few Romances which make any great Conscience; I see not how he could have perform'd more.*[82]

And from this we see also that Phillips was aware of the problem of *vraisemblance,* though *The Illustrious Shepherdess* is about as realistic as Cervantes' *Liberall Lover* or Congreve's own *Incognita.*

The story concerns the secretly born daughter of lovers plagued by parent trouble. It begins when an unwed girl leaves her baby with a shepherd named Albanius, but it does not really get under way until the child grows into a beauty named Silvia, who is espied by Don Francisco Osorio, a gentleman from Madrid.[83] Disappointed by Silvia's respectful coolness, Don Francisco resolves to leave for a while, then return as the long-lost Cardenio, son of a villager, thinking that this will remove the class barrier between Silvia and himself. But old Albanius, worried about Silvia's next move, tells her of her true identity. Now she is too good for Cardenio. The young man therefore resolves to woo her in his richest garments. But because it is the lowly Cardenio she really loves, Silvia will still have none of him. He next tries jealousy. But because the shepherdess he chooses to admire has other beaux, he becomes involved in a fight. This serves to arouse Silvia's sympathy, but at this point the girl's parents, fleeing from her still-irate grandparents, stop off to take her with them to Madrid. In huggermugger, unknown to Cardenio and against her wishes, she is rushed away. Each now thinks the other neglectful until at last Cardenio, returning to Madrid, engages in a street duel, seeks refuge in a nearby house, and discovers that the latter is the residence of—rare fortune! —his Silvia. It is then only a matter of paragraphs before the nuptials.

Although produced nearly half a century later, this story shows little advance over *Axa and the Prince.* Its basic design is pleasingly simple, but the work as a whole suggests lack of planning and lack of revision. Albanius, for example, who is early described as mourning for a deceased wife, is later and suddenly provided with a mate.

82. *Shepherdess,* A6.
83. The situation is not wholly incredible. Don Juan of Austria, bastard of Charles V, was reared in obscurity, ignorant of his origin and clad like any country boy. It bears repeating that unreality in some early fiction is traceable to treatment as much as to material.

Phillips' style is formal and copious, much what one might expect from a young writer who praised the prose of others for being "florid and ornate."[84] In fact Phillips was so ready to make changes and additions that his style is even more inflated than that of his flatulent original. It may be seen at its most full blown in the sentence which opens the work:

THE Heaven had newly display'd it's blue Canopie, besprinkled with innumerous flaming Gems; and that fair Star that leads up all the rest, and shines the glory of the Evening, was so profuse of her Rayes, that it might well have been thought that either the Sun was not set, or else that another Sun had succeeded in his room, and night, to whom he had surrendred his place, as to his lawful Successour, reposed in the bosome of her beloved silence; when *Albanius* leaving his little Flock of Sheep to feast themselves upon the sprouting dainties of the Field, retir'd himself to Contemplate the misfortunes of his past life.[85]

This one-hundred-ten-word grand opening is soon revealed to be so much glittering claptrap. Mere minutes after Albanius has left his sheep in this brilliantly starlit setting, he finds the new-born babe and its mother huddled against the "bleak violence of the night."[86]

When Phillips came to dedicate his second translation, his choice of dedicatee must have been easy, for it was the Countess of Strafford, sister to the Marchioness of Dorchester, who had asked him to undertake the task. After some more fulsome flattery he proceeds to relate the story of two brothers who compete with each other for a lady. The first brother, the good one, is Carlo. The second and imperious one is Alfredo, who is "more envious than

---

84. In his edition of the *Poems* of William Drummond of Hawthornden (1656) A3^v.

85. *Shepherdess,* p. 1. The word "shines" is substituted in the list of errata for "shares." When Silvia is informed that she must leave with her parents, Phillips (p. 67) turns out the following more typical sentence:

> This unexpected news of the necessity of her so sudden departure, affected *Silvia* in such sort, as that she wish'd Heaven had been so favorable to her, as that she might have been born to no other condition than that wherein she had lived all this while; since the advancement of her Fortune tended to no less a prejudice to her, than the depriving her of him whom she lov'd above all the world; constraining them to live so far apart, that her eyes should henceforth be debar'd the dearest object of their sight.

86. *Shepherdess,* p. 4. In trying to be impressive here, Phillips amplifies his source. The original Albanio, upon seeing the child, "Tomóle en los brazos, dándole algún calor con su pobre capa; porque los agravios de la noche no se atreviesen a su tierna vida . . ." (*La villana de Pinto,* in *Sucesos y prodigios de amor,* ed. Agustín González de Amezúa y Mayo [Madrid, 1949], p. 170).

for one of his quality might seem possible."[87] Because virtuous Carlo is afflicted with the most common of Spanish maladies, poverty and pride, he decides to physic himself by falling in love with a rich girl. As Phillips puts it, "to appear miserable, and in want, the greatness of his spirit made him disdain. . . ."[88] When he tells Alfredo of his plan to woo a lady named Stella, bad Alfredo, who is much more affluent, decides to win the lady himself. It is not until some sixty pages later, however, that Stella finally runs off to the country with Carlo. Then, in the village where they hide from Alfredo and Stella's father, a country wench falls in love with Carlo and promises to make additional trouble. But word comes next that Stella and Carlo are pursued, and in no time Carlo is captured and hustled off to prison, leaving fleet-footed Stella to seek refuge on her own. All works out well, of course. Stella's father is mollified, Carlo is freed, Alfredo becomes violently ill "from no other apparent Cause but a deep melancholy," and "within a few weeks he ended his wretched days."[89] Good fortune comes to Carlo, and envy kills his brother.

Both the slowest and most conscientiously exemplary of the four Montalván *novelas* which were translated, *The Imperious Brother* is still something of a fairy tale sans fairies. Like most of its kind, it ends in wealth and marriage, and, like many, it has a genuine if limited spontaneity. Though fashioned by formula and slowed by rhetoric, it nevertheless conveys an impression of being written impromptu. Stella's maid, for instance, whom one supposes to have fled to the country with her mistress, drops out of the reader's sight when back in the city she drops from Stella's balcony. Montalván seems, in other words, to have begun with a general idea, then to have filled in details as he wrote. Perhaps he learned the technique from his friend Lope, who reputedly was able to turn out a play after mass while waiting for his breakfast to be warmed, but unfortunately it was a technique which few save Lope or Cervantes could carry off.[90]

87. *Imperious Brother*, p. 2.
88. *Brother*, p. 5.
89. *Brother*, p. 83.
90. Amezúa y Mayo, ed., *Sucesos* . . . , p. xiv, has considerable praise for this last *novela*. Because of their relatively early date, Captain John Stevens' comments are also of interest. Like Stanley, apparently, Stevens finds *Aurora* "tolerable in contrivance, but absurd as to Geography"; *La prodigiosa* "has some good with such a mixture of bad, as would require much mending"; *La villana de Pinto* "is good except a soliloquy heard in another Room, which is absurd"; and *El envidioso castigado* "may be tolerable mending the beginning" (Robert H. Williams, "A Manuscript Document on the Translations from Spanish by Captain John Stevens," *RLC*, XVI [1936], 154–155).

Conclusion

The twenty-one *novelas* noted in the present chapter range all the way from the simple-hearted *Axa and the Prince* to the semi-realistic *Jealous Husband*. Taken altogether they suggest some of the elasticity and limits of the form as it was known in England. If one expanded the name *novela* to include San Pedro's old-fashioned *Arnalte,* with its slow and sentimental monologue-and-letter technique, presenting love as a purifier of the soul, worthy of comparison with a religion, then the limits of the genre would obviously be greater still, and one might see more clearly, by contrast, the essential and vastly different nature of *The Imperious Brother,* which is also rhetoric-ridden, but more flippant and vulgar, narrating more nimbly and presenting love as a means of spite or, at best, the practical solution of a financial problem. Whatever their differences, however, old or new, intercalated or separate, all are grounded on the subject of love. This and relative brevity are their chief common elements. Though they indeed offer delight in several shapes, Dr. Johnson's definition of "novel," seemingly anachronistic in his own day, is certainly applicable to the Spanish-English *novelas* we have considered: "A small tale, generally of love."[91]

As in the romances of the preceding chapter, it usually seems to be love itself more than characters in love that generates action in the *novelas*. The basic reason is simple: authors were not much interested in characters *per se*. As in picaresque fiction or Restoration drama or Byzantine mosaics, artistic conventions in the *novela* tended to freeze the "real" world in certain molds (just as the *novela* itself was molded by the aesthetic convention of which it was a part). Hence its characters seem capable only of a shrunken range of experience, an experience determined largely by love. Furthermore, within their limited range, characters are unlikely either to develop or to give the impression of being individuals in individual situations. Part of the reason for this thinness of characterization is a certain thinness when it comes to the mimesis of sense data. One can visualize Lazarillo and Don Quixote, but the details which might help us to see in the *novelas* are too often lacking, and when it is hard to see in fiction, it is sometimes hard to believe. Of course it is possible to claim that Cervantes, at his most romantic, was not even trying to present human beings, but archetypes. Such a view would certainly help to explain how the world's greatest satirist of romance could write not only *Persiles*

91. Vol. II of *A Dictionary of the English Language* (London, 1755).

but *The Liberall Lover.* Such a view would help us understand how he could create both Teresa Panza and the Spanish-English lady. If, however, we decide that finding some brand of Aristotelian realism in his work smacks of post mortem hindsight and is therefore best rejected, we may be left with only a very few palpable characters (such as Felipe de Carrizales) and an embarrassingly large number of puppets, the chief function of which is acting out amorous, adventurous plots.[92]

This word "plot" has become pejorative in our time. Nowadays there is a tendency to value most those stories with a Character or a Theme, perhaps even a Character or Theme presented not more or less explicitly but as a syndrome of images and symbols. Quite possibly we have gone too far toward forgetting that a narrative is none the worse for having a story. But even those die-hards who still like plenty of plot would soon be satisfied by the early Spanish *novelas.* The basic reason, once again, is simple: the *novela* writers were concerned primarily with spinning interesting yarns. In their stories, consequently, as in the romances of the last chapter, we find constantly shifting patterns of externalities. We find motion and rhetoric, but little knowledge of stillness.

Given compensations of some other kind, we should be less apt to complain. In the *novelas,* however, meager characterization and emphasis on plot are inseparable from poverty of theme. Just what have these stories to say about life? It would be unfair to analyze Alemán's fiction on the basis of *novelas* which, in good baroque fashion, seem meant to contrast to the work in which they are set. It would be unfair not to exempt Cervantes' best stories from comments more relevant to his worst. But the simple truth is that disappointingly little seems to spring from the individual consciousness of the *novela* writers. Even in Cervantes one too seldom feels that "Here is a personal impression of life." As for Pérez de Montalbán, one is inclined to apply Jonson's remark on certain other writers: "You may sound these wits and find the depth of them with your middle finger."[93] Auerbach discerns the basic problem clearly. In much early Spanish literature, he says, "There are passions and conflicts but there are no problems. God, King, honor and love, class and class decorum are immutable and undoubted, and the figures neither of tragedy nor comedy present us with questions difficult to answer." Hence, "we feel . . . , despite all their colorful and lively bustle, nothing of a

92. The problem is discussed by Arthur Jerrold Tieje, *The Theory of Characterization in Prose Fiction Prior to 1740* (Minneapolis, 1916).
93. *Timber,* ed. Felix E. Schelling (Boston, 1892), p. 25.

movement in the depths of life, or even of a will to explore it in principle and recast it in practice."[94] Cervantes, as I have said, may be partially excepted. His characters are sometimes their own men; Leocadia's father, for instance, forgives her for bringing dishonor to his house. Moreover, a theme-hunter may discover in Cervantes that revenge is not always the best policy, or that people are not to be treated as things. But too often in Cervantes and almost always elsewhere one feels that there is action without thought. There is no comment on life. There is only escape from life.

No wonder of it. Escape is an important function of the *novelas.* These adventurous stories were aimed chiefly at readers who could forget their own predicaments by reading about Aurora's, and surely the *novelas* did succeed in furnishing not only pleasurable excitement, but sheer delight in various artistic shapes. Certainly these are two important aspects of literary entertainment. As for pleasing by giving readers new insights, however, or by expressing individual feelings, the *novelas* are generally lacking.

Of the twenty-one examples mentioned here, the earliest ten were all inserted in longer works, the *Diana, The Rogue,* and *Don Quixote.*[95] An eleventh one, *Axa,* appeared in the *Galateo* in the same year as Mabbe's collection. Of the remaining stories, none of which were intercalations, some eleven editions and issues appeared in the seventeen-year span from 1640 to 1656. Excluding all intercalations (for the moment even *Axa*) because their fortunes were determined by the works in which they were embedded, there were ten stories translated by three Englishmen from the works of two Spaniards. Counting individual *novelas* in all eleven editions and issues, these stories made over two dozen appearances, or, after 1640, about one every six or seven months. This is no great total, but respectable enough if one considers that there was only a modest flow of brief fiction of any kind at the time. I would certainly hesitate to claim, as Lord Ernle does, that Mabbe's translation of Cervantes "popularised a shortened form of story, which in the last twenty years of the Stuart period became almost exclusively the fashion."[96]

94. *Mimesis,* tr. Willard Trask (New York, 1957), p. 292. George Ticknor long ago gave a Boston Unitarian's response. Observing that the Spanish were handed answers to all questions and instructed to memorize them, believe them, die for them, he concluded that in much of their art they "pleased themselves with brilliant follies that were at least free from moral mischiefs" (*History . . . ,* III, 18; preface to first ed. dated December, 1849).

95. I omit here the *novelas sentimentales* of San Pedro and Flores.

96. *The Light Reading of Our Ancestors* (London, n. d.), p. 158. To bring the present chapter back to its starting point, however, it might be of interest to add that Canby finds Congreve's *Incognita* "a replica in style and atmosphere, with

With the passing of the sixteenth century, nevertheless, England did turn from the Italian *novelle* to the Spanish *novelas,* and by the close of our period, translations of short Spanish stories had not only achieved the importance we have seen, but they were beginning to stimulate English counterparts. Before dying out, their fashion extended well on into the age of the Augustans, a lively little eddy in the swelling stream of eighteenth-century English literature.

added wit, if lessened vigor, of Cervantes' exemplary novel of the two students of Bologna and the unfortunate Cornelia" (p. 167).

Chapter VII

The World
Inside Out

Satiric and Realistic Fiction

I n his most famous play Calderón shows that surface reality is an illusion, and life is a dream. In vastly different ways, Spain's writers of satiric and realistic fiction achieved something similar. They depicted a world in which, as Quevedo put it, everybody lives on Hypocrisy Street, and the very sores of the beggars are false. Exposing hypocrisy in life and deflating romance in literature—romance such as we have considered in the last two chapters—the practitioners of this harsher kind of literature contrived to turn the world inside out. The unlovely sights which they exposed were of course not the whole truth. Indeed, the distorted fragments of their vision were sometimes no more faithful to "life as it is" than were the aureate visions of the romancers. But "realistic" still seems the best word for this sharper, harder writing, whether we use the term broadly to mean "relevant to life" or reserve it for narratives based on the details of everyday living. For the most part the works of the present chapter bid readers to open their eyes, whereas romance tries to close them. Perhaps it is significant, therefore, that in the two finest pieces of fiction in our period, romance is interwoven with its opposite. The later one, *Don Quixote,* we have already discussed but the *Celestina* remains to be considered.

The Spanish Bawd

A bout 1530 the *Tragicomedia de Calisto y Melibea,* usually known by the name of its central character, Celestina, was brought into English for the first time. As we have seen, it was changed into an interlude, probably by John Rastell, and thus conveyed beyond our range.[1] As we also have had

1. See Ch. IV, pp. 40–41.

occasion to note, it was translated in full a century later by the Oxford don, Diego Puede-Ser.

The Spanish *Celestina* is difficult to describe. Actually ageneric, the original work has been called both a novel and a play. (It is written entirely in dialogue and, in the expanded version that Mabbe used, divided into twenty-one acts.[2]) Whatever one decides to call it, however, it may also be considered a sort of latter-day *arte de amores,* a fact which tempts one to suggest that it is, in a sense, the highest development of, and the most searching comment on, the *novela sentimental.*[3] In France the literary depiction of the ceremonial of love had long since been frozen in the rhetoric of men like Guillaume de Lorris, and then thawed by the ire of Jean de Meun, with the result that the two parts of the *Roman de la Rose* are as different as they might be. In Spain the author of the *Celestina* dealt with similar elements but mingled them. As a matter of fact, because it consists entirely of the dialogue of various characters, his *Celestina* can convey a number of different views without overtly committing him to any one of them. The method is at once transparently simple and capable of leading to considerable subtlety. Stephen Gilman, for instance, has noted the striking and complex effect of putting certain traditional commonplaces on the lips of the old Spanish bawd:

Celestina does not betray any more than she confirms the inherited truths she utters. Rather the effect is one of irony, of simultaneous ironical vision of two kinds of truth, spontaneous and traditional, living and canonized, particular and general. And since simultaneous vision of two aspects of a situation or object is really another way of saying perspective, it is, I believe, fair to speak of Rojas' ironical separation from his work in much the same sense that we speak of Cervantes'.[4]

2. It may have appeared first in 1500. Previously, about 1499, there had been a sixteen-act form. Clara Louisa Penney, *The Book Called Celestina* (New York, 1954) lists numerous editions before 1635 and gives an extensive list of studies. See also Mack Hendricks Singleton's selected bibliography and survey of *Celestina* studies in the edition of his translation (Madison, Wis., 1958), pp. 283–299.

3. Edwin J. Webber, "The *Celestina* as an *Arte de Amores*," *MP,* LV (1958), 145–153, makes a case for regarding the work thus rather than as an imitation of Terentian comedy, as is sometimes done. As P. E. Russell remarks, there is likewise a real temptation to describe the *Celestina* as "an attempt to try out Petrarch's philosophical and moral views in terms of everyday life . . ." ("The Art of Fernando de Rojas," *BHS,* XXXIV [1957], 167). See A. D. Deyermond, *The Petrarchan Sources of La Celestina* (Oxford, 1961).

4. *The Art of La Celestina* (Madison, Wis., 1956), p. 123.

The *Celestina* admits that different attitudes are possible toward life and love, and, consequently, depicts the mad passion of its lovers as in some ways attractive, delicious, and even admirable, at the same time that it must be warned against as disruptive and dangerous, unworthy because of its denial of family and honor and duty. San Pedro's Lereano, it may be recalled, praised women so hyperbolically that the *Cárcel de amor* was banned by the Inquisition. In like fashion, Calisto, the Lereano of the *Celestina,* proclaims his sweetheart to be his god. Whereas the *Cárcel* is written strictly from a courtly viewpoint, however, with aristocratic characters, the lovers in the *Celestina* are complemented by tricksy servants and whores. In sum, although both works were written at about the same time, and although a careful reader should not overlook the *Celestina's* ecclesiastical, Greek, Latin, Italian, and other Spanish sources, it is possible to regard the story of Calisto and Melibea as constituting "the complete renovation" of the *novela sentimental* "through elimination of some elements, parody of others, and regeneration of still more."[5] That is, the *Celestina* may be thought of as being related to the *novela sentimental* in much the same way that *Don Quixote* is related to the chivalric romance. In broader terms (and broader terms are advisable because the *Celestina* is far more than an answer to San Pedro), it seems possible that the literary idealization of profane objects has in both instances resulted in a more or less realistic reaction.

As Gilman suggests, the fact that the *Celestina* is in dialogue is of major importance. It means that conversation is our sole means of learning the intricacies of the story—a story which is all the more compelling for being told by the characters themselves. Chiefly the plot concerns young Calisto's obsessive love for old Pleberio's ingenuous but inflammable daughter, Melibea. It all begins when Calisto's falcon flies into Melibea's garden. Upon seeing the young lady, the young man immediately begins to moon, too vociferously as it turns out, for Melibea huffily sends him away. Soon, however, he is being comforted by his rascally servant Sempronio, whose greatest service turns out to be the procuring of that wicked, wise, and thoroughly

5. Peter G. Earle, "Love Concepts in *La Cárcel de Amor* and *La Celestina,*" *Hispania,* XXXIX (1956), 92. Also of relevance is the unpublished Ph.D. dissertation by Margaret Eva Palmer, "An Interpretation of *La Celestina*" (University of Washington, 1955).

Among other Spanish sources perhaps the best known is by Juan Ruiz, Archpriest of Hita, whose *Libro de buen amor* (1330) introduced Trotaconventos, prototype of the bawd Celestina. See F. Castro Guisasola, *Observaciones sobre las fuentes literarias de "La Celestina"* (Madrid, 1924).

human old wretch, Celestina. Much else goes on in the story, including some business between two whores (Elicia and Areusa) and Calisto's servants (Sempronio and Parmeno), but the central plot involves the coming together of Calisto and Melibea; the ignominious, fatal, and perhaps symbolic fall of the hero from a ladder in his sweetheart's garden; and the girl's subsequent suicide.

Rather than plot, however, it is the revelation of character through dialogue that does most to give the work stature. It is trite yet true to say that the men and women in the *Celestina* are both individual and universal, possessed of dimensions comparable to those of the characters in some of Shakespeare's better plays. At this very early date in the history of modern literature, the creator—or the creators—of the *Celestina* somehow managed to garner a variety of materials from Spanish life and letters, and to fashion them into a book which remained unrivaled in excellence for a century.

Who the creator was—or who the creators were—we cannot be certain. Though students generally assign the composition of the work, or at least the major part of it, to a lawyer named Fernando de Rojas (*ca.* 1480?–1541), others have qualms about doing so. We do know that an anonymous "author" attributed the initial inspiration and first act of the work to someone else (he suggested the names of Juan de Mena and Rodrigo Cota), and we do know that some verses by an editor, Alonso de Proaza, call attention to an acrostic poem, ostensibly by the author, in which it is proclaimed that Fernando de Rojas completed the work. Whoever is responsible for the *Celestina*, however, students now tend to think that Rojas really did complete it, perhaps with some help, expanding it to the twenty-one-act length known to Mabbe.[6]

6. For a brief statement on the matter see D. W. McPheeters, "The Present Status of *Celestina* Studies," *Symposium,* XII (1958), 196–205. Recent criticism has made use of the fact that Rojas had Jewish blood (as is shown by Otis H. Green, "Fernando de Rojas, *converso* and *hidalgo,*" HR, V [1947], 384–387), suggesting that the love of Calisto and Melibea is doomed because Melibea, like Rojas, is of Jewish descent. The position is stated most persuasively by Fernando Garrido Pallardó, *Los problemas de Calisto y Melibea* (Figueras, 1957), and a good answer is given by Jerónimo Mallo, "¿Hay un problema racial en el fondo de 'La Celestina'?" *Cuadernos del Congreso por la Libertad de la Cultura,* No. 37 (1959), pp. 51–57. The suggestion seems unnecessary when we recall that the book claims to reprove any and all who are controlled by erotic appetite. Lesley Byrd Simpson believes that Calisto makes no move to marry Melibea because "Don Juan is not the marrying kind. He is a sex-ridden egotist" (*The Celestina* [Los

In England, after its presentation as an interlude, the *Celestina* seems to have lain quiet for a while. By 1580, however, it may have been appearing on the stage once again, at least according to the conjecture of some modern students. To Gustav Ungerer, "The fact that this play was quoted as a pattern for other comedies implies that it must have been one of the most prominent plays of the day."[7] With so few facts to go on, one cannot be sure. At least the next bit of evidence is less equivocal: about a decade later (1591), a Spanish version of the *Celestina* was recorded in the Stationers' Register.[8] And, perhaps most tantalizing of all, a license was issued in 1598 for a translation called *The Tragicke Comedye of Celestina*, though no copy of such a work is known.[9]

Whoever may have written *The Tragicke Comedye* of 1598, Mabbe's *Spanish Bawd* was not registered with the Stationers' Company until thirty-two years later. It did not take the town by storm. About two years after it appeared, Henry Reynolds was referring to the "trifling though extolled *Celestina*,"[10] and in 1634 the unsold copies were bound with a new edition of the more successful *Rogue*. Apparently no second edition of Mabbe's *Bawd* was ever called for. Although Captain John Stevens went back to the old story to make a tale called *The Bawd of Madrid*, which he published in *The*

Angeles, 1955], p. viii). Otis H. Green, carefully filling in the historical-literary background, shows that scorn of marriage was simply a conventional part of *amor-gentileza* ("Courtly Love in the Spanish *Cancioneros*," PMLA, LXIV [1949], 247–301).

7. *Anglo-Spanish Relations in Tudor Literature* (Berne, 1956), p. 35. Ungerer adds that "The intention of producing this new play would go back as early as 1569/70, if we identify it as *The most famous History of ij Spanesshe lovers* which was licensed at that date" (p. 36). Ungerer's chapter on "The 'Celestina' in England," pp. 9–41, is full of helpful data, but see also Gerard J. Brault's more conservative "English Translations of the *Celestina* in the Sixteenth Century," HR, XXVIII (1960), 301–312.

8. Edward Arber, ed. (London, 1875), II, 575.

The Delightful History of Celestina the Faire appeared in 1596, but tells the story of a princess of Thessaly who should not be confused with the old Spanish witch. Brault has discovered that this work is an unauthorized version of Bk. II of *Palmerín de Oliva* (p. 306).

One might add that in 1599 John Minsheu's *Spanish Grammar* extracted more words, phrases, and sentences from the *Celestina* than from any other work but the *Diana*.

9. Arber, ed., *A Transcript of the Registers of the Company of Stationers of London* (London, 1876), III, 127.

10. "Mythomystes," in *Critical Essays of the Seventeenth Century*, ed. Joel Elias Spingarn (Oxford, 1908), I, 146.

Spanish Libertines (1707), and although John Savage pilfered Mabbe's version in order to make a play in 1708, *The Spanish Bawd* seems to have been pretty much forgotten.[11]

The richly ornamented style of Mabbe's translation would have been more fashionable in Elizabeth's time. Perhaps this had something to do with the book's reception. Although Mabbe did not follow his source slavishly, as we shall see, he did retain and even enhance its highly rhetorical qualities, a point which is important here because students sometimes have tended to brush aside the *Tragicomedia*'s flowers of rhetoric in order to examine the picaresque brambles beneath. Rojas himself was greatly interested in style. Mabbe knew this, and Rastell before him had known it, and William G. Crane has tried to remind readers of today that

hardly any production in Renaissance literature is more elaborately embroidered with rhetorical ornament. It is farced with rhetorical devices of all kinds. Figures of syntax and words, such as, antithesis, repetition, translacing, and chiasma, are frequent. The rhetorical devices most characteristic of the romances and sentimental novels, those which depend upon appeal to the emotions, are abundant. The most prevalent of these are exclamation, interrogation, apostrophe, prosopopoeia, doubt, and concession. *Celestina,* contrary to what one might expect of a work of the sort, is thickly strewn with figures of thought, such as, proverbs, causes, similes, contraries, examples, and testimony of the ancients.[12]

Of course pedantry and a strained style are sometimes the spoiling vices of writers, and admittedly the parade of learning in both the *Celestina* and the *Bawd* is occasionally less than a virtue. In Act I the servant Sempronio prattles on about Nero, Nimrod, Alexander, Pasiphae, Minerva, Seneca, and Aristotle. But at worst such things are merely trappings of the time. At best, they actually serve to enhance what now seem to be the better qualities of the book. When Rojas (and, of course, Mabbe) has Calisto rhapsodizing over the glories of Melibea, he succeeds not only in displaying his own rhetorical virtuosity, but in conveying something of the character of Calisto. Moreover, the book has correctives for its own excesses. For example,

11. Recent interest among English-speaking students has been keen. Aside from many scholarly studies one now has not only the editions of Mabbe's translation by Fitzmaurice-Kelly (1894) and H. Warner Allen (1908 and 1923), but various original translations by Lesley Byrd Simpson (1955), Mack Hendricks Singleton (1958), and Phyllis Hartnoll (1959).

12. *Wit and Rhetoric in the Renaissance* (New York, 1937), p. 164. P. E. Russell thinks that "linguistic considerations as much as any others" led Mabbe to translate the *Celestina* ("A Stuart Hispanist: James Mabbe," *BHS,* XXX [1953], 82).

Sempronio is allowed to make dry comments and asides when Calisto is practicing his emotional scales. "What lyes and fooleries will my captiued Master now tell me," Sempronio asks in one place.[13] At another he laughs outright, ironically assuring Calisto that, oh yes, Melibea is a goddess—at any rate "As Goddesses were of old, that is, to fall below mortality, and then you would hope to haue a share in her deity."[14] By his response, Calisto assures us that he is not a puppet but a love-sick young man. "A poxe on thee for a foole," he exclaims; "thou makest mee laugh, which I thought not to doe to day."[15] The work, then, gains in vitality and strength not merely because its author and translator have mastered the art of verbal embroidery, and not merely because it is one of the great works of Spanish realism, but because it combines life and art in a literary whole.

Mabbe's version of the prologue and his dedication to Sir Thomas Richardson are interesting on several counts. For example, there is the old-fashioned style which Mabbe uses to express his own original thoughts. To imagine the esteem he must have had for the rhetoricians' art one need only turn to a single sentence on the *Celestina:*

It is not as many of your Pamphlets be, like a tree without sap; a bough without frut; a nut without a kernell; flesh without bones; bones without marrow; prickles without a Rose; waxe without honey; straw without wheate; sulfure without Gold; or shels without pearle.[16]

Obviously this might do equally well for any number of books. Another matter of interest is Mabbe's attitude toward the *Celestina*'s subject and style. He affirms that "Our Author is but short, yet pithy: not so full of words as sense. . . ."[17] And for all of Rojas' rhetoric, this is, to a degree, true enough. As Mabbe observes later on, the *Celestina* "is so concisely significant, and indeede so differing is the Idiome of the Spainish from the English, that I may imitate, [*sic*] it but not come neere it."[18] One quality of Spanish that virtually always is lost in English translations is concision, and the loss is particularly magnified in Mabbe's case because of his inclination toward euphuism. Of still greater interest, perhaps, is Mabbe's comment on the

13. *The Spanish Bawd* (1631), p. 9.
14. *Bawd*, p. 6.
15. *Bawd*, p. 6.
16. *Bawd*, A3ᵛ. It is hard to take him seriously, for he has just attacked "affected guildings of *Rhetorick*."
17. *Bawd*, A3.
18. *Bawd*, A5ʳ.

subject matter of the book. He advises that "when wee reade the filthy actions of whores, . . . wee are neither to approue them as good, nor to imbrace them as honest, but to commend the Authors iudgement in expressing his Argument so fit and pat to their dispositions."[19] Here is one of the relatively early points in the history of English criticism at which both realism and art for its own sake begin to seem important.

Admitting that Mabbe's work is a "brilliant achievement," Helen Phipps Houck has proceeded to demonstrate the many ways in which it differs from its source. Mabbe, she says, completely alters Rojas' style, which she characterizes as "sober, stark, forcible, intense, and concentrated."[20] Her chief aim, however, is to demonstrate that when it comes to Rojas' references to the Bible, religion, the church, or church doctrine, Mabbe with few exceptions "secularizes, classicizes, or expurgates."[21] Among other problems which confronted Mabbe was how to dispose of God.

He does it rather thoroughly, managing to eliminate all but seventeen of the literally hundreds of occurrences of the word in the original. The majestic God of fifteenth-century Spain frisks through Mabbe's pages as Cupid; he also takes the form of Jove, Jupiter, Mars, even Pluto; fate, fortune, destiny, heaven, Divine Essence, the deity, ye happy powers that predominate human actions, nature, the devil, the wind that blows. . . .[22]

19. *Bawd*, A4.
20. "Mabbe's Paganization of the *Celestina*," *PMLA*, LIV (1939), 422–423.
21. Houck, p. 424.
22. Houck, pp. 425–426. In view of such changes one wonders why, after making sure that Calisto goes to the myrtle grove to invoke the aid of Cupid (p. 101), Mabbe makes the slip of saying later that he has gone to church. In fact Parmeno even specifies that Calisto has gone to St. Mary Magdalene's (p. 109). Equally puzzling is Celestina's cry at the time of her murder, "Confession, Confession" (p. 147). Not only is her next cry for confession subverted to a non-sectarian "Oh, Oh, Oh!" but, equally interesting, all references to confession at the time of Calisto's death are suppressed. Did Mabbe slip, and, if so, why? Is it likely that he would have done such things when making his initial translation, when his eyes and mind would be most alert to details? Perhaps when he found himself in linguistic difficulties he turned to the French version, and, in so doing, forgot what had come shortly before. Then again, possibly in revising some lost ur-*Bawd* (did Mabbe himself have the 1598 Stationers' entry made?), he might have changed some details and failed to notice that still others would be necessary for consistency. (Fitzmaurice-Kelly, in his edition, p. xxxiv, notes Mabbe's use of a French translation; and Russell, "A Stuart Hispanist . . . ," p. 81, indicates that he also had recourse to an Italian one. The *Celestina* had been translated to Italian by Alfonso de Ordóñez as early as 1505, and, following an anonymous French translation in Paris [1527], a second French version was made [from the Italian] by Jacques de Lavardin [1578].)

In a sense it is true, as Miss Houck says, that Mabbe "paganizes" his story
—though even in the original, old Pleberio is scarcely religious. It is true also
that Mabbe confuses the issue of locale, making his setting seem sometimes
to be England, sometimes Spain, and sometimes a sort of classical never-never
land. In short, it is true that he blurs Rojas' suggestion of what Locke calls
the "principle of individuation." Locke held that ideas are made general
when divorced from circumstances of time and place. Conversely, fictional
characters are more readily made to seem individual when particularized in
terms of time and place.[23] It is not that Rojas, even in the Spanish, tells us
the name of the city where his story occurs, but he does give us details in
keeping with the fact that Parmeno was reared in Celestina's house on the
bank of the river near the tanneries.[24] Could Mabbe have been insensitive to
this aspect of his original? What was the purpose of his changes? Miss
Houck concludes that he "set himself to erase the vertical line of the Middle
Ages completely, . . . to make it represent the Renaissance spirit as he felt
it."[25] With no real proof, one might better imagine Mabbe shaking his head
and answering simply, "The captive here hath her head shorn." Not living in
an age of freedom, and perhaps aiming for a wider public than he could
otherwise reach, he secularized, classicized, and expurgated.

Quite in keeping with the work as Mabbe has re-created it are such resourceful and unfettered expressions as "slibber-slabbers" for female frip-
peries; "*Tom*-tell-troth"; "trimme and tricksie"; "fiddle-come-faddles" for
silly delays; and "pecke of troubles." When Melibea is speaking to her
mother about Celestina's bad reputation, she asks disarmingly, "Is shee one
of those, you know what?" And when Calisto dies, Sosia, the groom, exclaims that "hee is as dead as a doore-nayle."[26] Mabbe not only has the vigor
and vitality one likes to regard as Elizabethan, but, despite his words in the
Bawd's dedication, he transmits the same sort of carefree enthusiasm that
is found in the other great translators of the age. It is not that he could not
translate reasonably accurately, for his Spanish was good. It is not that
he was hobbled by the French or Italian versions, both of which he may

23. Ian Watt, *The Rise of the Novel* (Los Angeles, 1957), pp. 21–26, comments on Locke in connection with this aspect of early fiction.

24. Gilman writes: "From the first moment after his return home when Calisto
calls for Sempronio . . . , we know that we are in a realm of physical space, a
realm of rooms, houses, and the streets around and between them" (p. 105). Gilman also touches on the subject of time.

25. Houck, p. 422.

26. *Bawd*, pp. 79, 85, 88, 94, 137, 125, and 189.

have consulted. It is simply that in *The Spanish Bawd* he managed to produce, instead of a close translation, a work both excellent and new.

As an example of how the conventions of a southern love story can be brought to life, consider the impressionistic definition which Mabbe's Celestina gives of love: "And delight," she says,

is with friends, in things that are sensuall; but especially in recounting matters of loue, and communicating them, the one to the other. This did I do my selfe; this such a one told me; such a iest did wee breake; in this sort did I winne her; thus often did I kisse her: thus often did shee bite mee; thus I imbraced her; thus came wee neerer and neerer. O what speech, what grace.[*sic*] what sport, what kisses! Let vs goe thither, Let vs returne hither, Let vs haue musick, Let vs paint Motto's, Let vs sing songs, Let vs inuent some pretty deuices; Let vs tilt it; What shall be the Impresse? What the letter to it? To morrow shee will walke abroad; Let vs round her streete; Read this her Letter; Let vs goe by night; Hold thou the ladder; Guard well the gate; How did shee escape thee? Looke, where the Cuckold her husband goes; I left her all alone; Let vs giue another turne; Let vs goe backe againe thither.[27]

I submit that Renaissance fiction does not offer many such convincing glimpses into the excitement that was felt by the young women who actually stood in moonlit balconies, and by the idle young men who strummed gitterns beneath them. Diego de San Pedro, writing at about the same time, certainly did not have the knack of conjuring up life. Juan de Flores did not have it. But the creator of the old mender of maidenheads did. Consequently Celestina, with her beard and scotched nose, went trailing the tail of her gown through the narrow Spanish streets, raising a dust and muttering to herself, and incidentally achieving immortality. Standing as she does with Lazarillo, Don Quixote, and Don Juan among the greatest figures in the literature of Spain, it is no small tribute to Mabbe to say that his English version does her justice.

The Rogue

Because Spain's native artistic impulses often incline toward the basic realities of everyday life, it seems only natural that some of the qualities of the *Celestina* are similar to those of seventeenth-century picaresque fic-

27. *Bawd*, p. 27.

tion.[28] Both depict and attack real life, and both, to a lesser and less obvious degree, mock the highflown ideals of other fiction. It is no great surprise, at least in looking back, that Rojas' *Celestina,* published a hundred years before Mateo Alemán's *Guzmán de Alfarache,* endows Calisto's servants with the acquisitiveness, hard humor, and mercurial undependability that are typical of the later *pícaros.*

First of the great successors of *Lazarillo de Tormes, Guzmán de Alfarache* scored a hit both at home and abroad. Because it was composed by a man who had once been a government official under Philip II, an upright man who had damaged his health and spent his wealth in trying to maintain his position, one who had early come in contact with jail life (his father was a prison doctor), and felt the weight of debt, imprisonment, unhappy marriage, and Jewish blood—because it was composed by such a man, *Guzmán* would seem to be good evidence for those who hold that a strong book is apt to be a projection of what has fermented within its author.[29] No matter how its details differ from those of Alemán's life, *Guzmán de Alfarache* is certainly both a strong book and one that is tinged with autobiography. In fact these may be two of the reasons for its popularity. Few Spanish works have ever had greater immediate success. It is ironic, then, that at the height of the fame of Part I, Alemán was imprisoned for debt.

Since he cut the thread of his story before his whole web was woven, Alemán might have expected that someone would be tempted to take over his task. The predictable sequel was turned out by one Juan Martí, a Valencian lawyer who used the pseudonym Mateo Luján de Sayavedra. Alemán responded with a sequel of his own, and in its final and authentic (though still unfinished) form his *Guzmán* came to be known and admired in many lands. As Chandler remarks, however, Alemán's "alleged preference for being a poor philosopher rather than a rich flatterer was to be gratified to the letter."[30]

28. Among the most helpful books on Spanish picaresque fiction are Frank W. Chandler's *Romances of Roguery* (New York, 1899) and Fonger de Haan's *An Outline of the History of the Novela Picaresca in Spain* (The Hague, 1903). See also Angel Valbuena Prat's valuable *La novela picaresca española* (Madrid, 1943).

29. Alemán was born in 1547 in Seville, the city where God presumably let the devil work most extensively. On his Jewish ancestry, which he tried to conceal, see Francisco Rodríguez Marín, "Documentos hasta ahora inéditos referentes a Mateo Alemán," *Boletín de la Academia Española,* XX (1933), 216.

30. *Romances of Roguery,* p. 215. Possibly not without cynicism he set out for the New World, where the fame of his book had preceded him. The exploits of both Guzmán and Don Quixote were widely known in the Spanish colonies, where

In England, *Guzmán* was published by Edward Blount as *The Rogue*. It was the first of James Mabbe's three important translations of Spanish fiction, and in this case Mabbe's timing was good. Men were more concerned about Spain in 1622 than they were to be again for many a year. They were reading *Don Quixote, The Pilgrime of Casteele, Gerardo,* and the new sequel to *Lazarillo,* and the fact that *The Rogue* was in expensive folio form did not prevent their reading it, too. The book was issued again in 1622–1623, 1623, 1630, 1633–1634, 1655, and 1656.[31] Praised by Edward Burton, Leonard Digges, and Ben Jonson (who thought it bore the "noblest marke of a good Booke"),[32] and accompanied by John Fletcher's assurance that the Spanish rogue came not as a spy, though he made war "against sinne,"[33] the work was dedicated to "Don" John Strangwayes, with whom Mabbe was later to make his home, and signed with the pen name Puede-Ser, together with the significant flourish, "de Santa *Maria Magdalena.*"

The translation's eponymous rogue, of course, is young Guzman (in English, unburdened by an accent), the offspring of a Levantine usurer and a Spanish whore. Early in his story, after his family background has been established, times turn so bad that the boy resolves to visit some relatives in Italy. At first his adventures on the road are rather like Lazarillo's. He is fed nearly hatched eggs at an inn, and later eats mule meat for veal. After a while, however, he falls in with some wayfarers, one of whom tells the very un-Lazarillian story of Ozmin and Daraxa, the first of those inserted narratives touched on in the preceding chapter. Accepting employment as a stableboy, he begins to learn the tricks of the hosteler's trade (for example, how to steep barley in warm water to make it heavy). According to Alemán, however, Guzman is not yet a *pícaro.* It is only after he becomes discontent as a stableboy that he resolves to take up the "Trade *de la Florida Picardia.*" Then he serves a cook, learns to gamble, becomes a porter, robs a grocer,

---

they won and held a public which apparently exceeded that of any other fiction. (See Irving A. Leonard, *"Guzmán de Alfarache* in the Lima Book Trade, 1613," *HR,* XI [1943], 210–220). In Mexico Alemán brought out two minor books, then died about 1614, some six years after arriving.

31. "Gusmans Spanish rogue" is also said to be among books "printed in Oxōn two or three yeares before this present yeare of our Lord. 1630," but I know of no other record of an edition about 1627–1628. (Cited from *The Diary of Thomas Crosfield,* ed. Frederick S. Boas [London, 1935], p. 38.) An epitome, noted later, appeared in 1655–1656.

32. *The Rogue* (1622), I, A4ᵛ.

33. *Rogue,* I, A4ʳ.

and makes his way to Genoa. Maltreated by his relatives there, he decides to join a band of beggars, and soon acquires a repertory of beggar's tricks. As a consequence of rubbing his leg with an herb that produces a canker as pretty as you please, he is taken into the service of a compassionate cardinal. But the cardinal can stomach only so many of Guzman's knavish pranks, so Guzman enters the service of the French ambassador. For a while he serves the latter gentleman as a pandering page, but then, once again, he is dismissed, this time following an untidy mishap with a pig. Next he meets and befriends a certain Sayavedra, a character created so that Alemán might have some fun with the author of the false sequel. (Sayavedra's brother is named Juan Martí, and Sayavedra himself, drowning, has the hallucination that he is Guzman.) Then, returning to Spain, he is suddenly, in a single paragraph, chained to a wife. After he has served some six years in the marriage galley—and Alemán has some very bitter words for women—the rogue gains a widower's freedom and decides to pursue his formal education. For several years he lives virtuously at Alcalá, and is even ready to enter the priesthood when, throwing over his studies and plans, he suddenly marries a second time. Since other men are attracted to his new wife, and since he quickly learns when it is impolitic to be home, he and his helpmate become well-to-do. Then times grow bad again. Although his mother does her bit by acting the part of Celestina for her daughter-in-law, the girl eventually runs off with the captain of a galley. Guzman's last tumbling partner is a faithful "mulatta" slave, one whose favors he is still enjoying when the authorities finally carry him off, first to jail and then to a galley. In the closing scenes on shipboard he has some bleak moments. (He must, we are told, kiss the wads of rags and flax before passing them out to those who need them.) But at last he repents all his sins and is converted overnight, assuring the reader that he is now "so quite altred from that I was before, that I would rather suffer my selfe to be torne in a thousand pieces, then to commit any the least crime in the world."[34] Here the book ends. Since his punishments on shipboard give his conversion something of an expiatory quality, it is probably just as well that the promised third part of his story never appeared. In any case, not even Alemán could have imagined a good Guzman for more than a few paragraphs.

A summary as brief as this can do little more than convey a general impression of the kind of incidents found in the book. It is not so good for

---

34. *Rogue* (1623), II, 353.

suggesting Alemán's cynical tone. Equally or more important—and this brings to light a bone that critics have gnawed and nibbled for many a year —it ignores the great amount of moralizing in the book.

Alemán quite frankly admits that he does not cleave to his story. "I Haue made a long and a tedious digression," he says after one of his earlier sermons, "and am well witting thereof to my selfe. But I would not haue thee make it a matter of wonder; for the necessitie that enforced me therevnto, was very great."[35] In one place, as Miguel Herrero García has shown, he does not shrink from copying a passage verbatim from Alejo de Venegas' *Agonía del tránsito de la muerte*.[36] In another place he shows his hand still more clearly: "When shall I make an end of troubling thee with these, and the like discourses?" he asks ironically.

I know thou doest not looke for these Sermons from me, nor any other kinde of wholsome doctrine, but expectest only such things, as may serue to entertaine the time, or to bring thee asleepe. I doe not know how to excuse this terrible temptation, that I haue to talke in this fashion. . . .[37]

Alemán himself, then, raises the question of whether his sermons are out of keeping with his narrative. Peter N. Dunn's response is that

In this amazing work the analysis, the self-examination, the moral discourses do not impede the aesthetic effect of the work; in fact they rescue it from the futility and frivolity which permeate . . . so many other novels of the picaresque type. . . . Adventure and moralizing are complementary, directed towards a common end.[38]

James Mabbe, though, putting his own Spanish style to use, declares that the converted-rogue author aims at two targets by different approaches, giving us to understand one thing by his words and the opposite by his deeds.[39] Where Dunn emphasizes unity, Mabbe emphasizes duality. Mabbe does more. Although he does not himself agree, he says that some readers have

---

35. *Rogue*, I, 122.

36. "Nueva interpretación de la novela picaresca," *RFE*, XXIV (1937), 351. Not that Alemán tried to fool anyone on this score. In his introduction he confesses that *"These Arrowes are not all of mine owne Quiuer, nor this honey that I set before thee, all of mine owne hiue; much of their sweetnesse did I sucke from holy and learned men . . ."* (*Rogue*, I, *6ᵛ).

37. *Rogue*, II, 110.

38. *Castillo Solórzano and the Decline of the Spanish Novel* (Oxford, 1952), p. 7. Angel Valbuena Prat regards the fusion of doctrine and story as perfect (p. xxi), as does Julio Cejador y Frauca (*Historia de la lengua y literatura castellana* [Madrid, 1916], IV, 135).

39. *Rogue*, I, *2ᵛ.

complained that the subject matter of the book is confused and ill-digested (*maldigesto*).

Since it is clear at the outset that we are dealing with a dichotomous work, the real problem is whether the dichotomy is resolved into an artistic unity or whether the book remains dichotomous, with each major element at artistic odds with the other. Dunn and Mabbe hold the first view, and still other critics the second. Américo Castro, one of the latter, observes that

Mateo Alemán resorts to the trick of giving the events he relates a false perspective, false because its connection with them is not organic but forced and abstract. For example, after the anecdote of the omelet made with nearly-hatched eggs, and after the innkeeper's wife is sadistically punished . . . , the author launches into a theological and moral digression: "We are told in the Gospel according to St. Matthew, chapter five, and in St. Luke, chapter six: 'Forgive your enemies, and do good to those who hate you.'" In another case, after the reader is informed of the trickery of some pseudo-maidens, he is asked to consider "how devoutly, justly and reasonably the Council of Trent legislated regarding secret marriages". . . .[40]

Here, says Castro, artistry fails to reconcile the disparate elements which the author presents.

Good though it is in many respects, it seems to me that Alemán's book does lack that unifying tension which may be achieved in art with disparate elements. Because of their handling, the two chief components of *The Rogue*—narrative and moralizing—are at artistic odds, even though their purpose is complementary. First, as Castro implies, the story does not palpitate in the background while Alemán moralizes. Second, both the story and the sermon are set aside for the inserted *novelas*. And third, there is a weakening of some of the coherence which is possible in works where a narrator acts in his own story; since the book pretends to be the memoirs of its protagonist, and Alemán is thus prevented from moralizing in his own person, Guzman-narrator is reduced to admitting that sometimes his subject matter is "fitter to bee discussed by a *Preacher,* then a *Picaro.*"[41]

40. "The Prefaces to *Don Quixote*," PQ, XXI (1942), 71.
41. *Rogue*, I, 121. H. W. Allen describes the hero of *Guzmán* as "a composite monster, at one moment the respectable Alemán himself, at the next the embodiment of all that shocks him" (p. xlii). Enrique Moreno Báez believes the narrative and doctrinal elements are better fused in Pt. II ("¿Hay una tesis en el 'Guzmán de Alfarache'?" *Revista de la Universidad de Buenos Aires*, Ser. 3, Vol. III [1945], p. 271).

Despite its undeniable virtues, *The Rogue* would probably be more effective fiction without its overt moralizing. In the best satirical writing— and one ceases to have picaresque fiction if one leaves out the barbs—the desirable norms which the satirist would have us strive for are generally implied. To the extent that the satirist must look up from his story, take off his glasses, and say "Now what I *really* mean is thus-and-so," he undermines his efforts and deprives his reader of an important intellectual pleasure. The author of *Lazarillo* had let the facts themselves condemn his victims, and his book had gained in compression and force.

This is not to intimate that Alemán's form is altogether inartistic or nonfunctional. On the contrary, the relationship of form and meaning, important with regard to any fiction, is particularly significant with regard to both *The Rogue* and some of the other narratives that we are now approaching. As Arnold Kettle says, the form of any fiction enhances significance "in so far as it bears a real relation to, that is to say symbolizes or clarifies, the aspect of life that is being conveyed."[42] He goes on to say, however, not only that picaresque stories have haphazard form, but that this form lacks central significance. I hold that the form of narration in the Spanish picaresque novels, haphazard though it is, is capable of enhancing their significance. In these stories—and here I am switching the focus to include a larger area than the problem of relating action to sermon—a man's life is a chaotic series of events, a heap of broken images. "In and out," says Chandler, "the shuttlecock of fate bore the picaro, weaving his story in haphazard design. . . ."[43] But as Chandler also says, the real protagonist is not so much the *pícaro* as the world about him. In Castro's words, it is a world "which stubbornly affirms its unreality, its mere appearance in the face of the madman who tries to find a solider base in it."[44] In *Lazarillo* we saw an equivocal world in which values were dependent on external appearance, values epitomized in a toothpick or a secondhand fustian doublet. In *The Rogue* we see a kaleidoscopic world of false wives, false servants, false friends. "For, as a mans apparell

42. *An Introduction to the English Novel* (London, 1954), I, 15–16.
43. *Romances of Roguery*, p. 62.
44. *The Structure of Spanish History*, tr. Edmund L. King (Princeton, 1954), p. 452. Although Chandler makes the good observation that the rogue in life is a product of decadence, and the rogue in literature a protest against it (p. 42), Castro's ideas are more subtle than Chandler's. In brilliant fashion Castro analyzes the difficult problem of why picaresque writers depicted life as they did. Brief but also pertinent is R. A. del Piero's "The Picaresque Philosophy in 'Guzmán de Alfarache,' " *MLF*, XLII (1957), 152–156.

is, so is his esteeme," we are told.[45] And again: "All goes topsie-turuy; all Kim, Kam; all, is tricks and deuices; all Riddles and vnknowne Mysteries. . . ."[46] Alemán, in other words, is apparently concerned with things not for their own sake, but to show that they are not what they seem. It is therefore reasonable to think that the picaresque form he has chosen is no less satisfactorily symbolic of man's fragmented, illusory world than are the patches on the fool's costume, which symbolize the fragmented world of the fool. Despite their vast differences, Alemán, like the authors of the *Celestina, Lazarillo,* and *Don Quixote,* depicts life less in the "stable, ideal reality of the ought-to-be" than in the "problematical reality of its existence," and, perhaps adventitiously, the picaresque form helps to clarify his meaning.[47]

Both "ought-to-be" and "meaning," never so explicit in these three other works, are conveyed more directly in Alemán's moralizing. Doing all that he can to illustrate man's limitations and corruption, Alemán turns ultimately to the absolutes of the church. Through the autobiography of a regenerate sinner, he successfully exposes the confused, sordid, phantasmagorical world of everyday man, where things are judged by nonessentials, and then he goes on to offer hope. *"Blessed be the Name of the Lord,"* Guzman is told; "For euen in *Rogues* there is some vertue, some sparke of goodnesse; and this in thee shall bee thy Light."[48] Miguel Herrero García goes so far as to suggest that we have in Alemán's book the answer of the Counter-Reformation Spanish renaissance to the man-centered, pagan Italian renaissance.[49] Possibly so. It is interesting, at any rate, to think of Guzman as a sort of baroque

45. *Rogue,* II, 168.
46. *Rogue,* I, 128.
47. Castro, *Structure,* p. 397, uses these two suggestive phrases in his discussion of the *Libro de buen amor,* by Juan Ruiz, Archpriest of Hita.
48. *Rogue,* I, 119.
49. "Nueva interpretación . . . ," p. 353. This scholar has indicated the similarity between picaresque literature and religious reform writing. Also illuminating are Stephen Gilman's words on Counter-Reformation leaders: "To obtain converts, they must first convince them of the unsatisfactory nature of mundane existence and then demonstrate to them logically that acceptance of the Church was the only effective antidote" ("An Introduction to the Ideology of the Baroque in Spain," *Symposium,* I [1946], 93). It is necessary to recognize, too, the views of men such as Samuel Gili y Gaya, who believes that the moralizing is not the most significant part of the book, either with regard to the artistic effect or the author's intent. The narrative, he says, is the backbone ("Apogeo y desintegración de la novela picaresca," in *Historia general de las literaturas hispánicas,* ed. Guillermo Díaz-Plaja [Barcelona, 1953], Vol. III, p. VI).

Everyman. As Mabbe's friend Edward Burton puts it, *"Guzman,* is all the World. . . ."[50]

In the English translation, Mabbe gave his countrymen a real treat. Knowing him to have been one of the most articulate Hispanists of his day, however, one may be surprised to learn that the second part of his book contains passages that occur in none of the Spanish editions. Citing a handful of convincing passages, Fitzmaurice-Kelly concludes that Mabbe rendered Part II from Barezzo Barezzi's Italian translation.[51] In 1621, at the time *The Rogue*

50. *Rogue,* II, **7ᵛ. P. E. Russell, in "English Seventeenth-Century Interpretations of Spanish Literature," *Atlante,* I (1953), 72, protests the view that the novel is concerned with championing a purely Catholic thesis. Thinking particularly of the views of Enrique Moreno Báez (expressed in "¿Hay una tesis . . . ?" and *Lección y sentido del Guzmán de Alfarache* [Madrid, 1948]), and citing as evidence *The Rogue's* popularity in England, Russell writes:

> The greater part of the Christian moral doctrines whose truth is expounded in this novel were as acceptable to Anglican Englishmen—perhaps even to those of a more Calvinistic turn of mind—as they were to post-Tridentine Spanish Catholics. As for the occasions, relatively very few, when the backsliding Guzmán expressed opinions known to be at variance with Protestant teaching, doubtless Mabbe and his readers reflected that, after all, he was a Spaniard.

This is in keeping with the findings of James Russell Stamm ("Didactic and Moral Elements in the Spanish Picaresque Novel," unpublished Ph.D. dissertation [Stanford, 1959], p. 193), who says of *Guzmán:*

> The narrative element is in fact a series of instances of human error constructed to provide occasions for ethical discourse. The purpose behind Alemán's work is to provide an ethical guidebook to contemporary problems and experience, to give dramatic instances of possible human choice, and to show the predictable outcome of morally wrong choices. . . .
>
> That scholastic theology had failed to meet . . . popular needs is . . . evidenced by the successful emergence of major religious movements in the sixteenth century: the Protestant Reformation, the Counter Reformation, the Society of Jesus, and the revival of mystic theology. *Guzmán de Alfarache* supplements organized religious innovations by providing a secular morality based upon the experience of one man exposed to many facets of the society of his time.

Even tolerant readers were probably taken aback, however, to find Mabbe writing, "O *Spaine, Spaine,* my beloued Countrey, Faith's true keeper, God vphold thee with his hand . . ." (*Rogue,* I, 210). John Donne, in the following year, wrote thus of Spanish theologians: "Their authors in Divinity, though they do not show us the best way to Heaven, yet they think they do. And so, though they say not true, yet they do not lie, because they speak their conscience" (cited by Russell, pp. 67–68).

51. *Rogue,* tr. Mabbe, ed. Fitzmaurice-Kelly (London, 1924), I, xxxii–xxxvi. As Fitzmaurice-Kelly notes, "his use of an Italian text is not incompatible—as things were in his day—with qualities of loyalty. He was a scholar and a gentleman. It would be ridiculous to impeach his honesty of purpose" (I, xxxvi).

was being written, "This languag'd Man," as one friend called him, certainly knew Spanish.[52] Not only had he spent a number of years in Spain, but he included a Spanish dedication in this very work, and enriched the whole with dozens of explanatory notes translated directly from Covarrubias' *Tesoro de la lengua española* (1611). Possibly after returning to England he simply had difficulty laying hands on a Spanish copy of *Guzmán,* and, having rendered Part I, had to content himself with any version he could find of Part II. Fitzmaurice-Kelly postulates that some time later he gained access to the Spanish text and one of the French translations, and with these as aids touched up his work.

Whatever the process, the result is one of the notable prose monuments of a century known for its prose. In *The Rogue* as in *The Spanish Bawd,* Mabbe's style is broad and colorful, more so than that of his source. For instance, in describing rogues, he writes thus:

in blearing the sight, and picking a mans purse before his face, some haue the soule and conscience of your Gypsies, and will make of Iustice a matter of iuggling, with a hye passe, and a repasse, come off *Iacke* with a whim-wham; ordering things so, as they shall thinke good, and may make most for their profit.

The pages at the cardinal's home are "beetle-heads, dull-spirited fellowes, that had no wherry in them." Even "Necessity" is exuberantly described. She is "fierce, foule, fantasticke, furious, fastidious, faint, facile, feeble, false: only she failes of being a *Franciscan.*" Fortunately such unfettered fancies are not frequent enough to fatigue one. For the most part the prose is in keeping with the matter, and more often than not it is a fitting medium for the serious as well as the lighter parts of Alemán's book. Nothing could be simpler than this: "Twenty yeares of age, is a terrible beast: O how headstrong, and how wild it is."[53] Yet it has a rightness which rewording can only mar. Mabbe, to be sure, did make use of intermediaries; he did write more broadly and briskly, more genially, than Alemán; and he did expand a book which needed no expanding. Nevertheless, his *Rogue* deserves to be known as one of the best translations of its day.

In the two-part epitome of the book (1655–1656), an anonymous writer took Mabbe's version, removed practically everything but the plot, and produced a *Rogue* far different from Mabbe's, even more different from Alemán's, and yet, withal, fairly good reading.[54] Condensation itself is a

52. *Rogue,* II, **7ʳ.
53. *Rogue,* I, 8, 229, 190; II, 100.
54. The book is dedicated to "E. F." by "S. S."

hint of popularity, but more direct are the words of the publisher, Philip Chetwind, who claims that *The Rogue* up to that time has been *"much read, [and] as much liked."*[55] His statement is supported by a number of facts. Not only had there been several editions between 1622 and 1655, but in about 1633 Henry Reynolds praised the work for its wit, as did Thomas Nash in the same year.[56] In 1638 William Chillingworth found it sufficiently inoffensive to be quoted in his *Religion of Protestants,* and even the Archbishop of Canterbury owned a copy.[57]

Such a well-known book was bound to be influential. Seemingly the earliest English work inspired by the story of Guzmán was *The Little French Lawyer* (*ca.* 1619–1623), by Mabbe's friend Fletcher and Philip Massinger. In 1638 a translation of a Spanish work having nothing to do with Alemán was significantly disguised as *The Sonne of the Rogue.* A subsequent title of the same work—*Guzman, Hind and Hannam Outstript* (1657)—was another attempt to remind readers of Mabbe's book. Then, too, there were George Fidge's *English Gusman* (1652) and *The English Rogue Described in the Life of Meriton Latroon,* begun by Richard Head (1665), taken up by Francis Kirkman (1668), and continued by both (1671). (A fair measure of this last work may be taken from Kirkman's admission that among his reasons for writing, the "first and cheifest was to gain ready money.")[58] Springing from various sources and swelling the list still more were such stories as *The French Rogue* (1672), *The Dutch Rogue, or Guzman of Amsterdam* (1683), and *Teague O'Dively, or The Irish Rogue* (1690), and a number of plays—Thomas Porter's *A Witty Combat* (1663) and *The French Conjurer* (1678), Roger Boyle's *Guzman* (1669), and Thomas Duffet's *The Spanish*

---

55. *Rogue* (1656) I, unsigned leaf preceding A1.

56. Reynolds, "Mythomystes," p. 146. Nash (not to be confused with the more famous Thomas Nashe) makes his allusion in *Quaternio* (1633), quoted by Louis B. Wright, *Middle-Class Culture in Elizabethan England* (Chapel Hill, N. C., 1935), p. 407.

57. First reference noted by Douglas Bush, *English Literature in the Earlier Seventeenth Century* (Oxford, 1948), p. 53, and second by Ann Cox-Johnson, "Lambeth Palace Library 1610–1664," *Transactions of the Cambridge Bibliographical Society,* II (1954–1958), 109.

58. *The English Rogue* (1680), verso of leaf following title page. Chandler saw the book as "a mere debased copy that stole right and left three fourths of its matter from what was of least worth in its models. That it failed to reproduce more than the crudities was due to the brutality of its authors." In a word, it is "inferior in every way to the Spanish novels," though it amply attests their influence (*The Literature of Roguery* [Boston, 1907], I, 212, 214).

Rogue (1672–1673). Even if concerned chiefly with other problems, therefore, one may find enough clues strewn about to suggest that Mabbe's translation was among the well-known books of its time. Certainly it deserved to be.

The Pursuit of the Historie of Lazarillo de Tormez

I n the 1653 edition of *Lazarillo* there is to be found one of the rare early criticisms of Alemán's book. The initials "T. P." are appended to a poem which concludes thus:

> *No length with LAZARO prevails*
> *Till th' Readers eyes grow dim,*
> *GUZMAN & his Long-winded tales*
> *Are SPANISH ROGUES to him.*[59]

T. P. has a valid point. Even when accompanied by Juan de Luna's sequel, the *Lazarillo* is only about ten or fifteen per cent as long as Alemán's book.

Juan de Luna's *Segunda parte de la vida de Lazarillo de Tormes* had appeared first in Paris in 1620, and was translated into English only two years later.[60] As we have already seen, Luna was a Spaniard engaged in teaching Spanish in London. Though he recently had come over via Paris, he seems to have been originally from Aragon.[61] Furthermore, we have his own word for it that he left homeland, relatives, and property for a just and legitimate cause.[62] What this cause may have been, we do not know. The views in his *Pursuit of the Historie of Lazarillo de Tormez* are consonant with the guess that he required more religious freedom than Spain could afford him. In contrast to Alemán's book, Luna's is full of jabs at the clergy. For instance, he has the mother-in-law of a holy hermit inform Lazarillo that she has had three daughters by three fathers, "who (to the neerest coniecture) were a Monke, an Abbot, and a Priest, for I haue bin alwayes much deuoted vnto the Church."[63] Then, too, he may have left Spain with pecuniary motives. At

59. *Lazarillo,* Y7ʳ.

60. It was dedicated, incidentally, to the Hispanophilic friend of Donne and Drummond, Robert Carr (or Kerr) of Ancrum, who attended Prince Charles in Spain the next year.

61. José M.ª de Cossío, "Las continuaciones del *Lazarillo de Tormes,*" RFE, XXV (1941), 518.

62. *A Short and Compendious Art for to Learne . . . the Spanish Tongue* (1623), A4ʳ.

63. *Pursuit* (1622), p. 180.

the time he was living in France there was a great demand for both language teachers and language aids such as his *Diálogos familiares,* published in Paris in 1619.[64] In the following year, also in Paris, he brought out another textbook, a revision of the old *Lazarillo,* together with his own new sequel.[65] Perhaps in 1621 he arrived in London. In 1622, at any rate, there appeared not only the English version of his continuation, but also a translation of his dialogues;[66] and before another year had passed, a grammar which he had written in Spanish was translated, at his direction, as *A Short and Compendious Art for to Learne . . . the Spanish Tongue.* (It is in this bilingual text, by the way, that he identifies himself as a teacher of Spanish in London.) In other words, although we know relatively little about him, it at least seems sure that he was ready to take full advantage of both French and English interest in Spain.

If his sequel to *Lazarillo* was motivated in part by pedagogy, profit, and (one supposes) the hope to entertain, it also appears, like its original, to have had traditional, social, and literary inspiration. That the story was in part traditional is intimated by Luna himself. He says, *"I haue heard it a hundred times told by my Grandmother, and Aunts, by the Fires side in the Winter nights. . . ."*[67] According to Elmer Richard Sims, the book is constituted of "borrowings from all sides," including tradition, and Luna shows "considerable ingenuity in weaving the various threads into an artistic whole. . . ."[68] The whole, one must add, is sardonic. Luna's episodes, like those of the original *Lazarillo,* are implicit commentaries on society, especially on pseudo-religious hypocrisy. Yet Luna's prime inspiration, or so he claims, was literary. *"THe occasion . . . of Printing the Second Part of* Lazarillo de Tormes *hath beene, that there came to my hands a little*

64. This was a teaching manual for which Luna was indebted to Minsheu, and Minsheu to Stepney (see above, Ch. II).

65. Intending both sections to serve as new texts for his students, Luna modernized the old *Lazarillo* completely, removing what he considered an infinity of wretched words, constructions, and phrases. Actually the original demonstrates a fine use of idiomatic Spanish, but language changes were fairly rapid at the time, and by Luna's day the original *Lazarillo* doubtless seemed dated.

66. The latter appeared in a translation from César Oudin called *A Grammar Spanish and English.* According to a letter I have received from L. W. Hanson, Keeper of Printed Books at the Bodleian, *STC* 16926 (Luna's *Dialogues Spanish and English*) is a ghost. The Oudin-Luna volume is correctly entered as *STC* 18897.

67. *Pursuit,* A6ᵛ.

68. Ed., *La segunda parte de la vida de Lazarillo de Tormes* (Austin, Texas, 1928), p. xvii.

Pamphlet, which treats of his Life, without any likelyhood of truth." This refers to the work Englished by Phiston in 1596. Says Luna with distaste: *"The greatest part of it is stufft, with telling how* Lazaro *fell into the Sea, where he was turned into a Fish called a Tunny. . . ."*[69]

Luna capitalizes on the first sequel's shipwreck of Lazarillo, but then proceeds to quite a different series of events. According to his version, Lazarillo is rescued from the sea in the net of some fishermen, and then held captive and displayed through the country as a sort of sea monster. When he is finally taken to Toledo to be exhibited, he finds that his pregnant wife is just about to be married to another man, thanks to the efforts of the same archpriest who had procured her for Lazarillo in the original story. Lazarillo swoons at the news and is thought to be dead. In fact he is being carried to the river to be disposed of when he comes to and is rescued.

The book then sets off on a new tack. Lazarillo brings suit against his wife and the archpriest, loses all his money in the process, and finally must content himself with escaping to Madrid as a beggar. Here he sets himself up as a porter, has a number of misadventures with some lusty young folk and gypsies, and becomes a "Gentleman-Usher" to a flock of women, each of whom is too poor to afford an attendant for herself. At length, disgusted with humanity and without his last few teeth (it has long been his lot to lose teeth in beatings), he resolves to take up a more retired life. As luck would have it, he finds himself heir to the riches of a pious old hermit, including the latter's wench, and in the final scene, having been cozened by this quean, he is tied naked to a bed and threatened with gelding. While the reader holds his breath, however, Lazarillo manages to break loose and escape to a church. Here, like Guzman and Gerardo, he resolves to end his days in peace and quiet.

More plump and sophisticated than the anonymous first part, this fine little medley of mischief carries the reader along quickly through a variety of episodes, cleverly inserting a number of references to the *picaro's* early career. The only echo-sequence which clearly falls flat is that in which Lazarillo meets again the squire he once served in Toledo; the prideful, dignified squire of the first part is disappointingly converted here to a low and thieving rogue. In fact, none of the characterizations in the continuation—

---

69. *Pursuit,* A6ʳ. Another kind of source which Luna pretends is *"certain Scroules kept in the Treasurie of Records of the Beggars of* Toledo . . ." (A6ᵛ).

not even that of Lazarillo—measures up to the chief ones in the first part.[70] Luna's book is also different in that it places a greater emphasis on sex, a matter explained partly, perhaps, by its French provenance, and partly by Lazarillo's having passed beyond puberty at the outset. Furthermore, where the original story is mordantly humorous, Luna's sequel seems strident and ribald. As for similarities, Luna's lively mind, his ability to turn a phrase, his scorn for religious hypocrisy, and his love of a good laugh make his book alive and sprightly, just as the original *Lazarillo* had been. One can scarcely carp about a work which is so skilfully executed, and least of all because it fails to reproduce the dry, cutting tone of its model. After all, its special vitality is inseparable from Luna's own view of life.

The title page of the 1622 translation declares that the book is *"By* IEAN DE LVNA, *a Castilian. And now done into English,* and set forth by the same Author." The Stationers' Register concurs. The *Pursuit* is "By JEAN DE LUNA of Casteile, And by him Done into English."[71] It would appear, then, that the book is a unique example of a Spanish story translated into English by its original author. For three reasons one may be doubtful. First, the translation is more smooth than might be expected of a new arrival in the country. Consider such a random passage as that in which Lazarillo, "more content then a starued Cat with Gibblets," offers his services as a porter to a young girl "that simpered more than a new vayled Nun." After he has carried her bundle and asked to be paid, the "Rag-taile answered, That I wil very willingly; and with that, lifting vp her hand, she gaue me such a Boxe on the eare, that shee felled me to the ground, saying, Art thou such an Asse, as to aske Money of one of my Profession?" And "With that (as nimbly as a Grasse-hopper) shee leaped into the Waggon, and away she went. . . ."[72] These details all appear in the original, but here they are rendered, I think, with the skill of a true-born Englishman. A second hint that Luna is not the translator is that someone else, at about the same time, translated both his *Diálogos* and his Spanish grammar. Finally, in his own dedication, which is written in Spanish, one finds the contradictory words that Luna has *had* the work faithfully and literally rendered in order that it

70. Chandler, however, believes that the continuation is an advance over the latter because the anti-hero, not society, is of prime importance (*Romances of Roguery*, p. 285).

71. (London, 1877), IV, 83.

72. *Pursuit*, pp. 76–79.

might manifest its harmlessness and be known as a book in which there is nothing exceeding the bonds of decent, licit, laudable recreation.[73] Luna, therefore, is quite probably not the translator. Nevertheless, his story is unique among Spanish narratives of the time: no other was rendered at the request of its original author.

Who was the translator, if not Luna? The initials "J. W." in the *Dialogues* and in the 1639 *Pursuit* have led some students to name James Wadsworth, a Cambridge divine who was "perverted" to Roman Catholicism and later became the Spanish infanta's English tutor.[74] So far as I know, however, the puzzle remains to be solved. Suffice it here to say that where I have compared his English with the Spanish, I have found him fairly faithful. Whoever he was, the translator tells his story simply, strongly, and well.

After its debut in 1622, the *Pursuit* was put out again in 1631, 1639, 1653, 1655, 1670, 1672, and 1677. In 1677, therefore, its publisher could truthfully begin his remarks to the reader by saying, "YOu have often heard of the name of *Lazarillo*. . . ."[75] Sometimes published alone and sometimes with a version of the original *Lazarillo*, Luna's book found considerable favor in England.

The Sonne of the Rogue

A book which understandably found less favor was *The Sonne of the Rogue* (1638). Thanks chiefly to the venomous pen of an acquaintance, its Spanish source, *La desordenada codicia de los bienes agenos* (Paris, 1619), is now regarded as the work of Carlos García.[76] Marcos Fernández, the ill-

73. "He lo hecho traducir en Ingles, fiel, y literalmente, para que se manifieste su inocencia, y vea que en el no ay cosa que pase los limites de vna honesta, licita y loable recreacion . . ." (A4ᵛ–A5ʳ).

74. Hume, with customary abandon, writes that "Luna's continuation is almost as good as the original, and was immediately translated into English by James Wadsworth, and ran through numerous editions under the name of *The Pursuit* . . . , and Blakeston also translated it" (*Spanish Influence on English Literature* [London, 1905], p. 168). Elmer Richard Sims says more carefully in his helpful edition, p. 136, that the initials "J. W." in the 1639 edition are those of the translator.

75. *Lazarillo*, A3ʳ. The remark also appears in the 1653 edition (A6ʳ).

76. The best exposition of the problem of authorship is Alfredo Carballo Picazo's "El doctor Carlos García, novelista español del siglo XVII," *Revista Bibliográfica y Documental*, V (1951), 5–46. See also the same author's "Datos para la historia de un cuento. Una nota sobre el doctor Carlos García," *RBD*, I (1947), 425–466, and "Historia de un cuento. Una nota sobre el doctor Carlos García," *RBD*, II (1948), 225–241.

disposed acquaintance, was one of those self-styled maestros of language who, for some reason or another, made their way into France, and it is in his *Olla podrida* (1665) that one finds him not only referring to the *"Antipatía del Dotor garcias"* (by which he means García's *La oposición y conjunción de los grandes luminares de la tierra* [Paris, 1617]),[77] but also contemning García as a pseudo-doctor, a philosopher among the worldly, and a preacher of whatever he wished.[78]

García may not have been so bad as Fernández claims, but his *Desordenada codicia* does give reason for wondering if its author was ever in jail. Concerned chiefly with jail life and thieving, it is a mine of information about professional rogues. And, not surprisingly, the whole thing is ostensibly designed to teach the reader to eschew roguery. As the English translator says,

> if it be true that the wounds of Darts which are foreseene from farre, are not so hurtfull as those which are shot at us unawares, I assure my selfe that the Reader will use it as an instrument to avoide the snares which leud fellowes ordinarily lay for honest men.[79]

The first of the duodecimo's thirteen chapters opens with an extended simile comparing the misery and confusion of two places of punishment— hell and jail. One would naturally assume that the damned immortals had a hard row to hoe, but somehow it seems that all that keeps even mortal prisoners going is a wry sense of humor. This is interesting enough, though

---

77. *La oposición* concerns the antipathy of Spain and France. Although Spanish was important to many Frenchmen, the French "hatred & disdain against the Spanish nation" was so strong in some places, according to García, that he found it best to clothe himself in the French style (*The Antipathy Betweene the French and Spaniard,* tr. Robert Gentilys [London, 1641], H8ʳ). See Ludwig Pfandl, "Carlos García und sein Anteil an der Geschichte der kulterellen und literarischen Beziehungen Frankreichs zu Spanien," *Münchener Museum,* II (1913), 33–52; and Joaquín López Barrera, "Literatura francesa hispanófoba en los siglos XVI y XVII," *Boletín de la Biblioteca Menéndez y Pelayo,* VII (1925), 83–95, 152–164, 379–395; VIII (1926), 137–149; IX (1927), 137–143.

Although he is not altogether reliable, García has many interesting comments on the times. Those on Spanish pride might have appeared in a picaresque story: Spaniards "will fast two daies to have a handsome cloak, and a starched ruffe, to goe abroad in, and they will carry themselves so lustily, well disposed, and haughty, that you would thinke they had kept a very good house" (I4ᵛ–I5ʳ).

78. The passage is difficult to translate, but seems to say also that García was guilty of sodomy, had been in the Bastille, and was sentenced to the rack by Marie de Medici. It is quoted by Alfredo Carballo Picazo in *RBD,* V, 6–7.

79. *Sonne of the Rogue,* A6.

one comes to the end of the forty-seven-page chapter without finding any narrative. All so far has been in the nature of an essay.

The second chapter seems more obviously personal. Here the author relates that as he was sitting in the prison chapel one day, discussing the Ten Commandments, one of his "religious followers" came to him.[80] "Sir," said follower to narrator, "to day is my feast day, and they have made me a gift of a clarke of a harbour, with a Cardinalls Hat: what remedie shall I be able to finde for so great a mischiefe."[81] The speaker of this gibberish turns out to be one Andrew, the rogue-hero—or, rather, thief-hero—of the book. Before long he is explaining what his thieves' jargon means, and the chapter ends with his promise to relate his life story that afternoon. In the next chapter (the third), however, he merely warms up. He lauds the joys of thievery and declares that the most honest men are self-avowed thieves, for they, unlike doctors, preachers, and the like, own up to their villainy.

The fourth chapter, it turns out, is devoted mainly to Andrew's adventures as an apprentice to a cobbler. This traditionally picaresque matter is scarcely under way, however, when interrupted by Chapter 5, which is devoted to a history of famous thieves. Chapter 6 follows suit, telling how thievery has spread from the nobility down to the vulgar. Chapter 7 gives details concerning a variety of curious malefactors, including satyrs (who steal livestock), apostles (who carry keys, like St. Peter), and cigarets (who cut off parts of cloaks and gowns at public assemblies). Not until Chapter 8 is Andrew allowed to resume his life story, but by this time, after a three-chapter detour, it is almost a surprise to find him informing the narrator, "I will tell you a wittie tricke which I once plotted. . . ."[82]

At last and for the next five chapters the narrator proceeds to relay some of the adventures which Andrew has told him. The most elaborate of these concerns Andrew's theft of his mistress' pearls. It seems that for purposes of concealment he swallowed these treasures one by one, only to be found out by the lady, gawked at by some two hundred people who rushed into her chamber, and forced with a purge to divulge his prize. For about four hours

---

80. One wonders if Fernández is right in saying García was a sort of preacher. (Pfandl, by the way, is inclined to think so [pp. 35–36].) The narrator refers to the present discussion of religion as "continuing my no lesse accustomed than troublesome occupation" (p. 52).

81. *Sonne*, p. 54. The speaker later explains that the "clarke" of a harbor is one who receives those condemned to galleys, and that he himself has been condemned "To be whipt at the Carts taile" and placed in a ship bound for Marseilles (p. 63).

82. *Sonne*, p. 139.

Andrew goes on with his tales, finally telling the narrator how he has come to be in prison at the moment. By this time Chapter 13 is reached, the narrative is dropped again, and we are told of the statutes of thieves, their hierarchy, system of apprenticeship, weekly meetings, calendar of activities, and oath of allegiance. Then suddenly, with the observation that thieves are only half Christians because they love God but not man, and because they believe in confession and contrition but not restitution, the book comes to a stop.

Only six of its thirteen chapters, then, are directly concerned with Andrew's adventures. This means that more than half are devoted to essay-like digressions on various aspects of thieving. From the standpoint of narrative art, in other words, García does not try even as hard as Alemán to blend his disparate elements, "to the end," as Mabbe might put it, of "making it all one continued piece of worke, weauing it well and handsomely, running along in euen threds. . . ."[83] Still, notwithstanding his rather Spanish disdain for technique and continuity, García succeeds better than many early writers in conveying his own personal impression of life. Although he sometimes gets mired in scholastic cataloguing and exposition, his bitterness and pessimism come through. Life for García was made bearable, one would guess, by the sort of humor that makes prison life bearable. To the genuine religious ascetics of his day the world seemed a chaos where evil was to be exposed (not necessarily reformed) so that man might see a better life; but apparently to García, although he was perhaps a minister of sorts, the world was a chaos where evil was to be exposed for exposition's sake. An ascetic interpretation of *The Rogue* is possible, as is an Erasmian interpretation of *Lazarillo,* but, despite its claim to didacticism, García's book seems chiefly bent on discovering a world of thievery, venting its author's spleen, and entertaining with a handful of stories.

In 1638, when a translation of the book was first printed in English, interest in Spain was not great, and yet in this same year it seems to have appeared in three issues.[84] Its English title page, furthermore, advertises plainly that the work was "first written in *Spanish* by *DON GARCIA*" (though the translator, as a matter of fact, used a French intermediary, *L'antiquité des larrons* [1621], by the indefatigable D'Audiguier). The Spaniard García even gets better billing than his English translator, who signs only his initials, "W. M." (It does one little good, by the way, to

83. *Rogue,* II, 8.
84. Again I cite from Professor Jackson's notes for the revised *STC.*

learn that "W. M." is really William Melvin. At any rate, I have so far failed to uncover more than a passing reference to his name.)

In a subsequent appearance, which turns out to be a reissue instead of a new edition, the translation was appropriately disguised as *Lavernae, or The Spanish Gipsy* (1650) on the grounds that "the cunning . . . goddesse *Laverna* . . . was the Theeves Patronesse."[85] Doubtless the bookseller hoped to encourage sales by making the book seem a new one. In 1657 it made still another appearance, this time under the alias of *Guzman, Hinde and Hannam Outstript,* a name which linked Andrew not only with Guzman de Alfarache, as we have noted earlier, but also with two very real scoundrels.[86] In 1659 it bobbed up still a fourth time under the name of *A Scourge for a Den of Thieves.* The protean rogues whom the picaresque stories depict would have enjoyed this editorial ingenuity, just as they would have approved later on when Head and Kirkman highjacked a couple of García's episodes for their own *English Rogue.*[87] In view of all this deal of do, it is amusing to find William London listing in his book catalogue a work called *Antiquity of Thieves.*[88] Conceivably a volume actually came out with such a title, though I have found no other record of it. That London intends García's work, however, is unquestionable, for he gives as subtitle *The Son of a* [*sic*] *Rogue.*

The prose of *The Sonne* is clear enough and reasonably lively, especially considering some of the linguistic snares that Melvin faced; yet one is puzzled to say just how popular it was, for, despite its longevity, reissues generally indicate a slow sale. Chandler, who believes the book was well-received, offers the explanation that it

came closer than any other Spanish work to following the course suggested in the rogue-pamphlets of Harman, Greene, and Dekker, and but for its humor and satire was not unlike its contemporaries there, the *Essayes and Characters of a Prison and Prisoners* by Geffray Mynshul of 1618, or more nearly still, *The*

85. *Lavernae,* A3ᵛ–A4ʳ.

86. James Hind was the popular hero of a number of sub-literary works, a highwayman who specialized in robbing roundheads and ended his days in 1652 by being drawn, hanged, and quartered. Richard Hainam engaged in a variety of nefarious exploits in Paris and Rotterdam as well as at home, finally meeting his end at Smithfield in 1656.

87. Chandler, *Romances of Roguery,* p. 263, notes other borrowings in *The Complete History of the Lives and Robberies of the Most Notorious Highwaymen,* by Captain Alexander Smith (1714–1720).

88. *A Catalogue of the Most Vendible Books in England* (1657), T4ʳ. He lists it under "HISTORY With other Pieces of Humane Learning Intermixed."

Compter's Commonwealth, by William Fennor in 1617, reprinted in 1619 as *The Miseries of a Jaile.*[89]

In any case, García's book is an anachronistic and intriguing sort of halfway house on the road between the old-time beggar books and later, more artful low-life literature. In one sense, therefore, it is beside the point to complain of its author's awkward handling of narrative devices. Like many of the picaresque writers of Spain's Golden Age, García simply had a greater concern for the misdeeds of society than for those of his hero. Largely for their own sake, it seems, he presents the colorful and devious doings of a variety of thieves, offering his reader a story, yes, but using it merely as a partial means of providing a fascinating glimpse into a special and fascinating world.

Visions

The final writer we approach is Don Francisco de Quevedo y Villegas. Together with Rojas and Cervantes, Quevedo completes the trio of Spain's greatest Golden Age prose writers. Hailed, indeed, by Justus Lipsius as the chief glory of his land, Quevedo is an author whose breadth may be suggested by the fact that, like his Spanish peers and Shakespeare, he has appealed to readers of every class.[90] In addition to being a diplomat, he was a first-rate poet; he was the author of impressive political and religious works (in one of which he extols equality of civil rights, and in another of which he advocates that Jesus' teachings be applied to government); and, most important to us, he was one of Spain's greatest satirists. In view of his intrinsic interest and his comparative neglect by English-speaking students —few of whom know that Cervantes alone equals him in number of fictional works translated in our period—he merits special attention.

Quevedo's first writings to be Englished were his *Sueños,* called *Visions.* These are a group of satiric dream-pieces, similar to the dream-writing by Lucian of Samosata and a host of medieval writers, including William Lang-

---

89. *Romances of Roguery,* p. 264.

90. Cervantes called him the son of Apollo, but Edward Phillips, the Montalván translator, identified him merely as a *"Spanish* writer, of signal Fame and Credit both in Prose and Verse" (*Theatrum poetarum* [1675], II, 46). Edward M. Wilson notes that Spaniards still tell coarse stories which they attribute to Quevedo ("Quevedo for the Masses," *Atlante,* III [1955], 151–166).

land.[91] The realm of dreams, of course, had long since become a traditional means of expressing philosophical and moral ideas, but Quevedo's treatment of the subject is unique, a reflection of his own personal reaction to the decadence and corruption of Philip III's Spain. It is always dangerous to equate a satirist with his mask, and yet it certainly seems that the disgust which Quevedo expresses is his own disgust at Spanish decline, public and private, physical, moral, and spiritual. His *Sueños* seem to be a compulsive and emotional exposition, spontaneously conceived and composed, of a world that is frighteningly out of joint.[92] Some would say they are his masterwork.

Unfortunately their history is confused by the fact that a sixth *Sueño,* the *Casa de locos de amor,* became attached to the series fairly early. For some time it was thought to be the work of Quevedo's friend Lorenzo Vander Hammen, though actually it was composed by the poet-musician Antonio Ortiz de Melgarejo, a little-remembered writer who was much admired at the time.[93] A further cause of confusion is that Quevedo's *Infierno enmendado* (*Hell Reformed*) is sometimes erroneously included in the group, bringing the total to seven. Finally, muddling literary history still more, some of the *Sueños* circulated in manuscript for as long as two decades at the beginning of the seventeenth century, remaining unprinted until 1627, when Quevedo, during a period of enforced diplomatic unemployment, organized his papers and sent five of them off to the press. From that time on, Spain acclaimed them.

91. In their time it was said that they outdid Dante. Among other influences sometimes mentioned are Petronius, Cristóbal de Villalón, and the Dance of Death tradition.

92. H. Warner Allen, p. xlvii, speculates that Quevedo's virulence is traceable to the fact that he was half-blind and club-footed. It might also be traced to anguish from his inability to live up to the standards he believed in. Then again, he had plenty of external provocation. In 1618, e.g., at the request of Philip III, Pedro Fernández de Navarrete made a very realistic analysis of the causes of Spain's decline; and as Earl J. Hamilton reports, "all the inductive data at our disposal point to economic decadence" (*American Treasure and the Price Revolution in Spain, 1501–1650* [Cambridge, Mass., 1934], p. 304).

93. Ticknor remarks that "large portions" of the piece are "beneath the talent of Quevedo, and not at all in his manner" (*History of Spanish Literature* [1891], II, 342). Depicting a palace of lovers (whose porter is Beauty, and overseer, Time), and presenting such types as ladies who practice simpering before their mirrors, and bravely clad but penniless swains, it concludes: *"Love is nothing but meere and naturall folly"* (*Visions* [1640], p. 123).

In England, *Visions, or, Hels Kingdome* was licensed on February 12, 1639, and printed the following year. It includes *The Possessed Sergeant* (from *El alguacil alguacilado*); *Death and Her Dominion* (from *El sueño de la muerte*); *The Last Judgement* (from *El sueño del juicio final*); *The Foole Amorous* (from the pseudepigraphous fellow-traveler, *Casa de locos de amor*); *The World in Its Interior* (from *El mundo por de dentro*); and *Hell* (from *El sueño del infierno*—which has been called one of the greatest efforts of the human mind).[94]

In the phrase of its title page, however, the English version is indeed "Strangely displaied." Richard Croshaw, the obscure translator, produced a work quite different from Quevedo's, even fortifying his undistinguished prose with anti-Catholic barbs, and pretending to be the original author.[95] Despite Quevedo's fame in the peninsula, Croshaw felt sure enough of the Spaniard's obscurity to claim that "there is not any one in particular living, that I intend either by this or that. . . ."[96] Moreover, he claims that his visions are "the first fruits of a reformed life," and, with cool audacity, relates the book to *"mine owne deviation (still knowne to many),"* to the end that, *"seeing there is no stability in bubbling pleasure, nor no true content without*

---

94. Luis Astrana Marín, "Don Francisco de Quevedo Villegas," in *Historia general . . . ,* ed. Guillermo Díaz-Plaja, III, 533.

95. Croshaw declares himself to be "of the Inner Temple" and addresses an introductory letter to students at the Inns of Court. In November, 1628, twelve years before, a Richard Croshawe who was son and heir of John Croshawe of Heanor, Derbyshire, was admitted to the Inner Temple (*Students Admitted to the Inner Temple 1547–1660,* ed. W. H. Cooke [London, 1878], p. 257). There is no reason to confuse the translator with the poet Richard Crashaw.

Charles C. Mish finds Croshaw's style "inexcusably harsh and crude" ("English Prose Fiction, 1600–1642: A Survey," unpublished Ph.D. dissertation [University of Pennsylvania, 1951], p. 393), but this judgment itself may be a bit harsh. A random passage from *Death and Her Dominion* (*Visions,* pp. 71–72) reads thus:

> Counsellours and Lawyers, How doe they thrive? As nests of Ants, that from one breed a million. Justice that in ancient dayes went naked, as representing sincerity, is now so swadled with paper, as if she were a nest of Spices. And whereas heretofore we had but one booke of Lawes, there are now a thousand, the cause of so many squablings & divisions, being every ones private exposition. If you goe to some Lawyers, let your cause bee what it will, they will assure you good proceeding, and tell you, 'tis a faire *quaere,* and wants nothing but study, but that at that instant they are something busie, about a case betweene *Iohn Ash* and *Iohn Okes,* so that they cannot minde it.

96. *Visions,* A5.

a religious returne," the reader may profit by his precepts and example.[97] One wonders if Croshaw was chagrined the following year when Edward Messervy claimed to have translated not only six visions, but also a seventh, all composed by "that Noble Knight, *Don Francisco de Quevedo.*"[98]

A version as free as Croshaw's might almost be placed in Dryden's third category, imitation. The fact is not surprising, though. Quevedo is among the most difficult of Spanish writers to translate. He delights in neologism and subtle word-play, and alludes to matters which few non-Spaniards are apt to know. Furthermore, Croshaw based his translation on M. de la Geneste's French version of 1633, which had already modified its source rather considerably, playing up Quevedo as a source of humor.[99] It was inevitable that the English *Visions* and the Spanish *Sueños* would have striking differences. There is no hint in Croshaw's *Hell,* for instance, of the passage in *El sueño del infierno* where the narrator reports finding Luther in hell, arrogant as a toad and blaspheming.[100] On the other hand, there are additions in *Hell* which Quevedo would not have recognized. A bookshop is described as "a very Storehouse of Sedition," a "Stewes of licentiousnesse . . . , fraught with . . . obscene, scurrilous, prophane, railing, & popish Pamphlets, tending to the subversion of all good maners, & to the encrease of superstitious vanities."[101] Most interesting of all the spurious passages, however, is that in which a dead soul inquires about England and is assured that the virtue of that paradise remains unstained. In England, says Croshaw, one finds "Pietie in the Prince, Justice in the Magistrate, Religion in the Minister, and Obedience in the Subject." England is, forsooth, "the sparkling Diamond in the universall Ring."[102]

Despite the sea-change they suffered in traveling northward, the various visions have undeniable interest in both Spanish and English. In both, there

97. *Visions,* A2ʳ, A4.

98. *Hell Reformed,* A7ʳ. A possible exculpation for Croshaw is suggested by Messervy's words to his dedicatee: "Your *Name appearing in the Frontispice of this Booke, will serve to Protect it, from the malice of those, who would disallow the Authour for being a Spaniard . . .*" (A4ᵛ).

99. See Alfredo Berumen, "Un traductor de Quevedo," *Ábside,* XXI (1957), 306–315.

100. *Las zahurdas de Plutón* (variant title of *El sueño del infierno*), ed. Julio Cejador y Frauca, *Clásicos castellanos* (Madrid, 1916), XXXI, 181.

101. *Visions,* pp. 170–171.

102. *Death and Her Dominion,* in *Visions,* p. 74.

are two major themes: the pain of life and the decay of society, each of which points toward asceticism and neo-stoicism. Quevedo is concerned more with feeling than thought, however; more with depiction than reconstruction. Writing chiefly by intuition, he lashes out with Swiftian indignation at such subjects as women rather than at subjects which we, looking back, might think more apt. The value of the *Visions,* therefore, lies mainly in the manner in which he shows us that the world is a heap of grimy rubble, a street of false façades.

Structurally, in accord with the freedom of a dream-world, the *Visions* are very free. Quevedo simply proceeds from subject to subject as impulse dictates, firing grapeshot at all classes and types of people—women, clerics, doctors, lawyers, lovers, tailors, poets, and what-you-will. In fact, characters as different as Comedy, barbers, and Judas appear and vanish as soon as the author's attention is attracted to something new, with the result that the contents of the individual visions, including the one by Ortiz de Melgarejo, are as hard to remember as last year's clouds. A few images and ideas do stand out, of course: a devil of quality who raises an uproar at being constrained to live in the body of a catchpole; patients risen from the dead on Judgment Day, shoving toward The Throne the murdering doctors who dispatched them; and Death, "not a breathlesse trunke or bare anatomy," but a female creature with crowns, garlands, scepters, sickles, wooden shoes, bonnets, and diamonds, dressed in all colors, young on one side, and on the other, old, because "to bee borne, is to beginne to die; and the truest Image of *Death* is a mans own selfe. . . ."[103] But one lays down the book with a general impression of having walked through Bedlam in a nightmare. Everywhere there is twitching movement, yet little forward, narrative thrust. In short, the *Visions* are the inspired but disorganized improvisations of a genius. This is not to damn with faint praise. In the first place, Spanish art at its best is often improvisatory. In the second place, one need not complain that here, any more than in *The Rogue,* form obscures meaning, for the *Visions* succeed in nothing better than suggesting, as did Donne, a crumbling, mad world with *"all cohaerence gone,"*[104] a world which the author of *Lazarillo* long before had envisioned in a much quieter way, a world which all the king's men and the Inquisition could not put together again.

Whatever Croshaw's virtues, his little talent was scuttled by Quevedo's

103. *Death and Her Dominion,* in *Visions,* p. 52.
104. The famous phrase is from *An Anatomy of the World* (1611), B1ʳ.

genius, and his version never called for again. When Quevedo fell into later English hands, he fortunately fared much better.

Hell Reformed

The same year that Croshaw's *Visions* appeared, Mabbe's *Exemplarie Novells* and Style's *Galateo* were also published, but the next year, 1641, saw only one new piece of Spanish fiction. It was Edward Messervy's *Hell Reformed or A Glasse for Favorits,* based on the work which is occasionally regarded as Quevedo's seventh vision. Like Croshaw's book, it was printed by Edward Griffin for Simon Burton, so there can be little doubt that Croshaw's effort was fresh in the minds of both the translator and the bookseller.

Unlike Croshaw, Messervy informs his reader not only that Quevedo is the real author, but that he is "held amongst men of judgement, one of the ripest wits of this age, his writings being filled wth rich conceptions, and a thousand good conceits. . . ." Of course there is also the assurance that his work "tends to a good and holy reformation of life, representing Vice unto us, to the end we should abhorre it."[105] As we have just seen, Messervy was sufficiently impressed with Quevedo's abilities to translate his "other" *sueños,* too, although he adds, "for some reasons best knowne to my selfe, I have made a demurre of presenting them. . . ."[106] Perhaps Messervy had simply not appeared on the scene soon enough, and the bookseller refused to kill the sale of Croshaw's book by making competition for it.

Little is known of Messervy. In his dedication to Henry Jermyn, son of Thomas Jermyn (the governor of Jersey) and master of the horse to the queen, he at least gives the hint that *Hell Reformed* constitutes his "First-Fruits," and that Henry holds his *"small Patrimony and Fee."*[107] Apparently, then, the translator was a young man. Furthermore, he refers explicitly to Jersey as *"that Isle, where I tooke my first Breath."*[108]

This last bit of information is a clue to Messervy's immediate source, for Jersey was at one time part of the duchy of Normandy, and official documents from the island were still as often as not written in French.[109] One might therefore suspect that Messervy, like Croshaw, came to Quevedo via

---

105. *Hell Reformed,* A7^r.
106. *Hell Reformed,* A8^r.
107. *Hell Reformed,* A2^v, A4^r.
108. *Hell Reformed,* A3^r.
109. At one time boats arrived from the French mainland every day (*Calendar of State Papers, Domestic Series, . . . Addenda, 1580–1625,* XII, ed. Mary A. E. Green [London, 1872], 565).

La Geneste. The suspicion proves correct. Disregarding the book's reception in Spain, Messervy declares in his dedication that it has had *"Vniuersall Patronage"* in France, and at one point in the text he even inserts the otherwise meaningless comment that *"Pies in French signifies both pious and Meg-pies."*[110]

As its title suggests, *Hell Reformed* takes the reader on a tour of the infernal regions. In keeping with the *Sueños*, however, it is a tour which conveys less fascination for the after-life than for what Quevedo has seen in the bustling life about him. A revolution, it appears, has been brought on in hell by three archvillains—a secret accuser, a suborner, and a duenna. In fact, it has reached such proportions that Lucifer decides to investigate personally. First he is told of the old Caesar-and-Brutus affair;[111] then he is subjected to a long series of complaints from famous fallen favorites; next he is angered by an inept devil just returned without a single soul after a twenty-year tour of duty on earth; then he sees a flock of fleeing wives pursued by cuckolded husbands; and a little later there buzzes in a merry hive of foolish, painted old women so withered and dry that they are put in boxes to be used as tinder and matches. Thus the piece continues, until at last, having completed his inspection, Lucifer decides on a course of action. First he appoints Devil Prosperity as his chief aide, because *"they of the World, who obtaine and possesse all what they desire, turne their backes presently vnto* God. . . ."[112]

110. *Hell Reformed*, A5^r, p. 57. It is no surprise, then, that several identical rearrangements of subject matter are made by both Messervy and a translator who wrote after our period, Sir Roger L'Estrange (1667). Stevens tells us that L'Estrange translated from the French, and adds that the *Visions* have thereby "lost much of their bewty, being most consummate Peices in the Original, but much mangled in translating & several Things quite omitted especially in that the English calls the Vision of Hell" (quoted by Robert H. Williams, "A Manuscript Document on the Translations from Spanish by Captain John Stevens," *RLC*, XVI [1936], 151). As different as *Hell Reformed* is from its source, *Infierno enmendado*, it is disappointing to find Messervy claim not only that his translation is exact, but that any error in his book is "a meere defect in the impression" (A8^v).

111. Printed eight years before Charles's beheading, the words of Caesar's ghost seem prophetically ominous. He refers to the "bloody outrage" which brought on his death under the "pretext of the *liberty* of the *Countrey*," and protests that his murderers "did more harme taking away my *life*, then I did when I tooke away from the *Senators*, the Gouernement of the *Commonwealth*, since, I died *Emperour*, and my *Homicides* procured to themselves, the Title of *Traytors* during their life. . . . Cursed *blood-shedders!* . . . Many men full of Covetousnesse and Ambition ought they to be called *The* Fathers *of their* Countrey, and the generosity of One held for *Tyranny?*" And even: "the people . . . had rather be commanded by *Nero*, . . . then by Lawes and *Senators*" (pp. 9–11, *passim*).

112. *Hell Reformed*, p. 106.

Next he itemizes the ways in which hell is to be reformed. And finally he returns to eternal night, his auditors disperse, and an angelic voice is heard proclaiming, *"Whosoever shall have the understanding to comprehend the Morality of this Discourse may reape a most advantageous profit for his Soule. . . ."*[113]

Again, as in the *Visions,* there is a humorous but grim distortion which bespeaks hot blood, a fragmentation which hints of a yearning for lost coherence. Here also, as in the *Visions,* Quevedo fails to demonstrate that he is the man to offer a positive course of action. On the contrary, more artist than thinker, he seems—in the words of Gerald Brenan—to have

clung to the dream that, by some sort of miracle, the glories of the days of Charles V could be restored. This would happen, he thought, if men were more moral. But morality can only flourish if men are adjusted to reality, and such an adjustment required sacrifices to pride that neither he nor anyone else would hear of. . . . The great satirist belonged to that body of political idealists, so characteristic of Spain, whose utopia lies not in the future, but in the past.[114]

If hell is defined as a state in which there is no path ahead, only hopeless groping or painful fingering of what once has been, then Quevedo, or at least his persona, may be said to have discovered hell on earth.

The only commentator I have found on *Hell Reformed* is Charles Mish, who complains with some justice that "In spite of the attractiveness of presentation, . . . the material is, in both this and his other six 'visions,' pretty well worn. The stock subjects recur again and again for attack. . . ."[115] I would reply that unless one is surfeited with satire, Quevedo's works will seem no more threadbare than most other fiction of the day. True enough, there is repetition aplenty in the *Visions* and *Hell Reformed,* but one should remember that they were written over a period of many years and perhaps never meant to be read at a sitting. The best answer to Mish, however, lies in his own words, "attractiveness of presentation." The vitality of both books lies in Quevedo's anguished yet humoristic view of life. It is a view which has invited comparison with Bosch and Goya, with Donne and Swift, though my own suggestion is that it seems most like the view in Book IV of Pope's *Dunciad.*

---

113. *Hell Reformed,* p. 112.

114. *The Literature of the Spanish People* (Cambridge, Eng., 1953), p. 270. Quevedo hated commerce, detested Jews and Moors, and supported the renewal of war with the Netherlands.

115. "English Prose Fiction," p. 394.

Whatever our opinions may be, Quevedo's works were a hit in seventeenth-century England. Croshaw's was a weak if interesting beginning; Messervy's came along and bettered it; and following the 1667 debut of Sir Roger L'Estrange's version, after the close of our period, the visions gained great popularity, even leaving their mark on the *Tatler* and *Spectator*.[116] Remembering the reception of *Don Quixote* in England, one is better prepared to find hints of the nature of their reputation, to find Pepys, for instance, regarding L'Estrange's translation as "a merry satyr" with "many very pretty things."[117] At least L'Estrange himself, though obviously alert to the jocular strains in Quevedo, had described his book as *"full of* Sharpness and Morality. . . ."[118]

Pre-Restoration evidence about Quevedo is more difficult to come by. In the earlier seventeenth century, however, Englishmen, like Spaniards, were also skidding down the slopes of a golden mountain, with the fogs of political and moral disillusion growing thicker as they descended. Hall's *Mundus alter et idem* (ca. 1605) and Dekker's *Newes from Hell* (1606) might be brought forth as early Jacobean evidence of unpleasant rumblings of things to come. But only a few Englishmen can be thought to have read Quevedo before Croshaw's day. Later on, of course, they certainly did read him, and in 1649 the Hispanist Howell—who had no need of either Croshaw or Messervy—may well have been thinking of Quevedo when he published his *Winter Dreame* and *A Trance: Or Newes from Hell*. "O England, England . . . ," Howell exclaimed in the latter, *"let the torments of Hell deterr Thee, which are represented to the very life unto Thee in this ensuing Vision."*[119]

The Provident Knight

Bound with our terminal work, Quevedo's *Buscon* (1657), which was the last of the great picaresque books to be translated, there was a less

---

116. See W. S. Hendrix, "Quevedo, [Vélez de] Guevara, Le Sage and the *Tatler*," *MP*, XIX (1921–1922), 177–186.

117. *The Diary of Samuel Pepys*, ed. Henry B. Wheatley (London, 1895), VI, 355. He continues: "the translation is, as to the rendering it into English expression, the best that ever I saw, it being impossible almost to conceive that it should be a translation." Most striking of the British imitations was Ellis Wynne's *Gweledigaethau y Bardd Cwsg* (London, 1703), acclaimed the finest of Welsh prose classics.

118. *The Visions* (1667), A4r.

119. Howell, p. 2.

significant work which it may be well to consider first.[120] A rather Theo-
phrastan little sampler called *The Provident Knight,* it is based on the same
author's *Cartas del caballero de la tenaza* (1625). Now placed among
Quevedo's earliest notable works as a satiric and comic writer, the *Cartas*
is a series of letters whose point and humor lie in the skill with which the
presumed epistler, a preternaturally tightfisted gentleman, devises ways to
refuse any request or hint of a request to lure money from his purse.

Because both works, *The Provident Knight* and *Buscon,* came from the
pen of John Davies of Kidwelly, "the most active translator from the
French in his age," it is easy to predict that Davies, like Croshaw and
Messervy, was indebted to a French intermediary.[121] As a matter of fact, he,

120. Because it seems to have made its initial appearance subsequent to my terminal date, I omit an interesting satiric work which is sometimes said to have appeared in 1657. Chandler writes that "In 1657 Davies of Kidwelly had published
three tales out of Scarron, including 'The Hypocrites,' derived from [Alonso
Jerónimo Salas] Barbadillo's 'La Hyia de Celestina.' To these he added, in 1662, the
four from the 'Roman Comique.' The seven were issued together in 1667, and were
increased by an eighth three years later" (*The Literature of Roguery,* I, 206–207).
It is probable, however, that scholars who support these statements are giving too
much credence to Wood's *Athenae Oxonienses.* Joseph E. Tucker, who has looked
into the matter with care, quotes Davies in "The Earliest English Translations of
Scarron's Nouvelles," *RLC,* XXIV (1950), 558, as affirming in the first surviving
edition of his translation (1665) that "The three former of these novels were
printed here some four or five years since," which would mean about 1660. It is
difficult to say how long before 1660 the book could have been published. We do
know that Pepys, on October 15, 1660, was reading it, but whether it appeared as
early as 1657 would seem a bit doubtful.

The Hypocrites is of interest on several counts: (1) it was originally published
in 1612, before Cervantes' *Novelas ejemplares;* (2) its leading character is a *pícara,*
i.e., a female *pícaro;* (3) it has unity of plot such as is exemplified in no other
picaresque story we have discussed; and (4) it is the best work by "the subtlest
intelligence among the seventeenth-century short story writers after Cervantes"
(Caroline Bourland, *The Short Story in Spain in the Seventeenth Century* [North-
ampton, Mass., 1927], p. 47). Says Edwin B. Place: "Scarron followed the original
quite closely, merely changing a few names, and in the *dénoûment* permitting Elena
[the heroine] to escape to the Indies instead of undergoing the death-penalty for
having poisoned her paramour" ("Salas Barbadillo, Satirist," *RR,* XVII [1926],
241).

Published with *The Hypocrites* were two other translations by Davies through
Scarron: *The Fruitless Precaution* (from *El prevenido engañado*) and *The Innocent
Adultery* (from *El juez de su causa*), both by María de Zayas Sotomayor. (See
Place's "María de Zayas, An Outstanding Woman Short-story Writer of Seventeenth
Century Spain," *University of Colorado Studies,* XIII [1923], 1–56.)

121. See Joseph E. Tucker, "John Davies of Kidwelly (1627?–1693), Translator from the French," *PBSA,* XLIV (1950), 119; and Henry Thomas, "The English

too, was indebted to the French of M. de la Geneste.[122] Son of a Welsh yeoman, Davies was born about 1627, shortly after his friend Thomas Stanley. In 1641 he entered Jesus College, Oxford, then transferred to Cambridge when Oxford was garrisoned, and in the latter university learned French. After living in France for a time (1649–1651), he finally settled in London, and there, as Wood says, "did make it his livelihood to translate Books from *French* into *English*. . . ."[123] A review of these books shows that he was no mere hack. In fact, Tucker offers the opinion that his

contributions were almost all significant *per se* and brought to the English public a considerable number not only of France's most distinguished writers but also, through his use of French intermediaries, of outstanding figures from several other lands.[124]

The dedicatee of the volume at hand is "T. P.," Davies' "much Honoured Friend."[125] "T. P." is a person who deserves this present honor, we are told, because of an interest in Spanish literature. Says Davies, "*I Had no sooner boarded the Adventure, but I thought my self bound to send you the Prize; She's* Spanish, *and so your own, whose approbation set me first out to scowr those Coasts. . . .*"[126] Though it is dangerous to guess at identities behind initials, it is also tempting to suggest Thomas Porter, who was a son of Endymion Porter, and hence had Spanish blood in his veins. The Restoration dramatist could scarcely have helped being affected by Spain. Himself indebted to Spanish fiction, as we have seen, perhaps it was he who drew Davies' attention to Quevedo.

In Davies' English, the letters of the parsimonious knight bear such titles as "A Pleasant Denyal to an Importunate Lady of Pleasure" and "In Answer to a Curtisan That Desired Some New Fashioned Dressing of Him."[127] All the recipients but one are mistresses—Florence, Messaline, Flora,

---

Translations of Quevedo's *La vida del buscón*," *RH*, LXXXI, Pt. 2 (1933), 282–299.

122. La Geneste had published his version together with *L'Aventurier buscon* in 1633.

123. II, 902.

124. "John Davies . . . ," p. 140. He died in 1693, "leaving then behind him," according to Wood, "the Character of a genteel, harmless and quiet Man . . ." (II, 904).

125. *Buscon*, A2ʳ.

126. *Buscon*, A2.

127. One letter (pp. 301–302) reads as follows:

Florence,

AFter a due consideration of what Answer I should give you in return of

Phil, Gilian, Lais, etc. (Quevedo's original knight had addressed his letters to a single woman.) Except for one railing missive from a mistress to the knight, each billet-doux refuses something to a lady.

The knight's ingenious husbandry, either in its original or its modified form, is a good example of Quevedo's technique of distorting life. Probably because his kind of realism, even more than Alemán's, is the realism of caricature, the *Cartas* have sometimes been regarded as merely comic. If we regard them thus, though, we may find it difficult to explain Quevedo's comment in *The Possessed Sergeant* that none are damned but those who covet the goods of the world.[128] As in the *Visions* and *Hell Reformed*, I think, Quevedo's grotesque magnification of folly—in this case miserliness—is itself a sort of moral act.

There is reason enough that such a work should have gained renown in Spain. First, Spain's romances and *novelas* are usually concerned with love, and her satiric-realistic literature, with money or its lack. When the two subjects are combined, as here and in the *Celestina*, one possible result is parody.[129] Since Golden Age fiction is strewn with saccharine love missives,

---

those many things you desire me, I have found no style more proper then the Laconique, or indeed more fit then the usual answer we make unto poor Beggars, *God keep you, I have not at present any thing for you.* I was at first much surprized at the novelty of this encounter, I knew indeed there was a kind of Friers Mendicants abroad in the world, but I never yet heard of any such order of Nuns. I pray therefore cease giving your self the trouble of making any more such requests unto me, which will assuredly work no other effect then that of making me shun your company, there being nothing in the world of more power to keep me chaste then when I am constrained to part with my money; And so God keep you my friend, I have not at this time any thing to bestow upon you.

The question may arise as to whether a group of such letters constitutes a "character" or fiction. At least it has the coherence afforded by a single epistolizer, and it has unity of theme. For a glimpse of the pedigree of epistolary fiction in Spain see Charles E. Kany, "The Beginnings of the Epistolary Novel in France, Italy, and Spain," *UCPMP*, XXI (1937), 1–158. Though not concerned with Spanish literature, some helpful insights are also to be found in Godfrey Frank Singer's *The Epistolary Novel* (Philadelphia, 1933). Robert A. Day lists nearly two hundred epistolary works which appeared in England between 1660 and 1740 (preface to Mary Davys' *Familiar Letters Betwixt a Gentleman and a Lady* [Los Angeles, 1955]).

128. *The Possessed Sergeant*, in *Visions*, p. 36.

129. Especially since Quevedo apparently had a noble concept of love (Otis H. Green, *El amor cortés en Quevedo* [Saragossa, 1955], p. 137). The knight admonishes one mistress as follows: "instead of calling me in your Letters, *My Life, my Joy, my Heart, and my Eyes,* express me by those things you most affect: call me thy *Twenty shillings piece, thy Jacobus, thy half Crown, and thy Angel* . . ." (p. 317).

the contemporary reader, especially one familiar with courtly artifice, might well have been amused by the ungallant evasions of a closefisted knight.

Second, the work's popularity may be related to the number of impoverished gentry in Spain at the time. That is, the *Cartas* may be regarded as a satire on those out-at-heels and pseudo-gentlefolk whose pride prevented their seeking advancement by labor. To understand the book fully one might do well to recall not only the general historical importance of Spanish pride, but the specific example of the squire in *Lazarillo*.[130] The squire, it may be remembered, comes to the city gaunt as a greyhound, hoping to serve one of the chief nobles of the place, but because he finds none who will have him save gentlemen of a mean sort, he is reduced to existing on food that Lazarillo begs for him. Particularly pertinent is the scene in which Lazarillo, watching his master talk with two light ladies of the town, hears him recite more sweetness than Ovid ever wrote, but, when the ladies ask for breakfast, sees him faint dead away. Analogously, in his own *Buscón,* Quevedo's hero is assured by a needy, would-be hidalgo that, no matter how pretty they are, fancy ladies must be foregone. Having noted Quevedo's willingness to reiterate, one may suppose such a passage to be the result of thinking like that which produced the *Cartas*. It was a mode of thinking which stayed with him. Years later, in 1645, he wrote: "There are many things which, while seeming to exist and have being, are now nothing but a name and a shape."[131] Castro suggests that "the world around him seemed like a tapestry turned wrongside out; but he clung to his cult of bravery and boldness, the only railings his unsteady soul could lean upon as it looked into the abyss of nothingness."[132]

130. Every student of the period knows that the literature by and about Spaniards is pervaded by the subject of pride. Américo Castro concludes that the Spanish Christian "did not believe in his own superiority for the same reasons as the nobility of feudal Europe—not, that is, because he was doing what the commoner could not do . . . —but because he was possessed of a better belief. This explains why the Christian had more a sense of caste than of class." He felt superior because he was a Christian rather than a Moor or Jew. "The humblest peasant sensed that he was a member of the seignorial caste, a potential *hidalgo*" (*Structure,* pp. 609, 611). See Miguel Herrero García, *Ideas de los españoles del siglo XVII* (Madrid, 1928), pp. 45–59.

131. Quoted by Castro, *Structure,* pp. 6–7.

132. *Structure,* pp. 194–195. Of course he also sought support in the church, but because it is impossible to distinguish between the satirical artist and the man, one cannot say to what degree he found or failed to find it. Otis H. Green, for one, is convinced that to Quevedo, ultimately, the grave was an entrance to eternal life ("The Concept of Man in the Spanish Renaissance," *Rice Institute Pamphlets,* XLVI [1960], 53).

Not, of course, that the *Cartas* creates an impression of despair. Captain Stevens, who himself translated the work as *The Retentive Knight,* remarked that it was "pleasant enough, but not so solid as the Visions."[133] Davies' version, dependent on La Geneste's, is pleasant, too, but only moderately successful. Compared with the prose of his *Buscon* in the same volume, Davies' prose in *The Provident Knight* seems rather quiet and mild, though the sentences, built similarly, proceed with the same mysterious punctuation and ramble in the same free fashion.

I find no evidence that the work made much of an impression on Englishmen. Its subtitle, *Sir Parsimonious Thrift,* suggests the use which dramatists might have made of it, but, so far as I know, it simply dropped into an out-of-the-way cranny and has remained virtually undisturbed to this day.

Buscon

Quevedo's *Historia de la vida del buscón* was written early in the seventeenth century, circulated in manuscript, printed in 1626, acclaimed in some dozen French editions, and translated by Davies in 1657. Ludwig Pfandl says that it is the purest type of picaresque novel, faithful to its kind, yet marking the limits to which the genre may be extended.[134] One might add that in Davies' English it became an octavo that is sprightly, vivid, biting, humorous, and unflaggingly interesting.

The book gets off to a rapid start that sets both tone and pace:

GEntle Readers, I was born in *Segovia,* a City of the . . . Province of *Casteele,* in the Kingdom of *Spain:* My Fathers name was *Ysidore,* Native of the same City, and by Trade a Barber; but such was his courage, that he was much troubled, when any one called him Barber, and would reply, he was a Circumciser of Hairs, and a Metamorphoser of Beards: His Wife, who as I believe, was my Mother, was called *Roguille.* It was the opinion of most of the Neighbourhood, that she was of the race of the *Jews:* she was of indifferent good behaviour, and tolerably handsom, and for that reason, most of the Poets and Rimers of *Spain* made Copies of pleasant Verses upon her. When she was first married, as also some time after, she had many vexations; for some of our Neighbours tongues were so lavish as to report, that she had changed the Roman I of my Fathers name into a Greek Y. He poor man was accused, and in fine convicted, that at any time when he shaved his Customers, or dress'd his Patients, about the

133. Quoted by Williams, p. 151. *The Retentive Knight* appeared in Stevens' *The Comical Works of Don Francisco de Quevedo* (1707).

134. *Historia de la literatura nacional española en la edad de oro,* tr. Jorge Rubió Balaguer (Barcelona, 1952), p. 310.

Groin, holding up their noses aloft, a young Brother of mine about seven years old, was wont very dexterously to pick their Pockets; but that poor little Angel, (Peace be with him) dyed in Prison, under the pennance of a discipline which was applied to him with a little too much rigour. My Father was very much afflicted at it, for that he drove a pretty Trade with him: he had often times before his death, and never so much as once after, been Prisoner; but as I have been told, he always was delivered with a great deal of honour, accompanied by people of all conditions. I have heard too, that the women used to be Spectators at their windows of this Comedy; I speak it not by way of vain glory, for every one knowes, I am not that way inclin'd.[135]

The background is laid, and the story of Buscon ("Pablo" in the original) begins. The boy's first fight at school is caused by his schoolmates' opinion of his mother, who, we are told, is able to "soder up a crack'd Mayden-head" with Celestinian finesse. When Don Diego, Buscon's best friend, is sent away to study, she and Ysidore permit their son to go along, and it is then that he begins to understand the meaning of hunger. For a glimpse not only of his plight but of Davies' colorful, run-on style and Quevedo's hyperbolic humor, consider this famous description of the schoolmaster, known in English as "Ragot":

He was broad-shoulder'd, his head form'd like a Sugar-loaf, his hair red, from which colour God deliver us: His eyes were so sunk into his head, and withall so hollow, that their stations would have been very proper to have made shops for Brokers, who cheat the world by selling in the dark; his nose like a Saddle, you would have imagined, some one had broken the bridge of it with a clap; his Beard like a Palisadoe, not so much with age, as with fear, for being so neer his hunger-starv'd mouth, which seem'd perpetually to threaten the devouring of him. He had not full six teeth in his mouth, his Throat was as long as a Cranes, his Arms lean, his Hands like a Skeleton, if he stirred never so little, all his bones ratled within him, just like a wicker bottle at a Dogs tail; he never cut his beard, that he might loose nothing of it, and used to say, he would as soon loose his life, as suffer a Barbers hands to come upon his chopps; he wore a cap which the rats had all to be-eaten, for the Grease sake; it was now worn stuffe, though once called cloath; he had a Cassock, some called it miraculous; for that no one could tell of what colour it was, or ever had been; some seeing it, and that it had no napp upon it, concluded it to be made of Frogs skins; othersome said it was an illusion, at a distance, you would have sworn, it had been black, and neerer at hand blew, he had no Coller, girdle nor Sleeves; in a word, so accoutred, that every one would have taken him for a Scar-crow. In his house was neither Rat nor Mouse, he had a trick to conjure them away, least they should eat up the Crusts of bread, which he always kept in his Pockets: his bed

135. *Buscon*, pp. 1–3.

was the bare ground, and he ever lay on one side, for fear of wearing out his clothes, to conclude, he was an arch Villain, and a miserable Hound.[136]

On the basis of such works as the *Vida del buscón,* Henry Edward Watts maintains that "Not more unquestioned is Cervantes' claim to be the first of Spanish humorists than that of Quevedo to be the second."[137] The humor of the two men is of course very different. Cervantes' humor is like Shakespeare's in that it often arises from a sympathetic conception of human character, whereas Quevedo's, as we have seen, is that of the caricaturist. Compared with the humor of *Lazarillo* (which is lean, dry, and wry) and *Guzmán* (which is diffused by moralizing), the humor of the *Vida del buscón* seems fast, direct, and violent. Written by a young man, it sometimes has, not surprisingly, the harsh and smutty qualities of collegiate humor. Perhaps in the "sick" comedians of the mid-twentieth century, sociologists might find an even closer parallel, symptomatic of a more recent decay of values.[138] Whatever its analogues, however, Quevedo's humor has kept some readers from enjoying his book. We might note right here, as an instance, that Ragot's table is so meagerly set that when Buscon asks a servant the way to the "house of Office," he is plainly told that there is none in that house and "you may do it where you please; for during two months that I have been here, I never went to Stool but once, and then too, it was the effect of what I brought in my belly from my Fathers house. . . ."[139] This is but one of numerous passages which provoked Fitzmaurice-Kelly's opinion that Quevedo's wit is "a strange personal secretion, stimulated into activity by a constant vision of tragic details, sordid and repugnant in the highest degree."[140]

---

136. *Buscon,* pp. 21–23; a turned "n" has been righted. Quevedo based the character of the schoolmaster ("Cabra," not "Ragot") on a real person (Aureliano Fernández-Guerra y Orbe, *Obras de Don Francisco de Quevedo Villegas,* I, in *Biblioteca de autores españoles* [Madrid, 1923], XXIII, 489). The whole Ragot episode is reminiscent of Lazarillo's life with the miser-priest.

137. Ed., *Pablo de Segovia* (New York, 1926), p. 3. Some scholars hold that the *Buscón* is an example of pure literary diversion (e.g., Valbuena Prat, p. lviii; Gilman, "An Introduction . . . ," p. 104; and Francisco Maldonado de Guevara, "La teoría de los géneros literarios y la constitución de la novela moderna," *Estudios dedicados a Menéndez Pidal,* III [Madrid, 1952], 304–305, 313–315).

138. As *Time* put it, "What the sickniks dispense is partly social criticism liberally laced with cyanide, partly a Charles Addams kind of jolly ghoulishness, and partly a personal and highly disturbing hostility toward all the world" (LXXIV [July 13, 1959], 42).

139. *Buscon,* p. 28.

140. *"La vida del bvscon,"* RH, XLIII (1918), 8.

For its wit and humor, notwithstanding, one may pick up Davies' *Buscon* as a holiday book. In fact, despite its serious overtones, many modern readers might find its humor, together with its style, length, and tone, better suited to their taste than is that of Cervantes' rambling masterwork.

When his friend Don Diego is sent to the university at Alcalá, Buscon tags along. At first, like Lazarillo and Guzman, he is not really a rogue so much as a naïve boy who is put upon by all he meets. For example, he is the target in a spitting contest at school. When he finally resolves to become a rogue, however, he becomes a good one, and as he sinks morally, he begins to rise in the esteem of those about him. The *pícaro's* world is an inverted one.

When Buscon gets a letter from his Uncle Grimpant, an executioner, saying that he has just had to hang and quarter Buscon's father, the boy decides to go to Segovia for his inheritance. On the way he meets a number of fascinating fools. The first is an engineer who proposes to capture Ostend by drying up the sea with sponges. The second is a swordsman who fences according to mathematical rules (an interesting commentary on a fencing master whom the lame, myopic author once defeated). And the third is a schoolmaster-poet who has composed nine hundred and one sonnets in praise of the feet of the lady he loves, though he has never yet glimpsed those inspirational members. After a time in Segovia, Buscon leaves for Madrid, is taken in by a band of thieves, finds himself clapped into prison, escapes, falls in love with a wench called Annetta, joins a company of actors for whom he writes plays, falls in love with a girl named Rozelle, tricks her into thinking him a fine gentleman, and weds her. And thus Davies' version ends.

Perhaps because of its mocking laughter, opinions regarding the original story have varied greatly. Hannay decried it as

> stripped of the last rag of whatever could disguise its essential hard brutality. If you can gloat over starvation—if the hangman expatiating joyfully over halters and lashes seems a pleasant spectacle to you—if blows, falls, disease, hunger, dirt, and every form of suffering, told with a loud callous laugh, and utterly unrelieved, seem to you worth reading about,—then *Pablo de Segovia* is much at your service.[141]

According to Fitzmaurice-Kelly,

> there are few characters so odious, so uniformly base, so devoid of any pleasing, redeeming vice. Quevedo writes the epic of famished roguery, sparing no detail however loathsome and defiling. Swift himself does not dwell more fondly on

---

141. David Hannay, *The Later Renaissance* (New York, 1898), pp. 144–145.

the obscene squalor of existence, and Quevedo has an individual love of the ghastly which holds him still further aloof from common humanity.[142]

To me, however, it is amazing to find readers who think that Quevedo is merely laughing at a hangman's halter. To think thus is to miss the point. It is almost as if one should denounce Defoe for wanting to hang all dissenters, or damn Swift for wanting to cook Irish babies. Either it is true that inhumanity, callousness, and brutality are things which Quevedo deplores, or he is a canting, two-tongued hypocrite. It should be remembered that he elsewhere champions the teachings of Jesus, even advocates that they be put to use in government. It should be remembered that he writes of Paul the apostle as well as Paul the sharper. In a word, one must not be led by Quevedo's vivacity and wit into thinking him tolerant of the evil he depicts. To be sure, he lacks restraint. He carries to extremes the Spanish penchant for the hard and grotesque. But his probing stare at sordidness is not proof of his love of it, and as Fitzmaurice-Kelly could see, he does not lapse into pornography.[143]

Does he give us nothing positive? Does he give us nothing to cauterize the sores he exposes? It is possible to interpret *Buscon* as a product of the most rigid religious orthodoxy,[144] and yet, as in the *Visions,* it is Quevedo's astringent wit and his indignation at man's degradation, rather than any positive philosophy, which give his story vitality. He offers a stop sign, not a map. Sometimes he is spoken of as a defender of the old traditions, and sometimes as one whose religion and philosophy were inadequate answers to his desperation. Possibly both views are right, but of one thing we may be sure: in 1605, at about the time he wrote the *Vida del buscón,* he was deeply concerned about the condition of Spain. To his Belgian friend Lipsius he wrote, "I cannot speak of her without pain. If you are the prey of war, we are the prey of idleness and ignorance. . . . Here we ruin ourselves. There is no one who may speak, but many who lie."[145]

142. *"La vida del bvscon,"* p. 7.

143. *"La vida del bvscon,"* p. 8. T. E. May writes: "To those of his contemporaries who eagerly seize on any picaresque tale that appears, it is meant to spare nothing of the truth as to what they are enjoying, and to make them uneasy about it" ("Good and Evil in the 'Buscón': A Survey," *MLR,* XLV [1950], 335). In any case, as William Webbe wrote in 1586, literature "is not debarred from any matter which may be expressed by penne or speeche . . ." (*A Discourse of English Poetrie,* in *Elizabethan Critical Essays,* ed. G. Gregory Smith [Oxford, 1904], I, 249).

144. May, p. 322.

145. Quoted by Antonio Papell, *Quevedo* (Barcelona, 1947), p. 285.

It has been observed more than once that the principal vice of modern literature is its attempt to arouse violent emotion;[146] that the vulgar want to feel, not think, and an inferior book will invite them to do just that. It is necessary to add, though, that any work of fiction has failed if it fails to touch the feelings of the reader for whom it is designed. That Quevedo can use his intellect to give squirming, living form to his hatreds is a tribute to his genius commensurate with the fact that by his distorted images of reality he can simultaneously arouse in his reader both thought and feeling. In fact, by using each to fortify the other, his satire is considerably intensified. An abstract dissertation on man's inhumanity to man is quite unlikely to approach the effectiveness of Quevedo's ostensibly objective yet completely damning treatment of Buscón's Uncle Grimpant. That hideous passages such as this are underlined in Quevedo with humor makes them all the more strong—the humor all the more cutting, and the intellectual implications all the more effective. If the seventeenth century was right in believing that one of the purposes of art is to teach, using the word in its broadest sense, then Quevedo should have been able and should still be able to teach an important lesson in an impressive way.

I maintain that Quevedo does teach. As he puts it in his preface to *Don Reymundo el entremetido,* the author of a story can alert readers to their own vices—to which they are blinded by pride—by making these same vices seem loathsome in fiction.[147] In the text of the *Buscón,* economy of artistry has precluded the moral meanderings of an Alemán, but Quevedo does manage to say in his prologue that a reader will find not a little fruit in the book if he heeds the examples it gives.[148] I think that this is more than conventional lip service. For all of his slogging through details of degradation, I think that

146. William Dean Howells long ago noted that Valdés had made the observation (*Criticism and Fiction* [London, 1891], p. 65).

147. The passage is quoted by Ernest Merimée, *Essai sur la vie et les oeuvres de Francisco de Quevedo* (Paris, 1886), pp. 168–169. *Don Raimundo* is a little-known picaresque story by Diego Martín de Tovar y Valderrama.

148. He writes: "no poco fruto podrás sacar dél si tienes atención al escarmiento; y, cuando se lo hagas, aprovéchate de los sermones, que dudo nadie compre libro de burlas para apartarse de los incentivos de su natural depravado" (*Vida del buscón,* ed. Luys Santa Marina, in *Clásicos castellanos* [Madrid, 1951], V, Pt. 1, 7). James Russell Stamm, noting this passage, writes that "The references to 'fruto podrás sacar', to the 'escarmiento' and to 'los sermones' leave no doubt that this work shares a kinship with Quevedo's nonfictional didactic works" (p. 82). Like the *Buscón,* the terse *Lazarillo* had earlier used the fruit image to suggest seriousness of purpose. One is also reminded of the old advice, when reading a book, "do not turn the leaves only, but gather the fruit."

Quevedo's book adds up to more than the sum of such details. In fact its underlying essence is finally made overt in his very last sentence, which may be translated as, "he never betters his state who changes only his place, not his life and habits." It is a maxim pregnant with meaning. If one could change one's way of life, it implies, one might improve one's lot and, by extension, take at least an infinitesimal step toward making the race better and kinder. The Augean stables to be discovered and cleansed are within ourselves. In other words, I would submit that Quevedo, though sometimes his control is imperfect, succeeds not only in arousing strong feelings in his reader, but for the most part is arousing them purposefully. Were it merely a comic, dirty book, his *Vida del buscón* would no more be entitled to as much consideration as it has received than would the work of Francis Kirkman or Richard Head. On the other hand, if Quevedo had succeeded merely in writing a witty fantasy on the baser realities of his time and place (something Kirkman and Head could not rise to), he still would deserve our regard. The point is, he has done this and more. Even in its modified English form, Quevedo's picaresque story is valuable, interesting, and entertaining not only because of its appeal as a museum-piece and its ability to convey a biting humor, but because it is one of the means by which an intelligent artist has succeeded in presenting the ills of life as he sees it. The mirror which Quevedo holds up to nature is a cracked one, to be sure, but men of his day might have found themselves in it if they had bothered to look with any care.

"Will you buy a Glass, a Mirror that flatters not?" John Davies asks the reader in the preface to his translation. "Bid fair, here 'tis that will show you your whole proportion; for it represents the greatest part of the world Fools and Knaves; and 'tis two to one but you may see your self here." The result will be edifying: "Here you may . . . be taught as Dancing-Masters first teach Bumpkins, by laughing them out of their old Garb: You'l say, 'tis too light; no, you are too grave: Nothing but hath something of lightness. . . ."[149] True enough, so far; but unfortunately Davies was dependent for his views on what the French translator, La Geneste, had seen. Likening his translation to a ship, Davies declares that *"Her main burthen is mirth. . . ."*[150]

As we observed earlier, the concluding passages of La Geneste and Davies are totally different from those of Quevedo.[151] Quevedo's own last chapter,

149. *Buscon,* A3ʳ–A4ʳ.
150. *Buscon,* A2ᵛ.
151. See Ch. III, p. 34.

so difficult as to defy translation, has its hero assist in a couple of drunken murders, sends him off to the Indies with a whore, and comes to no good anchorage.[152] The English version, sweetened with amorous feeling and marital bliss, implies that Buscon, like Guzman, is capable of mending. It can therefore have him say that "there are few men in the world, who for happiness may compare with my self."[153] One might argue for the superiority of either ending. The revised version will seem best to those who, in Henry James's words, think the ending of a novel should be "like that of a good dinner, a course of dessert and ices. . . ."[154] Quevedo thought no such thing.

Davies turned out a good book, if not a good translation. Considering Quevedo's style, perhaps we should be grateful. Quevedo's Spanish was sometimes more complex than that in his picaresque story, but, as Fitzmaurice-Kelly observes,

even the direct and forcible prose of the *Bvscon* has an individual savour which is almost impossible of reproduction in any language but Spanish; . . . Quevedo . . . purposely eschews the obvious, fabricates expressions at need, plays disconcerting tricks with syntax, abounds in "conceits", distorts the natural meaning of words and throws on them a burden greater . . . [than] they can bear.[155]

Perhaps the English book reads as well as it does precisely because it is not a good translation. Though it is sometimes awkward, it is always colloquial and colorful, lively as a lizard in a sack with a cat. It differs in a thousand ways from Quevedo's, and does not even transmit La Geneste's with great accuracy, and yet one may rationalize in this case with John Selden, who thought it good to have translations because they serve as comments as far as the judgments of the translators go.[156]

152. In *El celoso extremeño* Cervantes calls the Indies a decoy of loose women and a refuge for the desperadoes and homicides of Spain.

153. *Buscon*, p. 287. Lazarillo had concluded his autobiography in "my chiefest time of good aduenture."

154. Henry James, "The Art of Fiction," in *The Art of Fiction and Other Essays* (New York, 1948), p. 7.

155. "*La vida del bvscon*," p. 4.

156. *Table Talk of John Selden*, ed. Frederick Pollock (London, 1927), p. 23. In Davies' book the chief epic hero of Spain appears as the "Syd," a famous "marquess"; we find that prisoners let down a cord from a window "with an old Hat at the end of it, such as Prisoners use in New-gate . . ."; and the Portuguese who loves Annetta never comes near her without sighing "like a *Presbyterian* at a long Lecture" (*Buscon*, pp. 128, 144, and 222). Also interesting in view of the practices of other translators is Davies' willingness to write that the "Popes . . . are Gods Viceregents, and the Keys of the Church . . ." (p. 76).

How was the book received in England? After 1657, the *Short-Title Cata-logue* lists a second edition, an octavo sold by Simon Miller in 1669–1670, and another "second" edition for Henry Herringman, 1670. In 1683, to-gether with *The Famous History of Auristella* (from a tale in *Gerardo*), a truncated version appeared as *The Pleasant Story of Paul of Segovia*. (Al-though the translator, "W. B.," had the advantage of working with the orig-inal Spanish, his book is still a far cry from Quevedo's.) Later still, in the first years of the next century, Captain Stevens found the book "witty & di-verting," and brought out the most accurate of the early translations, calling his effort *The Life of Paul the Spanish Sharper* (1707).[157] Such is the biblio-graphical evidence. On such bases one is not tempted to say that Quevedo's narrative was a best-seller, and yet, excepting only the *Visions,* it was the best known of his works in England.

Conclusion

All told, some eight satiric-realistic books were newly translated into Eng-lish between the time of the completed *Quixote* (1620) and that of *Buscón.* (Earlier there had been only *Lazarillo,* its anonymous sequel, and *Don Quixote* itself.) Of all these, judging by editions alone, one would have to conclude that Alemán's *Rogue* and Luna's *Pursuit* were the most popular in the pre-Restoration period. Though not even these works appeared in any great quantity in comparison with the true best-sellers of the day, they must have reached a sizable body of English readers.[158]

Their appeal has been explained in various ways. First of all, in England as elsewhere, the popularity of Spanish satire was not so much a matter of new subjects as the interesting treatment of basically familiar ones. Awdeley, Har-man, Greene, Dekker, and Rowlands had clearly proved that England was rich in low-life material, yet somehow their kind of writing never ripened and matured.[159]

A second reason for the popularity of the Spanish imports is offered by Er-

---

157. It was printed in his *Comical Works of Don Francisco de Quevedo.*

158. See Charles C. Mish, "Best Sellers in Seventeenth-Century Fiction," *PBSA,* XLVII (1953), 356–373.

159. Chettle, Breton, and Nashe created rogue-heroes, but "just when the romance of roguery seemed fairly established in England it somehow went bankrupt, and for fifty years no one would again venture faith in it" (Chandler, *The Literature of Roguery,* I, 205).

nest Baker: "The economic and social condition of England late in the sixteenth century was not altogether unlike that of Spain—or, indeed, of the
Continent in general."[160] The parallels between Falstaff's world and Guzman's would be difficult but intriguing to pursue. Both Shakespeare and Alemán depict characters who disdain the old-fashioned ideals of honor and love,
men who fail to find any rule better than "self first." Still it is dangerous to
overemphasize and especially to antedate the popularity of Spanish picaresque
fiction. *Guzmán de Alfarache,* the earliest surviving romance of roguery
printed by a Spaniard after *Lazarillo* and its first sequel, did not appear in its
original language until the turn of the century, nor was it translated into English until 1622. If rogue biographies were relatively numerous in Elizabethan
England, then, this is more apt to have been a reflection of local conditions
than of admiration for Spanish works. Later on, however, according to at
least one scholar, the Spanish *pícaros* were welcomed fairly warmly because
Counter-Reformation Spain and Protestant England were akin in their hopes
to return life to sounder bases.[161]

Third and last, Rowland had originally claimed to present *Lazarillo* to Sir
Thomas Gresham in the hope that it would be useful for disseminating
knowledge of Spain. It was natural for curious Englishmen, both then and
later, to turn to any sources available to learn something about their long-
time enemy and sometime friend.

But the first answer still seems the best. Be he Protestant or Catholic, it was
tempting for an Englishman to read about Lazarillo and his descendants simply because these raffish rascals were the heroes of some very good stories.

Looking back on them all, one is tempted to make some generalizations.
For one thing, the authors of the fiction considered here dealt widely in humor. Their inclination toward humor might even be thought pervasive
enough to demonstrate an important affinity between humor and what we
have called realism. Nevertheless, by harping on the physical and magnify-
ing the gross, they created an unlovely and loveless world which, whatever

---

160. Baker continues: "True, she was not a defeated nation; but she was over-
strained by warlike effort, the social system had been unhinged by the suppression
of the monasteries, agriculture was depressed, unemployment general, and the land,
especially in the neighbourhood of towns, was swarming with discharged soldiers
and sailors, and others hard put to it to make a living, who were easily induced to
join the regular army of vagrants and criminals" (*The History of the English Novel*
[London, 1929], II, 50).

161. Herrero García, "Nueva interpretación . . . ," p. 362.

their intent, was often hard to smile at.[162] One may even feel sometimes that in reading these works he is watching Spanish writers awaken from the golden dream of the Renaissance—the pastoral and chivalric dream—to find life itself a bad dream, a labyrinth of illusion and error.

Most important, these books usually seem to be saying something. No matter how hard it is to understand them, one generally has the feeling that their authors are purveying something besides entertainment. *The Spanish Bawd,* for example, is finally unlike *The Rogue,* which champions orthodoxy, and yet both voice the lament of Pleberio: "O life fulfill'd with griefe, and accompanied with naught but misery! O world, world!"[163] Man at his best is no better than dust, says Alemán.[164] And Cervantes, whose *Don Quixote* might have been placed in a chapter like the present one, has a character exclaim,

> *Oh, the vain hopes we cherish all life long!*
> *Thinking at last to find the rest we seek,*
> *But shadow, smoke, and dreams are our reward.*[165]

Like the picaresque writers, in other words, Cervantes is concerned in his masterwork with the illusion of appearance, the relativity of everything, and the need for care in determining values. Life to him is not the hell it seemed to Quevedo, of course. On the other hand, even Quevedo, who created a nightmare world, seems to have seen both that world and the world of the romances and the *novelas* (as well as the corresponding elements of each in life) at once and as one, a sort of jeweled pomander filled, like the merchant's box of sugar cakes in *Buscon,* with offal and stones. Duality is present, at least by implication, in all the works considered here, most clearly in the skilfully rounded *Spanish Bawd,* but also in the *Visions* and *The Provident Knight.* In his *Novelas ejemplares,* especially the ones translated by Mabbe and considered in the preceding chapter, Cervantes sometimes offers little more than sops of honey steeped in rose water, but he, too, understands the danger as well as the attraction of mere romancing. No one has phrased this better than Maynard Mack: to Cervantes, Mack writes, the danger "lay in diverting moral idealism into tilts with sensational or merely apparent evils

---

162. Baker writes: "The crudity and coarseness of the witless compilations that were intended to compete with the Spanish article are enough to persuade us that the acrid comedy of genuine picaresque fiction was little appreciated" (III, 43).

163. *Bawd,* p. 199.

164. *Rogue,* II, 64.

165. Since Shelton bungles a bit, I quote here from Samuel Putnam's translation, *Don Quixote* (New York, 1949), I, 462.

—giants who are only windmills—when all about real evil walks unchallenged in homelier shapes."[166]

The technique of this fiction is sometimes belittled. Incidents might well be rearranged, it is said. And of course, with the exception of *The Spanish Bawd,* the stories *do* tend to have a rope-of-onions sort of structure, though this is not to say that they lack central significance. I would not grow hot in a cold cause, and yet it does seem important to say that these segmental stories do succeed in presenting man cut loose from his traditional values; that decay of meaning is their common theme, whatever specific answers a writer may offer, imply, negate, or ignore; and that technical "crudity" (the climaxes are "not prepared for") serves to enhance the fragmentary nature of the world depicted. Some of the picaresque stories—*Lazarillo, Guzmán,* and *Buscón*—even stop with the promise of a sequel, a fact which says as plainly as anything, *Here is a fragment.*

Then, too, although there are snatches of character revelation, there is, outside *The Spanish Bawd,* little or no character development. Is this not a sign of primitive fiction? Lack of characterization deprives the picaresque stories of a major kind of depth, without doubt, but the concentration on man's "external" rather than "internal" aspects must sometimes be regarded as a matter of approach, not success or failure, as we may see by glancing at Fielding. In the picaresque stories from Spain, such a concentration is a means of throwing into relief the importance of social conditions. Though it is true that the *pícaros* are more often types than individuals, this fact is balanced by the fact that society is the basic subject of the works in which they appear. The *pícaros* are metonymic expressions, one might say, of their environment. We are meant to smile at their wiles, to be sure, but we are also meant to be alerted to the ills of their world. It is as if the magnification of vice and folly in the *pícaros* and their world were the first step in the process of exorcising.

Along with jocularity, at any rate, the satiric books from Spain provided various examples of what abominations may be brought to light when an imaginative writer reaches down the "real" world's windpipe and pulls it inside out. Quevedo has given us a phrase to label the whole lurid, chaotic, Bosch-like vista he has seen—*el mundo por de dentro,* the world from within, or, as it has also been translated, the world inside out. It is an indelicate but important vision in the history of Spanish letters. In England, whatever else it did or did not do, Arnold Kettle says that "It made impossible

166. Introd. to Fielding's *Joseph Andrews* (New York, 1957), p. x.

any serious attempt to move back to the pastoral and courtly traditions of the early romances."[167] It clarified the fact that actual life is the most vital source and subject of fiction.[168]

167. *An Introduction to the English Novel* (London, 1954), I, 62.

168. Charlotte Morgan amplifies this idea: "The great contribution of the anti-romances . . . was not so much actual material or structure, as the training of readers and writers of all classes to appreciate the humorous or comic view of life, the cultivating of a taste for robust animalism as opposed to the etherial sentimentalism of the romances, the revealing of the possibilities of low life and bourgeois material, the realistic depiction of a definite, concrete background, and the developing of a vigorous, colloquial style for purposes of narration, although not as yet for the expression of emotion" (*The Rise of the Novel of Manners* [New York, 1911], pp. 48–49).

Chapter VIII

Conclusion

Considering them altogether and returning to the *sergas* metaphor of Garci Rodríguez de Montalvo, we may envisage the Renaissance English versions of Spanish Golden Age stories as constituting a large and varied tapestry. Because the panels of this fictitious fabric were woven by so many hands over so long a period, thus encouraging the salpetrous damps of time to eat holes in it here and there (its most recent part is over three centuries old), and because it has been mended and patched somewhat unevenly by modern students, our knowledge of it is lamentably incomplete. Nevertheless it is possible not only to gain an over-all impression of some of the tapestry's qualities, but also to make an estimate of the reception accorded its various parts.

A Statistical Analysis of Translations

Before concluding with a few words of general criticism, let us consider briefly what may be learned about the matter of reception. Including strong stories and weak ones, the preceding chapters have touched on some forty non-chivalric works between Clerc's *Arnalte* (1543) and Davies' *Buscon* (1657).[1] If we count all the various known editions and issues of these books, their total number of appearances is raised to approximately seventy.

Naturally a chronological survey embracing all of these Spanish stories shows increases and decreases in certain years. Less obviously, as Edith Klotz's survey of all English books during the same period reveals, the total number of literary works increased more steadily than did that of Spanish translations.[2] Such a fact is meaningful if it does no more than suggest that the

1. Individual *novelas* by Cervantes and Montalván have been counted separately, but not those intercalated in longer narratives.

2. In 1500 there were some fourteen works which might be deemed literary; in 1550 there were twenty-one; in 1580, forty-four; in 1600, eighty-four; in 1620, eighty-seven; in 1630, one hundred and seventeen; and in 1640, one hundred and fifty-six ("A Subject Analysis of English Imprints for Every Tenth Year from 1480 to 1640," *HLQ*, I [1938], 418).

Focusing strictly on narratives, both Spanish and English, from the beginning of our period to the end of the sixteenth century, we find at first that each ten-year

relatively sporadic interest in Spanish literature may not have been an image in small of general literary interests. Spanish books seem instead to have been capable of an independent existence which could be modified by factors not quite like those which determined literary interest in general. What these factors were is not easy to determine. Certainly they sometimes seem to have been related to England's current concern or comparative lack of concern for Spain as a nation. Underhill would say that

The dissemination of Spanish books in [Tudor] England . . . was absolutely dependent upon the course of politics and commerce. It followed their development closely in volume and in kind. The rise and power of Castilian culture in the home of the Tudors were determined by and sensitive to the successive phases of the political contest between the English and Spanish nations.[3]

Unqualified as it is, however, this generalization is a bit difficult to accept, even if we restrict our attention to the Tudor period. It implies, after all, that the phenomenal and sustained popularity of the moralist Antonio de Guevara may be traced to purely political or commercial sources; and if the view were extended to include the Stuart period (not that Underhill attempts to do so), it would ignore that a book such as *Lazarillo* could find readers even when general interest in Spain was low. Therefore it is best to soften Underhill's statement and say simply that the kind of reading matter made available by the early English booksellers was often a good indication of the importance of the Anglo-Spanish political and commercial climate of the moment.

An analysis of English imprints suggests also that Spanish fiction, by not

---

period shows a marked increase. Sterg O'Dell's *Chronological List of Prose Fiction in English Printed in England and Other Countries 1475–1640* (Cambridge, Mass., 1954), a work which is swollen because of its author's rather loose definition of fiction, yields the following data: 1550–1559, thirty; 1560–1569, forty-two; 1570–1579, fifty-six; 1580–1589, ninety-nine; 1590–1599, one hundred and sixty-two. The first half of the seventeenth century is a different story. There is a long-range increase in number of imprints between 1600 and 1655; in 1600 there were nine titles, and in 1655, twenty-five (Charles C. Mish, *English Prose Fiction, 1600–1700: A Chronological Checklist* [Charlottesville, Va., 1952]; O'Dell, less conservative than Mish, lists fifteen for 1600). But these facts alone are deceptive. The years 1600–1609 witnessed the publication of ninety works; 1610–1619, sixty-two; and 1620–1629, eighty. In other words, there is no long, gradual curve from 1600's nine titles to 1655's twenty-five. Instead there is a very jagged line of progression and regression. In 1607, an unusually productive year, the number of titles jumped from nine to sixteen, and for 1643 (just one hundred years after Clerc's *Arnalte*) Mish does not list a single work of fiction.

3. John Garrett Underhill, *Spanish Literature in the England of the Tudors* (New York, 1899), p. 16.

increasing along with other literature, may have been decreasing as far as proportional popularity is concerned. If this is true, then interest in Spain (which would seem relatively more steady if we examined only the works translated from Spanish) was apparently, in the long run, really undergoing a decline. If we take two decades such as the 1620's and 1640's, the matter will become more clear. Between 1620 and 1640 the number of literary imprints in England nearly doubled, yet the decade of the 1620's saw just about twice as many Spanish translations as did the decade of the 1640's. If we consider only these years (neglecting the fact that the 1650's saw an apparent renewal of interest in Spanish fiction), it would seem that interest in Spain faded considerably more than we could guess from studying the translations alone. Conversely, Hispanic interest in the 1620's was the greater.

The same general view may be seen from another vantage point—and an important vantage point it is, for it reminds us of the many translations of Spanish books beyond those we have considered. Using the bibliography of E. G. Mathews, it is possible to estimate that in the first decade of the seventeenth century about twenty-five non-fiction works appeared; in the years 1611 to 1620, thirty-five; in 1621 to 1630, fifty-five; in 1631 to 1640, twenty; in 1641 to 1650, eight; and in 1651 to 1660, eleven.[4] Most striking, the important years from 1615 to 1625 saw about sixty editions of non-fiction works translated from Spanish, or roughly a third of the non-fiction Spanish works which were to appear in the entire sixty-year span between 1600 and 1660. What kinds of books are included? There is a sprinkling of hard-to-classify titles such as *Prose Against Painting by Women* (1616) and *A Curious Treatise of the Nature and Quality of Chocolate* (1640), but most fall under two main headings—first, religion; and second, current events and history. Current events and history account for between forty and fifty titles in the list, but the really important category, religion, accounts for over ninety, most of which were published at St. Omer, Douay, Paris, or somewhere else on the Continent.[5] Obviously, then, a considerable amount of translating was

4. The figures in this passage are derived from Mathews' "Studies in Spanish-English Cultural and Literary Relations, 1598–1700," unpublished Ph.D. dissertation (Harvard, 1938), pp. 588–635.

5. Probably most of these books were intended for the edification not only of exiled Englishmen, but of Roman Englishmen anywhere. Then, too, Spanish religious books could be modified for non-Roman English consumption. As Mabbe put it, one could remove the colocynth and make the broth fit for tastes at home. P. E. Russell, after considering both fiction and non-fiction, writes that "the really important conclusion which may be drawn from a study of the reception given to Spanish literature in seventeenth-century England is that, in that age, Spanish literature was

being done aside from the fictional works on which we have been concentrating. We should err in estimating the significance of both fiction and non-fiction were we to ignore such a fact.[6] The main point at the moment, however, is that the years when interest in the Spanish match was greatest were also the greatest years for various sorts of translation from Spanish.

Adding in the chivalric romances sprinkled throughout the period, we may observe matters of significance in the 1590's, 1620's, 1630's, and 1650's. In the first of these periods far more fiction was printed in English than had been printed in any previous decade in English literary history, in fact more than had been printed in the entire period before 1570.[7] Among other reasons it was the Indian summer of the Spanish chivalric romance. In those post-Armada years when Sidney's *Arcadia* was but recently in print, when Spenser was working on the *Faerie Queene,* and the not totally dissimilar *Diana* was attracting much attention, the fame of the Knight of the Sun was approaching its meridian. Furthermore, although only four works of non-chivalric Spanish fiction appeared at the time, this was as many (setting aside Guevara) as had appeared in the preceding twenty years. Clearly there was mounting interest in fiction in general, but that emphatically included Spanish fiction.

In the early 1620's, when interest in Spain was high again, the number of Spanish titles mounted again, while the total number of fiction titles remained relatively constant. It is worth remembering that it was in this decade that Middleton's *Game at Chesse* played for nine days—longer than the initial run of any other drama in the pre-Restoration theater[8]—not because it was an artistic success, but because it was a topical satire concerned with the Anglo-Spanish alliance. Here we seem to have corroboration not only of

---

still—by and large—a universal literature whose message was capable of transcending not only the geographical frontiers of the Iberian Peninsula, but also the theological frontiers which the sixteenth century had created" ("English Seventeenth-Century Interpretations of Spanish Literature," *Atlante,* I [1953], 77).

6. Slightly more than two hundred works of prose fiction were published in Spain in the seventeenth century (Willard F. King, "Literary Academies and Prose Fiction in Seventeenth-Century Spain," *DA,* XVIII [1958], 590), but literary books in Spain, as in England, were a small part of the printers' total output. Américo Castro, *The Structure of Spanish History,* tr. Edmund L. King (Princeton, 1954), pp. 663–664, presents the following data from the indexes of the *Bibliotheca hispana* (1672) of Nicolás Antonio: "48 pages of titles of religious works; 40 of historical works of largely religious character; 13 of jurisprudence and law; 8 of profane literature; 7 of humanistic learning; 6 of medicine and natural sciences; 5 of philosophy (in support of theology and religion); 4 of mathematics, astronomy, music, geography, nautical science, engineering, and architecture all together; 3 of political science."

7. The figures in this paragraph are based on O'Dell.

8. Gerald E. Bentley, *The Jacobean and Caroline Stage* (Oxford, 1956), IV, 877.

J. G. Underhill's observation on Tudor translations, but of the tentative conclusion just drawn from Edith Klotz's survey of literary works in general.

In the 1630's the number of English imprints varied considerably, then rose sharply in 1639 and 1640. Meanwhile the Spanish titles, nowhere to be seen in 1635–1637, also began to multiply. From this it seems that there may have been a positive correlation between the two. At this time, in other words, the demand for Spanish fiction may have been part of the general demand for fiction. Then finally, after some lean years prior to the execution of Charles, when Englishmen seem to have had little time for fiction of any sort, there was a considerable increase in editions in the 1650's. Suddenly there was as much Spanish fiction as there had been in the 1590's—and this time with a far smaller percentage of chivalric romances. If we superimpose the curve of Spanish works on that of all fiction during the 1650's, we find that this time, too, the increase in books of Spanish origin was apparently part of a general reawakening of interest in fiction.

From such facts we may conclude that in the 1590's a broad interest in things Spanish flowed over into every field, including literature. Later on, at the time of the projected Spanish match, people were again reading Spanish fiction at least in part to satisfy their curiosity about Spain. Later still, they seem to have read it more because it was fiction than because it was Spanish, and, at the end of our period, both because it was fiction and because Spanish interests were rising again.

At best, however, bibliographical statistics such as these are suggestive rather than conclusive. By chance we know that Wilson and Paston translated from the *Diana*, and young Charles Stewart from the *Amadís*. But how many other translations remained in manuscript? Surely there were some. At the turn of the century Francis Meres observed that "As cheries be fulsome when . . . they be plenty: so bookes be stale when they be printed in that they be common."[9] Then again, some printed translations may simply have disappeared. Again, our knowledge about sizes of editions is scant. And again, as in the case of the single edition of Yong's *Diana* and the variant issues of *Aurora* and *The Prince*, a book's number of appearances may prove to be a confusing kind of evidence. This does not prevent an estimate of the general success of Spanish fiction in England. It means only that we had best be careful about making categorical statements.[10]

9. *Palladis Tamia* (1598), p. 266ʳ.

10. Although it does not specifically concern translations, one of the gaps most vexing to me is pointed out by James Howell's advice that Englishmen should read Juan de Mariana and José de Acosta as "the most authentique *Annalists of Spaine,* and *Alvares* for the moderne story, *Lope de Vegas* works wil give good entertain-

On the one hand, though Spanish books were known, read, admired, and imitated, the evidence indicates that their popularity should not be exaggerated. On the other hand, of the nineteen fictional books which Mish accepts as bona fide best-sellers during the seventeenth century, several in the years 1600–1660 had careers comparable to that of Alemán's *Rogue*.[11] For instance, Richard Johnson's *Seven Champions of Christendom* and Thomas Deloney's *Jack of Newbery* both made about six appearances, and Emanuel Forde's popular *Parismus*, seven. *The Rogue,* then, with its seven or so appearances, was moving in relatively fast-selling company. Pretty clearly Alemán's book is the seventeenth-century star of the Spanish company, though with its Luna sequel *Lazarillo de Tormes* managed to catch up.

William London, a Newcastle bookseller who wasted no affection on fiction, included at least thirteen Spanish stories in his *Catalogue of the Most Vendible Books in England,* a work which he issued in 1657. Some of these he did not regard as fiction, hence scattered elsewhere in his list, but in the section set aside for "Romances" he recorded fifty-nine works, of which eight (some fourteen per cent) are from the Spanish.[12] Since London's catalogue appeared in our terminal year, it may serve as a good key to contemporary interest in the years just prior to the Restoration.[13]

---

ment for *Verse,* and *Guevara* for pure Prose . . ." (*Instructions for Forreine Travell* [1642], ed. Edward Arber [Westminster, 1903], p. 39). If Howell does not use the phrase *"Alvares* for the moderne story" to refer to a contemporary historian (e.g., Juan de Álvarez Serrano), then he refers to a "moderne" writer of fiction who is totally unknown to me.

11. None, English or Spanish, came close to the approximately forty editions achieved by Aesop's fables. For some interesting comparative data see Charles C. Mish, "Best Sellers in Seventeenth-Century Fiction," *PBSA,* XLVII (1953), 356–373.

12. He includes Gayton's *Pleasant Notes.*

13. Limiting our view to translations, we have necessarily neglected other ways by which Spanish stories became known. First, there were a few "home-bred *Spaniards"* (*Rogue* [1623], II, **7^r) who would have had little or no trouble reading them in their original form. Second, more than a few could have read the same stories in French translations. Third (and admittedly farther afield), a considerable number of Spanish plots were presented to the English in dramatic form, the most deeply indebted playwright being John Fletcher, who apparently found material in the work of Flores, Cervantes, Alemán, Céspedes y Meneses, and Lope de Vega. Information on Spanish fiction in English drama is still scattered and likely to remain so, since many dramatists could say, as did Dryden at the end of the century, *"where ever I have lik'd any story in a Romance, Novel, or forreign Play, I have made no difficulty, nor ever shall, to take the foundation of it, to build it up, and to make it proper for the English Stage."* But when it was completed, *"there scarce remain'd any Plank of the Timber which first built it"* (*An Evening's Love,* preface [1671], a3^v).

Some Generalizations on Technique

Turning finally to the qualities of the fiction that was translated, one is perhaps struck most forcibly by its range. Moreover, though all generalizations are at best partial truths, one might be inclined to begin by agreeing with V. S. Pritchett that "The Spanish genius is for excess, for excesses of austerity as well as excesses of sensual decoration."[14] In any case, the fine art of Spain, like the Eastern art from which it borrows, is often one of embellished surfaces, of elaborate but largely two-dimensional complexity. In literature the interest in embellishment seems to have been transmuted into a fascination for rhetoric. (Not that rhetorical intricacy was limited to Spain, of course.) Flattering ourselves that we have passed beyond the artificial refinements of *Arnalte* and *Euphues,* we tend nowadays to regard rhetoric more as a mode of illustration than as subject matter itself. Hence the books of *Diana* and especially the *novelas sentimentales* are apt to strike us as too preoccupied with surfaces. In a very different way and with vastly different effect, the later but conceit-spangled prose of Quevedo is also a case in point—though one must immediately add that most of Quevedo's stylistic devices have been lost in translation. In other cases, where a translator's stylistic awkwardness has been added to an original work's stylistic complexity, as in the translations of Clerc, Berners, and Lawrence, the Spanish stories are simply not very appealing.

The other half of Pritchett's generalization is also suggestive. Some students have argued that the more highly decorated works in Spanish literature are not ultimately Spanish in temper because Spain's native muse is, for the most part, austere and simple, preferring hard fact to chimera.[15] Perhaps so. At any rate, some of the most attractive pages of Golden Age fiction are those which deal with everyday subjects in a plain and unaffected style. Appropriately, then, translated into the English of David Rowland, *Lazarillo de Tormes* has a plainness, a hardness, even a roughness which are somehow more faithful than the smoother kinds of plainness which could have been offered by the more flexible prose of the eighteenth century.

If we seek the colloquial color and stylistic bravado sometimes associated

14. *The Spanish Temper* (New York, 1954), p. 51.
15. E.g., Arturo Farinelli, *Divagaciones hispánicas* (Barcelona, 1936), I, 93. Guillermo Díaz-Plaja points to Don Juan Manuel (1282–*ca.* 1349) as the first Castilian writer to give his ideas on literary style. According to him, a good style is characterized by sobriety, economy, and simplicity (*Historia de la literatura española* [Mexico City, 1955], p. 62).

with Elizabeth's reign, we may of course find it readily enough in the translations of Rojas, Cervantes, and Alemán—that is, in Mabbe's *Rogue* and *Bawd,* and Shelton's *Don Quixote.* For colloquial vigor of a later sort, we may turn to Davies' version of Quevedo's *Buscón.* Elsewhere, for the most part, we are apt to find that the Renaissance translators were more often journeymen than masters, producers of interesting but not outstanding books.

Structurally, too, the Spanish stories offer considerable variety. In the non-chivalric romances, pastoral and Byzantine alike, a reader finds his wit challenged by a superficial intricacy such that he may easily forget the main plots altogether while his attention is fixed on some wonder of the moment. In spite of the fact that the mazes may have plans, a reader is likely to be less aware of these than of a series of surprises, a succession of scattered incidents. All the evidence indicates that the artificers of the mazes tried to please by using as many interlocking pieces as possible.

In the picaresque stories, also, a reader's attention is focused on the event of the moment, but here he is not confused by relationships between story elements. Here, as occasionally in the chivalric romances which they may mock, an episode is often simply slipped onto the string and placed next to the last one. The effect, therefore, is a gradually cumulative one. Though some passages might be omitted without serious loss, and though a reader may have trouble finding such things as rising action, turning-point, or resolution (except in individual episodes), the rogue stories and even Quevedo's *Visions* do, nevertheless, have ways of achieving unity: they have a narrator, a consistently hard and comic tone, and sometimes, I believe, an underlying theme.

Different from both the labyrinthine form of the non-chivalric romances and the rope-of-onions form of the picaresque stories are the varying patterns of *The Spanish Bawd,* the *novelas* of Cervantes, and, to a lesser degree, *Don Quixote.* The interlocutory *Spanish Bawd* interweaves plebeian and patrician strands to make a varied but satisfyingly coherent whole, meanwhile conveying a comparatively simple love story with a beginning, climax, and end. Cervantes' *novelas* such as *The Force of Blood* and *The Jealous Husband* exemplify narratives of less scope. In these, as in Rojas' work, details are not generally used gratuitously nor as matters interesting largely for their own sake, but as ways of developing plots which are basically simple. In contrast, Cervantes' masterwork has elements of various kinds of fiction. Like a picaresque narrative, for instance, it is something of an incident book, and yet by its mingling of various themes and subjects (especially in Part II, where the seams are best concealed) it attains a higher kind of unity and a deeper significance than may be found in any of the picaresque fiction we have considered.

Intimately related to the structure of the early Spanish stories is the incessant movement they depict. Except in the *novelas sentimentales* and *The Spanish Bawd,* travel is found almost everywhere—in romances, *novelas,* and picaresque books alike. No one need be told, of course, that travel has been an important literary device since the time of Homer, perhaps even before, but a recent study has shown that it was particularly important in the fiction of Golden Age Spain, both as a means to adventure and as a vehicle for satire.[16] In the picaresque stories, travel is obviously a mechanical boon to satirizing different elements in society; and in *Persiles,* Cervantes himself observes explicitly that travel is a source of adventure.[17] Quite possibly it is also a reflection of the spirit of the time, of actual adventures and adventurousness. As travel is treated in picaresque books, it might even be regarded as a means of indicating that life itself is rambling and unstable, and, in the long romances (chivalric, Montemayoran, and Byzantine), that life is a series of unreflective moments, adventurous hours of valor, melancholy, or splendor. Whatever the reasons or results in individual works and genres, the Spanish stories are generally full of movement. The imposing number of sequels and promised sequels might even suggest a momentum that carries on beyond the limits of the printed page.

A Brief Criticism

D espite their historic importance and brilliant patches, and despite their incidental pleasures, the stories we have touched on are at some points —and naturally—disappointing. Their finest effects, for one thing, seem to be the product of spontaneous invention, and yet they sometimes suffer because of their creators' apparent disdain for correcting errors. The price of this method was contradiction and repetition.

A deeper criticism has to do with what this art says or refuses to say about

16. Jess Lee Gerding, "Spanish Travel Fiction in the *Siglo de Oro,*" unpublished Ph.D. dissertation (University of Texas, 1957).

17. *Persiles and Sigismunda* (1619), p. 274.

life. Quite simply, it is too seldom concerned with ideas. Why should this be true? It has been said that the Spaniard is more a man of passion than thought; that his quixotic expulsion of the Jews was a rejection of the most viable intellectual element of his society; that his genius was allowed to exercise only in an area circumscribed by the Inquisition, the Council of Trent, and the Index.[18] Perhaps all of these statements have certain attractions as explanations, but they overlook some of the facts. For one thing, other stories of the same time—English stories, for instance—were not faring nearly as well; and for another, however tempting the Holy Office is as a scapegoat, its period of greatest influence corresponded to Spain's literary, artistic, and political Golden Age.

Whatever the causes, as I have said, the surface of some of this art seems more important than its center. Conflicts tend to be external or rhetorical. Protagonists act and feel, but do not think.[19] If Hamlet had been limited thus,

---

18. Américo Castro is among those who regard the Inquisition as "a long calamity," but he also takes the view that "The *Celestina,* the picaresque autobiographies, the pastoral narratives, . . . and, finally, Cervantes' novel—none of this could have come to be in an atmosphere of placid religious and intellectual tolerance where the tranquillity of economic well-being would have permitted the luxury of critical thought about man and nature" (pp. 648, 640).

Of course many Roman Catholic strands are found in the Spanish fiction of the time. Sometimes these show forth clearly enough in the English translations, but more often they are hidden or blurred. Persiles and his sweetheart, for instance, go on a pilgrimage to Rome in the 1619 English translation, at about the same time that Céspedes y Meneses' Fernando is deprived of witnessing a "papisticall" miracle and Lope's Pamphilus is kept from watching religious plays. In reworking Quevedo's *Sueños,* Croshaw rejects the pleasure of seeing Luther and Calvin in hell, and Cervantes' Ricaredo, even in Mabbe's sympathetic hands, is prevented from going to Rome to fortify his faith and do homage to the pope. In striking contrast, then, the English *Buscon* affirms the pope to be the head of the church, which in Elizabeth's day would have been enough for any owner of the book to be regarded as guilty of treason and liable to execution (George Haven Putnam, *The Censorship of the Church of Rome* [New York, 1907], II, 258).

Unfortunately the number of stories translated is too small and their treatment too varied to allow safe generalizations about trends. We can only surmise the views of an individual author or translator and remind ourselves that then, as now, different groups with different ideals were more readily discernible than any Spirit of the Age.

19. Nor do they invite thought in a reader. Sidney Zink believes that "The highly generalized emotional proclivities toward charity, bravery, etc., or the conventional intellectual formulas about these virtues (which [Sir Philip] Sidney represented art as furnishing) are indeed positively dangerous to reflection. . . . If art is to contribute to the best life [i.e., moral reflection as well as action], it must be used deliberately by the moral agent for his own good, not practiced on him by some ministerial authority who acts in his interest. The former is the only way in which

Claudius certainly would have made his quietus long before Act V, from which it would seem that the crucial struggle in Shakespeare's tragedy may lie as much in reaching a decision as in applying it. Perhaps a generalization based on *Hamlet* is unfair, and yet it may help to indicate that what fiction often neglected was a matter of both characterization and the problematical nature of values.

A great work of literature not only draws attention to itself, but in some way illumines its surroundings. Moreover, it casts light on something perennial in the human situation, if only by reflecting a single ray on some aspects of life which we might have overlooked without the artist's help. Too many Spanish stories are rather like lighted Christmas trees drawing attention to themselves and little else. Of course there is real value in a skilful work of this sort, a well-juggled handful of balls or a cameo. Certainly there is pleasure in such things, and certainly this sort of pleasure is one gauge of value. In the finest works of the Spanish Renaissance, however, there is also a further pleasure. In the *Celestina,* Rojas gives us life-in-the-round by presenting a simultaneous view of different kinds of truth. In *Don Quixote,* notwithstanding an impulse toward slapstick, Cervantes is willing to pose problems; in his masterwork, it may be said, he creates an ironic compound of ideas which evoke further ideas in his reader. In Alemán's *Rogue* we watch the painful probing of a mind caught between the ideal standards of orthodoxy and the real standards men live by. And the anguish which may have derived from Quevedo's inability to shed reservations about either the Renaissance, the Reformation, or the Counter-Reformation has resulted in a series of works which are always provocative and sometimes potent even in their modified English form. Since the vitality of any fiction is dependent on its author's view of life, these are important matters. I do not mean at this point to indicate the attitude of early English readers, nor am I trying to single out every Spanish writer of worth. I mention Rojas, Cervantes, Alemán, and Quevedo because these men are writers whose works are more than cream-bowl deep. Whatever else the English translators did or did not do, they translated such Spanish authors as these, and consequently succeeded sometimes in bringing forth better books than their more original countrymen.

One hundred and thirty-seven years after William London issued his catalogue, the Hispanophile Robert Southey could say that "Don Quixote, the Vi-

---

respect can be shown for the moral agent, just as it is the only way in which justice is done to the work of art" ("The Moral Effect of Art," *Ethics,* LX [1949–1950], 270–271).

sions of Quevedo, the Spanish Rogue, and the Lazarillo de Tormes . . . are almost the only Spanish books that we have naturalized. . . ."[20] In other words, when the eighteenth century was drawing to a close, time already had begun its sorting, carelessly laying waste to some parts of the tapestry while putting other parts in storage, but fortunately choosing, by and large, fairly well. Though Southey omits some important ones, he lists four of the works that are really best worth remembering. Even the most soporific of those he omits, however, must be sought out and brought forth for any complete judgment of the age which produced it, since, as the Spanish proverb says and as the student comes to see, the least, like the greatest, is a means by which the dead may open the eyes of the living.

20. *Letters Written During a Short Residence in Spain and Portugal* (Bristol, 1797), pp. 122–123. In London in 1818, Angel Anaya produced *An Essay on Spanish Literature* in which he made "An Inquiry into the Causes of the Prejudice Existing Against Spanish Literature." Note, however, Southey's "almost." Pleading the Affective Fallacy, I would add, first, *The Spanish Bawd,* and then Cervantes' *Jealous Husband,* Quevedo's *Buscon,* and Luna's *Pursuit.*

Appendix A

A Note on Those Who Learned Spanish

It would be interesting but impossible to catalogue the names of those in England who knew Spanish. The most one can do is gather evidence. For example, in his famous *Description of England,* the chronicler William Harrison reminds us that the noble learners of Spanish were not all men. He writes: "And to saie how many gentlewomen and ladies there are, that beside sound knowledge of the Greeke and Latine toongs, are thereto no lesse skilfull in the Spanish, Italian, and French, or in some one of them, it resteth not in me. . . ."[1] Apparently beginning with the apex of the social pyramid, Elizabeth herself, both ladies and gentlemen studied Spanish, though then, as now, there were probably many people who were satisfied merely to flavor their writing with exotic scraps.[2] Florio complains that when they have mastered two words of Spanish, they think they have enough and stop studying.[3]

If a courtier had a need for Spanish but no desire to learn it, he could hire a foreign secretary. In a work where he lays down rules for the government of an earl's house, Richard Brathwait includes a section on the secretary in which he says that the latter "is to understand the Latin and Greek Tongues; also the Italian, French, and Spanish, with other Languages, but also to speak and write well in them, thereby he shall be the better able to discourse with other Noblemen's men and Strangers."[4] The Earl of Leicester was lucky enough to have as secretary the cosmopolite Welshman James Howell, a man who thanked God that he had "this fruit of my foreign Travels, that I can pray to him every day of the week in a several Language, and upon Sunday in seven. . . ."[5] Perhaps

1. (1587), I, 196.
2. Gustav Ungerer, *Anglo-Spanish Relations in Tudor Literature* (Berne, 1956), pp. 43–44, cites several sources to indicate Elizabeth's knowledge of the tongue, and to these may be added the words of Roger Ascham, her tutor, who refers to "her perfit readines, in . . . Spanish . . ." (*The Scholemaster* [1570], p. 21). Among other ladies who knew Spanish were Katherine Parr, Jane Grey, and Mary Sidney, Countess of Pembroke. After Elizabeth's death, however, learned ladies were less in vogue (Myra Reynolds, *The Learned Lady in England 1650–1760* [Boston, 1920], p. 23).
3. Cited by Kathleen Lambley, *The Teaching and Cultivation of the French Language in England During Tudor and Stuart Times* (Manchester, 1920), p. 65.
4. Quoted by Foster Watson, *The Beginnings of the Teaching of Modern Subjects in England* (London, 1909), p. 485.
5. *Epistolae Ho-Elianae,* ed. Joseph Jacobs (London, 1890), p. 336.

most grateful of all, however, was Sir William Cecil, whose secretary was the lexicographer Richard Perceval. At any rate, Perceval deciphered for him the Spanish packets telling of Philip's Armada. (To assist in translating Spanish documents and help turn out "pamphlets of official anti-Spanish propaganda," Cecil hired a staff which included Perceval, Richard Eden, and Ruy López.)[6]

Among English businessmen traveling to Spain and learning her language was John Frampton, who, after being tortured by the Inquisition, lived to return home and translate several Spanish books.[7] James Howell first went into Spain as a steward in search of beryllia for use in the glassworks of Robert Mansel. Peter Mundy, who traded in olive oil and pilchards, learned Spanish while staying with an English weaver in San Lucar, and Paul Ricaut, the translator of Gracián's *Criticón,* was sent by his father to Madrid to collect a large commercial debt.[8]

The religion of Spain was sufficient cause for still others—sympathetic Englishmen, some of them trained abroad—to learn the Spanish tongue; but as Edward M. Wilson points out, even the English clergy included men who knew it. Both Bishop Ken and Archbishop Sancroft "could read Spanish enough to find edification in it. . . ."[9]

Among men of letters who knew the language one finds a number of well-known figures: Philip Sidney (named after Spain's Philip II when the latter was king of England); Gabriel Harvey, who scribbled Spanish phrases in his copy of Corro's *Spanish Grammer;* William Drummond of Hawthornden, who read Spanish with such delight that he adapted several compositions by Juan Boscán and Garcilaso de la Vega;[10] Ben Jonson, who read at least part of Mateo Alemán's *Guzmán de Alfarache* in the original; John Donne, whose knowledge no longer seems to be in doubt;[11] George Herbert, who "had learnt to understand the *Italian, Spanish,* and *French* Tongues very perfectly . . .";[12] and Andrew Marvell,

6. Ungerer, p. 48.

7. See Lawrence C. Wroth, "An Elizabethan Merchant and Man of Letters," *HLQ,* XVII (1954), 299–314.

8. For further evidence of merchants and merchants' factors in Spain see Gordon Connell-Smith, *Forerunners of Drake: A Study of English Trade with Spain in the Early Tudor Period* (London, 1954), and Julian Paz and Ricardo Magdaleno, *Documentos relativos a Inglaterra* (1254–1834) (Madrid, 1947).

9. "Spanish and English Religious Poetry of the Seventeenth Century," *The Journal of Ecclesiastical History,* IX (1958), 47. Among other sources on this topic is Anthony F. Allison and David M. Rogers, *A Catalogue of Catholic Books in English Printed Abroad or Secretly in England, 1558–1640* (Bognor Regis, England, 1956).

10. L. E. Kastner, "The Italian and Spanish Sources of William Drummond of Hawthornden," *Miscellanea di Studi critici in Onore di Vincenzo Crescini* (Turin, 1927), pp. 151–182; and Matthew P. McDiarmid, "The Spanish Plunder of William Drummond of Hawthornden," *MLR,* XLIV (1949), 17–25.

11. Evelyn M. Simpson, introd., *The Sermons of John Donne,* ed. George R. Potter and Evelyn M. Simpson (Berkeley, Calif., 1959), IV, 39–40.

12. Izaak Walton, *The Life of Mr. George Herbert* (1670), p. 27.

whom Milton described as having "gained" Dutch, French, Italian, and Spanish, along with Latin and Greek.[13] The list might be extended backward to include Barnabe Googe—who translated from Montemayor and Santillana—and forward to Samuel Pepys, who was sometimes to be seen, he says, in Duck Lane and Paul's Churchyard "at the foreign Bookseller's looking over some Spanish books, and with much ado keeping myself from laying out money there. . . ."[14]

Despite its sketchiness, such a roster is imposing. Harking back to a time when many Englishmen still signed their names with an X, it serves to remind us that at least some were capable of reading Spanish fiction in its original form.

13. Noted by Watson, p. 524. For Milton's own knowledge of Spanish see pp. 155–156 of the present work.

14. *The Diary of Samuel Pepys,* ed. Henry B. Wheatley (London, 1893), III, 78.

Appendix B

A List of Translations and Translators of Non-chivalric Spanish Fiction with Dates of Editions through 1657[1]

N.B. Bracketed titles are some of those which, for various reasons, I have finally rejected. For further information see *Appendix D,* "A Brief Commentary on Some Peripheral Works."

Acuña, Hernando de.
> *El caballero determinado* (1553), from Olivier de la Marche's *Chevalier délibéré.*
>> [*The Resolved Gentleman*] (1594), tr. Lewis Lewkenor.

Alemán, Mateo.
> *La vida del pícaro Guzmán de Alfarache* (I, 1599, II, 1604).
>> *The Rogue: or The Life of Guzman de Alfarache* (I and II, 1622), tr. James Mabbe. Also I, 1622, and II, 1623; I and II, 1623; I and II, 1630; I, 1634, and II, 1633 (with *The Spanish Bawd;* see Rojas, Fernando de); I and II, 1655; I and II, 1656.
>> *The Rogue: or, The Life of Guzman de Alfarache* (I, 1656, and II, 1655), epitomized by S. S.

Blakeston, James. *See Lazarillo de Tormes.*

Bourchier, John, Lord Berners. *See* Guevara, Antonio de, *and* San Pedro, Diego de.

1. For bibliography of the period after 1657 consult Charles C. Mish, *English Prose Fiction 1641–1660* and *English Prose Fiction 1661–1700* (Charlottesville, Va., 1952); Arundell Esdaile, *A List of English Tales and Prose Romances Printed before 1740* (London, 1912), and William H. McBurney, *A Check List of English Prose Fiction 1700–1739* (Cambridge, Mass., 1960). For the chivalric romances, see *Appendix C,* and, for more detailed listing, Sterg O'Dell, *A Chronological List of Prose Fiction in English Printed in England and Other Countries 1475–1640* (Cambridge, Mass., 1954), and Mish, *English Prose Fiction 1600–1640* (Charlottesville, Va., 1952).

Caxton, William. *See* Lull, Ramón.

Cervantes Saavedra, Miguel de.

El ingenioso hidalgo Don Quijote de la Mancha (I, 1605; II, 1615).

> *The History of the Valorous and Wittie Knight-errant, Don-Quixote* (I, 1612), tr. Thomas Shelton. Both parts, 1620. Subsequent ed., 1652.

Los trabajos de Persiles y Sigismunda, historia setentrional (1617).

> *The Travels of Persiles and Sigismunda, a Northern History* (1619), an anon. tr.

Novelas ejemplares (1613).

> *Exemplarie Novells; in Sixe Books* (1640), tr. James Mabbe. Also issued as
>
> *Delight in Severall Shapes* (1654).

[*The Troublesome and Hard Adventures in Love*] Falsely attributed to Cervantes. *See* Montemayor, Jorge de.

Céspedes y Meneses, Gonzalo de.

Poema trágico del español Gerardo y desengaño del amor lascivo (I, 1615; II, 1617).

> *Gerardo the Unfortunate Spaniard* (1622), tr. Leonard Digges. Also 1653.

Croshaw, Richard. *See* Quevedo y Villegas, Francisco de.

Cuevas, Francisco de las, pseud. *See* Quintana, Francisco de.

Davies, John, of Kidwelly. *See* Quevedo y Villegas, Francisco de; Salas Barbadillo, Alonso Jerónimo; *and* Zayas y Sotomayor, María de.

De Sainliens, Claude. *See* Hollyband, Claudius, *under* San Pedro, Diego de.

Digges, Leonard. *See* Céspedes y Meneses, Gonzalo de.

Flores, Juan de.

Los amores de Grisel y Mirabella (1495).

> *The Historie of Aurelio and of Isabell, . . . Nyeuley Translatede in Foure Langagies* (1556 *bis*), anon. tr. Also [1586?], [1588?], 1608 *bis*.
>
> *A Paire of Turtle Doves, or, The Tragicall History of Bellora and Fidelio* (1606), anon. tr. sometimes attributed to Robert Greene.

García, Carlos.

La desordenada codicia de los bienes ajenos (1619).

> *The Sonne of the Rogue* (1638, three issues), tr. William Melvin. Also appeared as
>
> *Lavernae* (1650), a reissue of 1638 ed., and
>
> *Guzman, Hinde and Hannam Outstript* (1657).

Gil Polo, Gaspar. *See* Montemayor, Jorge de.

Gracián Dantisco, Lucas.

Galateo español (1582?).

> *Galateo Espagnol* (1640), tr. William Style. Contains intercalated *novela, Axa and the Prince.*

Greene, Robert. *See* Flores, Juan de.

Guevara, Antonio de.
> *Epístolas familiares* (1539–1541).
>> [*The Familiar Epistles of Sir Antony of Guevara*] (1574), tr. Edward Hellowes. Also further eds. In the succeeding year, Geoffrey Fenton brought out his [*Golden Epistles*], which also had subsequent eds.
> *Libro áureo de Marco Aurelio* (1527).
>> [*Golden Boke*] (1535 *bis*), tr. John Bourchier, Lord Berners. Also further eds.
> *Libro llamado reloj de príncipes* (1529).
>> [*The Diall of Princes*] (1557), tr. Thomas North. Also further eds.

Hollyband, Claudius, pseud. *See* San Pedro, Diego de.

Lazarillo de Tormes (1554?), anon.
> The Pleasaunt Historie of Lazarillo de Tormes (1586), tr. David Rowland of Anglesey. First ed. (1576) no longer extant. Also 1596, 1624, 1639, 1653. (N.B. This work sometimes issued with Luna's sequel, q.v.; James Blakeston's "new" *Lazarillo* based on Rowland's made its debut in 1653.)
> *Segunda parte de Lazarillo* (1555), anon.
>> The Most Pleasaunt and Delectable Historie of Lazarillo de Tormes. The Second Part (1596), tr. William Phiston.
> *La segunda parte de la vida de Lazarillo de Tormes* (1620), Juan de Luna.
>> The Pursuit of the Historie of Lazarillo de Tormez (1622), anon. tr. Also 1631, 1639, 1653, 1655.

Lodge, Thomas.
> [*Margarite of America*] (1596).

Lull, Ramón.
> *Libre del orde de cavayleria* (ca. 1275).
>> [*The Book of the Ordre of Chyvalry*] (1484), tr. William Caxton.

Luna, Juan de. *See Lazarillo de Tormes*.

Mabbe, James. *See* Alemán, Mateo; Cervantes Saavedra, Miguel de; *and* Rojas, Fernando de.

[*Margarite of America*]. *See* Lodge, Thomas.

Melvin, William. *See* García, Carlos.

Messervy, Edward. *See* Quevedo y Villegas, Francisco de.

Mexía, Pedro.
> *Silva de varia lección* (1540).
>> [*The Foreste*] (1571), tr. Thomas Fortescue. Also subsequent borrowings by other writers.

Montemayor, Jorge de.
> *Los siete libros de la Diana* (1559); anon. story of *Abindarráez y Jarifa* (sometimes attributed to Antonio de Villegas) inserted in later eds.
> *La segunda parte de la Diana* (1564), by Alonso Pérez.

Diana enamorada (1564), by Gaspar Gil Polo.
> *Diana* (1598), tr. Bartholomew Yong.
> [*Diana*] (*ante* 1583), partial tr. by Edward Paston.
> [*Diana de Monte Mayor*] (1596), tr. Thomas Wilson.
> [*The Troublesome and Hard Adventures in Love*] (1594?), by R. C.,
> borrows heavily from the above, especially Gil Polo.

[*Morindos, The Famous & Renowned History of*] (1609), anon. work. No
Spanish source known.

Núñez, Nicolás. *See* San Pedro, Diego de.

Ortiz de Melgarejo, Antonio.
> *Casa de locos de amor,* in *Sueños* (1627). *See* Quevedo y Villegas, Francisco de.

Ortúñez de Calahorra, Diego.
> *Espejo de príncipes y caballeros* (1562).
>> [*The First Part of the Mirrour of Princely Deedes and Knighthood*]
>> (1578), tr. Margaret Tiler.[2]

Paston, Edward. *See* Montemayor, Jorge de.

Pérez, Alonso. *See* Montemayor, Jorge de.

Pérez de Montalván, Juan.
> *La hermosa Aurora* and *La prodigiosa,* in *Sucesos y prodigios de amor*
> (1624).
>> *Aurora, & The Prince* (1647), tr. Thomas Stanley. Also 1648 (in
>> 1647–1648 *Poems and Translations*), 1650 *bis* (two separate is-
>> sues), 1651 (reissue of 1650, in *Poems and Translations*), 1652 *bis*
>> (1652 *Poems and Translations* made up sometimes of sheets of
>> 1647 ed., sometimes of 1650 ed.).[3]
> *La villana de Pinto,* in *Sucesos. . . .*
>> *The Illustrious Shepherdess* (1656), tr. Edward Phillips.
> *El envidioso castigado,* in *Sucesos. . . .*
>> *The Imperious Brother* (1656), tr. Edward Phillips.

Phillips, Edward. *See* Pérez de Montalván, Juan.

Phiston, William. *See Lazarillo de Tormes.*

Quevedo y Villegas, Francisco de.
> *Cartas del caballero de la tenaza* (1625).
>> *The Provident Knight, or, Sir Parsimonious Thrift* (1657), tr. John
>> Davies of Kidwelly, bound with *Buscon.*
> *Historia de la vida del buscón* (1626).
>> *The Life and Adventures of Buscon* (1657), tr. John Davies of Kid-
>> welly, bound with *The Provident Knight.*

---

2. This work is included to mark the entry of the Spanish romances of chivalry.
See first note to present list.

3. For this entry I depend entirely on Margaret Flower, "Thomas Stanley (1625–
1678) . . . ," *Transactions of the Cambridge Bibliographical Society,* I (1949–
1953), 139–172.

Infierno enmendado (1628).
> *Hell Reformed or A Glasse for Favorits* (1641), tr. Edward Messervy.

Sueños (1627).
> *Visions, or, Hels Kingdome* (1640), tr. Richard Croshaw. *See also* Ortiz de Melgarejo, Antonio.

Quintana, Francisco de.
Experiencias de amor y fortuna (1626).
> *The History of Don Fenise* (1651), anon. tr.

Rastell, John. *See* Rojas, Fernando de.

Rojas, Fernando de.
La Celestina (*ca.* 1499–1502).
> [*A New Cõmodye in Englysh in Maner of an Enterlude . . .*] (*ca.* 1530), tr. John Rastell.
> *The Spanish Bawd, Represented in Celestina* (1631 *bis*), tr. James Mabbe. Also issued with *The Rogue* in 1634.

Rowland, David. *See Lazarillo de Tormes.*

Sainliens, Claude de. *See* Hollyband, Claudius, *under* San Pedro, Diego de.

Salas Barbadillo, Alonso Jerónimo.
La hija de Celestina (1612).
> [*The Hypocrites*] (*ca.* 1660), tr. John Davies of Kidwelly. Published with *The Fruitless Precaution* and *The Innocent Adultery*. *See* Zayas y Sotomayor, María de.

San Pedro, Diego de.
Cárcel de amor (1492).
> *The Castell of Love* (*ca.* 1548), tr. John Bourchier, Lord Berners. Contains sequel by Nicolás Núñez (1496). Further eds. in 1552, *ante* 1560.[4]

Tractado de amores de Arnalte y Lucenda (1491).
> *A Certayn Treatye Moste Wyttely Devysed . . .* (1543), tr. John Clerc.
> *The Pretie and Wittie Historie of Arnalt & Lucenda* (1575), tr. Claudius Hollyband (pseud. of Claude de Sainliens). Also 1597, 1608.
> *A Small Treatise Betwixt Arnalte and Lucenda Entituled The Evill-intreated Lover, or The Melancholy Knight* (1639), tr. Leonard Lawrence.
> [*Arnaldo, or, The Injur'd Lover*] (1660), tr. T. S. from a modified Italian version by Girolamo Brusoni.

Santa Cruz, Melchor de.
Floresta española de apotegmas (1574).
> [*Wits Fittes and Fancies*] (1595), tr. Anthony Copley. Also further eds.

---

4. Dating editions of this translation is particularly difficult.

Shelton, Thomas. *See* Cervantes Saavedra, Miguel de.

Stanley, Thomas. *See* Pérez de Montalván, Juan.

Style, William. *See* Gracián Dantisco, Lucas.

Teixeira, José.

(Though the work named below may derive from a Castilian original, I have found only a French version entitled *Adventure admirable, par dessus toutes autres des siècles passez et présent . . .* [1601]).

[*The Strangest Adventure That Ever Happened*] (1601), tr. Anthony Munday.

Tiler, Margaret. *See* Ortúñez de Calahorra, Diego.

Torquemada, Antonio de.

Jardín de flores curiosas (1570).

[*The Spanish Mandevile of Miracles*] (1600), tr. Lewis Lewkenor.

Vega Carpio, Lope Félix de.

El peregrino en su patria (1604).

The Pilgrime of Casteele (1621), anon. tr.[5] Also 1623 *bis*.

Villegas, Antonio de. *See* Montemayor, Jorge de.

Wilson, Thomas. *See* Montemayor, Jorge de.

Yong, Bartholomew. *See* Montemayor, Jorge de.

Zayas y Sotomayor, María de.

El juez de su causa, in *Novelas ejemplares y amorosas* (1637).

[*The Innocent Adultery*] (*ca.* 1660), tr. John Davies of Kidwelly. *See next entry.*

El prevenido engañado, also in *Novelas. . . .*

[*The Fruitless Precaution*] (*ca.* 1660), also tr. Davies. Both stories published with *The Hypocrites. See* Salas Barbadillo, Alonso Jerónimo.

5. In the copy at Worcester College, Oxford, according to Professor Jackson, a handwritten note names William Dutton as the translator.

A List of Chivalric
Romances

The following résumé of the Spanish chivalric romances translated into English has been carefully compiled, but it is (understandably, I hope) offered
with bibliographical misgivings.

With the aim of partially clarifying a complicated matter, generic names are
given as general headings, beneath which are listed Spanish authors and Spanish
titles, and then data relevant to the English translations. To set them apart, I
have placed brackets around references to two works: (1) Charles Stewart's unprinted but historically significant translation from the *Amadís,* and (2) Part III
of *Palmerin of England,* which seems to have originated outside the peninsula.

Amadis

Rodríguez de Montalvo, Garci.
> *Amadís de Gaula* (1508).
>> Part I, *Discoursing the Adventures and Love of Many Knights and
>> Ladies* (1590), tr. Anthony Munday.
>> [Also an unprinted fragment, tr. Charles Stewart (1571).]
>> Part II (1595). tr. "Lazarus Pyott."[1]
>> Parts I–II (1619), tr. Munday ("Pyott").
>> Parts III–IV (1618), tr. Munday.
> *Esplandián* (1510).
>> Part V (1598), anon. tr.

Páez de Ribera, Ruy.
> *Florisando* (1510).
>> Part VI (1652), tr. Francis Kirkman.

Bellianis

Fernández, Jerónimo.
> *Don Belianis de Grecia* (1547).
>> *The Honour of Chivalrie* (1598), tr. L. A. Also 1650.

---

1. Celeste Turner Wright has been good enough to inform me that she has recently discovered evidence proving "Lazarus Pyott" was really Anthony Munday
himself.

Mirrour of Princely Deedes

Ortúñez de Calahorra, Diego.
   Espejo de príncipes y caballeros (1562).
      The First Part of the Mirrour of Princely Deedes (1578), tr. Margaret
        Tiler. Also 1580, 1599.
      The Second Part of the First Booke (1583), tr. R. P.[2] Also 1585, 1599.
      The Third Part of the First Booke (1586), tr. R. P. Also 1599.
Sierra, Pedro de la.
   Espejo de príncipes . . . Segunda parte (1580).
      The Second Part of the Myrror of Knighthood (Books IV–V) (1583),
        tr. R. P. Also 1598.
Martínez, Marcos.
   El caballero del Febo (1580).
      The Sixth Booke (1598), tr. R. P.
      The Seventh Booke (1598), tr. L. A.
      The Eighth Booke (1599), tr. L. A.
      The Ninth Part (1601), tr. Robert Parke (?).

Palladine

Don Florando de Inglaterra (1545), anon.
      Palladine of England (1588), tr. Munday. No relation to *Palmerin*
      cycle.

Palmerin

Palmerín de Oliva (1511), anon.
      Palmerin d'Oliva, Part I (1588), tr. Munday.[3] Parts I–II (1597).
      Also 1615–1616, 1616, 1637.
      The Delightful History of Celestina the Faire (1596), tr. William
      Barley.[4]

---

2. John Weld, "Studies in the Euphuistic Novel (1576–1640)" unpublished
Ph.D. dissertation (Harvard, 1940), pp. 40–41, offers reasons for doubting that the
R. P. who worked on this cycle was Robert Parry, who is sometimes named in connection with the work; and Dorothy F. Atkinson makes a good case for identifying
him as Robert Parke ("One R. P." and "The Authorship of *The Mirror of Knighthood,* Part Nine," two articles in *MLQ,* VI [1945], 3–12 and 175–186, respectively).

3. A 1586 edition of both parts is listed by Samuel A. Tannenbaum, *Anthony
Mundy . . . (A Concise Bibliography)* (New York, 1942), p. 10.

4. Gerard J. Brault, "English Translations of the *Celestina* in the Sixteenth Century," *HR,* XXVIII (1960), 306, indicates that this is an unauthorized version of
Bk. II of *Palmerín de Oliva.*

Primaleón (1512), anon.

> *The Honourable, Pleasant and Rare Conceited History of Palmendos*
> (1589), tr. Munday. Also 1637, 1653.

> *Primaleon of Greece,* I (1595), "first foure sheetes" tr. Munday; re-
> mainder anon.; Part II (1596), tr. Munday; Part III (1597), tr.
> Munday (perhaps a ghost); Parts I–III (1619), tr. Munday.

Moraes, Francisco de.

> *Palmerín de Inglaterra* (1547–1548).

> > *Palmerin of England,* Parts I–II (between 1581–1587), tr. Munday.
> > Part I also 1609. Parts I–II also 1596, 1616, 1639.

> > [Part III] (1597), tr. Munday, this version probably from a French
> > translation of an Italian original.[5]

---

5. [Julia] Celeste Turner [Wright], *Anthony Mundy: An Elizabethan Man of
Letters* (Berkeley, Calif., 1928), pp. 144–146, 182.

Appendix D

A Brief Commentary on Some Peripheral Works

We have already seen how a conservative definition of fiction will lead one to regard as non-fiction (or at best semi-fiction) *The Booke of the Ordre of Chyvalry*, the first *Celestina*, the *Golden Boke*, and *The Diall of Princes*.[1] To enable a reader to make up his own mind regarding still other peripheral works, it may be helpful to offer some further titles and reasons for their omission.

An additional "Guevara" piece in this category is the story of Sinorix and Camma, which appears in the well-known *Petite Pallace of Pettie His Pleasure* (1576). Evidence indicates that Pettie took it not from Guevara's *Reloj* nor from Plutarch's *Moralia,* where it was also available, but from Hoby's translation of Castiglione called *The Courtyer.*[2]

William Painter's *Palace of Pleasure* (I, 1566; II, 1567), upon which Pettie modeled his more petite work, borrowed not only from Guevara, as we saw in Chapter IV, but from Pedro Mexía—specifically, from the latter's encyclopedic and popular *Silva de varia lección* (1540). One Mexía "Nouel" that Painter included, however, is simply a character sketch of the misanthrope Timon (I, no. 28); another is an anecdote about a man and woman, "he being the husbande of .xx. wiues: and she the wife of xxii, husbandes" (I, no. 29);[3] and a third is devoted largely to a description of the Amazons (II, no. 1).

Also derived from Mexía's *Silva* are Thomas Fortescue's *The Foreste* (1571), Thomas Milles's *The Treasurie of Ancient and Modern Times* (I, 1613; II, 1619), and John Baildon's *The Rarities of the World* (1651). It is with some reluctance that I reject Mexía, his *Silva,* and all his English translators because his miscellany is crammed, among other things, with hundreds of brief and interesting pieces which it may seem cowardly to call anecdotes. Many of these are apparently of classical or Italian origin, hence not pertinent here; but among his selections there are some based on Spanish history, for example the passage in Book III of *The Foreste* which tells how the Lady Marie tricked "the Lorde

1. See Ch. IV, pp. 39–43.
2. Douglas Bush, *"The Petite Pallace of Pettie His Pleasure,"* JEGP, XXVII (1928), 162.
3. *Palace* (1566), p. 59ʳ. This is based on an epistle by Jerome, although Painter cites both Jerome and "Pietro Messia." It may serve as an example of the danger of being too certain of Renaissance sources. See also J. C. Maxwell, "William Painter's Use of Mexía," NQ, CXCIX (1954), 16.

Peter Counte of Barcelon, afterward by succession the seuenth kyng of Aragon. . . ."[4]

Much easier to reject is *The Resolved Gentleman* (1594). This work was translated by Sir Lewis Lewkenor from *El caballero determinado* (1553), which in turn was a translation by Hernando de Acuña. The latter was a soldier, courtier, and poet, traditionally said to have rendered his *Caballero* from the prose of Charles V at the emperor's own request. Whether or not this is true, Acuña's version was ultimately based on a long French poem, *Le chevalier délibéré,* by Olivier de la Marche.

Also relatively easy to cross off our list is Anthony Copley's frequently reprinted *Wits Fittes and Fancies* (1595), a transformation of Melchor de Santa Cruz's *Floresta española de apotegmas* (1574).[5] Along with its witty sayings, proverbs, and jests, this book includes characters and incidents and bits of dialogue, but none of these is sufficiently developed for the work as a whole to merit the name of fiction.

In the following year, 1596, Thomas Lodge introduced his violent *Margarite of America,* maintaining that "it was my chance in the librarie of the Iesuits in *Sanctum* [Santos, Brazil] to find this historie in the Spanish tong, which as I read delighted me, and delighting me, wonne me, and winning me, made me write it."[6] Though the book is no doubt fiction (it is a euphuistic romance), there is considerable question as to what particular Spanish work it might be derived from.[7] Until our information is fuller, we may suspect it is Lodge's own invention.

Other works may be rejected for other reasons. In 1600 came Sir Lewis Lewkenor's *Spanish Mandevile of Miracles,* the varied substance of which (anecdotes on the variety of nature) is given a certain cohesion by its presentation in the form of colloquies. The framework, at least, smacks of fiction. Moreover, some of Lewkenor's little stories approach the outer limits of anecdotal length. Nevertheless I believe that both Antonio de Torquemada's *Jardín de flores curiosas* (1570) and its English translation are not so much fiction as fascinating gropings toward fiction.

In the following year appeared Anthony Munday's *The Strangest Adventure*

---

4. *Foreste,* p. 138ᵛ. See also René Pruvost, "The Source of George Turbervile's *Tragical Tales,* Nos. 2, 5, and 8," *RES,* X (1934), 29–45.

5. The rather roguish Copley asserts that he has included a number of things of his own invention, "& that without any iniury I hope to my Authour: the which are easily to be discerned from his, for that they taste more Englishlie: Neither haue I vsed his Methode therein, but haue set downe one of mine owne, which I take to be better" (A2ᵛ).

6. Prefatory address to *Margarite* in *The Complete Works of Thomas Lodge* (Glasgow, 1883), III, 4.

7. As a matter of fact, its Italian flavor has struck a number of students. See especially L. E. Kastner, "Thomas Lodge as an Imitator of the Italian Poets," *MLR,* II (1907), 155–161; and Thomas F. Crane, *Italian Social Customs of the Sixteenth Century* (New Haven, 1920), pp. 545–551.

That Ever Happened, professedly from the Spanish of José Teixeira through the French of an anonymous translator.[8] This work was the earliest in a series which purport to give more or less current news concerning Don Sebastian, the missing king of Portugal. Because they tend to be romantic and untrue they raise the question, when does unreliable reporting become fiction? Not quite in these tracts, I would submit.

A further work to be rejected is the little-known *History of Morindos* (1609), which tells of a preternaturally wicked Spanish king. So vile and vigorous that he has a different bed-mate every night in the year, Morindos is at last tricked into marriage by Miracola, a witch. Not one to waste time, Miracola meets and marries the king in a single night, and, at the moment of procreation, sees him devolve into a shapeless lump of flesh. In due time she takes to her childbed, repines for some twenty years, and at last brings forth seven daughters. These turn out to be none other than the seven deadly sins. To each of these a chapter is then devoted, her evil adventures and sad end being related with obvious relish. The Spanish would have liked all this. Ever since the time of Prudentius' *Psychomachia* they had turned out allegories personifying vices and virtues, but with no evidence beyond this and the sin-drenched little composition itself, one well might hesitate to affirm whether or not *Morindos* is a translation—from Spanish or any other language. I should guess that it was composed by an Englishman who wanted to astound, horrify, and (as a by-product) edify his fellow Englishmen. At any rate it would seem dangerous, evidence lacking, to list the book among translations from Spanish.

Last is *Fragosa King of Aragon* (1618), the handiwork of one W. C. Despite its name, this rather popular story does not seem to be a translation either from Spanish or any other tongue. John Weld, one of its rare modern readers, reports that it is indebted to *Euphues, Rosalynde,* and *Pandosto.*[9]

8. Miss Clara Louisa Penney has kindly given me the suggestion that Teixeira's original text may have been in French. Not only is his title always listed in its French form, even in Portuguese bibliographies, but Teixeira lived in France for many years.

9. "Studies in the Euphuistic Novel (1576–1640)," unpublished Ph.D. dissertation (Harvard, 1940), pp. 113–126.

Index